Stronger

Stronger

My Life Surviving Gazza

SHERYL GASCOIGNE

MICHAEL JOSEPH
an imprint of
PENGUIN BOOKS

MICHAEL JOSEPH

Published by the Penguin Group

Penguin Books Ltd, 80 Strand, London WC2R ORL, England

Penguin Group (USA) Inc., 375 Hudson Street, New York, New York 10014, USA

Penguin Group (Canada), 90 Eglinton Avenue East, Suite 700, Toronto, Ontario, Canada M4P 2Y3
(a division of Pearson Penguin Canada Inc.)

Penguin Ireland, 25 St Stephen's Green, Dublin 2, Ireland (a division of Penguin Books Ltd)

Penguin Group (Australia), 250 Camberwell Road, Camberwell, Victoria 3124, Australia
(a division of Pearson Australia Group Pty Ltd)

Penguin Books India Pvt Ltd, 11 Community Centre, Panchsheel Park, New Delhi – 110 017, India

Penguin Group (NZ), 67 Apollo Drive, Rosedale, North Shore 0632, New Zealand
(a division of Pearson New Zealand Ltd)

Penguin Books (South Africa) (Pty) Ltd, 24 Sturdee Avenue,
Rosebank, Johannesburg 2196, South Africa

Penguin Books Ltd, Registered Offices: 80 Strand, London WC2R ORL, England

www.penguin.com

First published 2009

1

Copyright © Sheryl Gascoigne, 2009

The moral right of the author has been asserted

Set in 12.75/15 pt Monotype Garamond
Typeset by Rowland Phototypesetting Ltd, Bury St Edmunds, Suffolk
Printed in Great Britain by Clays Ltd, St Ives plc

A CIP catalogue record for this book is available from the British Library

ISBN: 978-0-718-15560-5

For:

Bianca, Mason and Regan
There really is 'No mountain high enough'
I love you, love you, love you
Up to the moon and back again a million,
trillion, zillion times
xxxxxxxxxxxxxxxx

and

Nanny, my beautiful, elegant, kindest Nanny
The only other person who could possibly share this page
Not a day goes by that I don't think of you or ask
for your approval
I love you and miss you with all of my heart
xxxxxxxxxxxxxxxx

An Apology

There are several reasons why you may have picked up this book. Perhaps you have experienced or been on the receiving end of alcoholism, drug addiction, mental-health issues or domestic violence – or probably, like me, a dangerous concoction of them all. If so, and you are looking for support, understanding and compassion, then please read on. I firmly believe you will find those things in the pages of this book. Then, again, you may have missed your train and are standing in the bookshop and they've run out of anything by Jordan. Or you might have picked it up expecting a hatchet job on Paul Gascoigne, or his alter ego 'Gazza', in which case, put it down. This is not that book.

It may have started in that way, when I was full of rage over the injustice of having spent nearly twenty years taking beatings and cruel insults while I tried to help him – only to be labelled a 'wicked vulture' by Paul and his family – but as I wrote I changed. Yes, Paul did many hurtful things but the person who has to apologize, it turns out, is me. Thanks to some incredible people who helped me up from the floor and held on to me until I was strong enough to stand on my own two feet, I have learnt the fundamental difference between taking the blame, and taking responsibility. I take responsibility for everything that has happened in the pages of this book. I do not blame Paul, and I do not blame myself either, though I'm only too aware that I have many things to say sorry for.

First and foremost, I would like to apologize to my precious children. I put them through years of uncertainty, conflict and pain under the misapprehension that in taking Paul back I was doing the right thing for them. I wasn't. I would like to apologize to my parents. It would kill me to see another person injure a hair on one of my children's heads, yet they had to stand by and watch while Paul annihilated my confidence. I know they love me in their own way. The fact that it is not my way is no reason to condemn them — as I learnt while writing this. They had suffered deep pain of their own that lay buried under years of silence. Lastly, I would like to apologize to Paul: I know that you believe my writing this book was the ultimate betrayal, but it has finally set me and the children free from a cycle of violence that you and I set up two decades ago, so, for no other reason, it had to be written. I am just so sorry that I didn't have the strength to walk away before it came to this.

In publishing my book I hope it will help the many others who live with violence and addiction in all its ugly and cruel forms. So, over to you. This is my story, but it may also be yours. If it is, know this: you do not have to listen to one more insult, take one more beating, or accept one more false promise. There is a way out, but you have to find it, choose it, then walk it. Here's how I found mine and I'm still walking.

This is the Big-headed Blonde Bitch signing out.

Prologue

The first time I met Tracy Towner, a psychologist, I couldn't stop staring at her, she looked and sounded just like my beloved sister Vicki who we'd lost to cancer five years previously. Immediately I sensed her warmth and understanding. I sat down opposite her.

'How can I help?' she asked.

This was new territory for me. Help was not something I had ever asked for – I didn't know how to ask for it – so I started telling her about the terrible state that Paul was in and how desperate we all were that he wasn't getting the help he needed. She interrupted me and asked me to start from the beginning. So I did. After I finally reached the infamous Gleneagles incident and told how I'd gone back to him yet again, she stopped me: 'And that still wasn't enough?'

All I could do was shake my head. I was embarrassed to admit it, but no, it hadn't been enough to make me see sense. If I mentioned any of the rehab centres Paul had visited, she would say, 'So was that the *first* time?' or 'Was that after the *second* time?' or 'The *third* time?' I started to hear how ridiculous it sounded and when I told her he had only recently come out of yet another six-week stint of rehab I began to see what she saw. Since then Paul had come home to us, disappeared, only to re-emerge a week later pissed again on the Iron Maiden tour. Now we believed he was somewhere in Portugal in a critical state.

Then she got down to the bare bones of it. She was pretty tough on me but I truly appreciated it. When I'd finished talking she looked at me and said, as only an American can, 'Gee, I'm exhausted!' Then she leant forward. 'Have you had enough yet?'

ix

'What do you mean?' I'd thought she was going to help me – give me some answers as to what to do next, and how to do it! Here was my sister's doppelganger asking me if I'd had enough. I was confused and couldn't respond.

'You have a pattern here of opening up your house, letting him come back only to have him leave you. That's what you do.'

I was taken aback again. *I* was doing this? *I* was letting him come back only to have him leave me? I'd had eighteen years of Paul telling me it was all my fault, and now she was doing the same? She changed tack. 'If you had your ultimate fantasy, what do *you* want?'

Who? Me? I couldn't get my head round the question. Then, from somewhere, the answer came. 'I want to shut the front door.'

Weird, I know, but that was what I felt. I wanted to shut the door and not have to open it again.

She nodded. 'We could do that. You can do that.'

I was terrified. What would Mason and Bianca say? How could I give up on him? It was tantamount to giving up on them! 'I can't,' I said.

'You've done so well to leave a man who abused you, but you haven't shut the door. You've left it open just a crack, so he can always come back in. You're entitled to a life, you know.'

But what about Mason and Bianca? They'd been brought up by Paul and wanted him home. He was their father as far as they were concerned. Our youngest son Regan needed him too – someone to come and watch the plays, see him dance, stand proudly like the other dads did.

'Do they know much about addiction?'

'Yes,' I replied. But they didn't really.

'Do they know that a lot of people die, and most people don't get better from getting help and this is what happens?'

'I know what they'd say if they were sitting here. That we can stop him.'

'Do they think they can?'

'I think they think I can. By keeping him here and stopping him drinking.'

'Yeah, you can lock someone in the house and become a babysitter for the rest of your life, but at some point somebody becomes responsible for their own behaviour.'

Did she mean Paul? Or me?

'A good part of me wants to say you've done enough, and that if you continue to do this, you will lose more and more of yourself.'

I knew that was true: our lives revolved around one person. Paul. And I didn't want to live like that any more, but I didn't know how to stop it. Tracy was patient, but firm. There was nowhere to hide from her, so I came out into the open with my hands up, defeated. I had failed. And it was okay. I started crying. Tracy thought it was because Mason would be so angry with me if I said Paul couldn't come home again, but the tears weren't from sadness: they were tears of relief. No one had ever told me I didn't have to go on living like this. It struck me to my core. Eighteen years I'd been trying to help 'fix' Paul – his bad turns, his twitches, his jealousy and mood swings, his anger, his violence, his drinking, his drug-taking. I had carried a weighty responsibility for the football industry to keep him playing, for his family to keep him happy and for the children to keep him alive. 'No one's said to me before that it's okay if I don't help him.'

Where had it all gone so wrong? I thought I'd been doing the right thing for the children by letting him back into our lives over and over again. It was an enormous blow to discover I'd been doing the opposite. The one thing I'd always wanted to be above anything else was a good mother, but I'd put my children in both emotional and physical harm's way. That was not what a 'good' mother did. I believed that if I could fix him, they'd have a father, I'd have a husband and we'd have a family that could live happily ever after. Tracy looked me right in the eye. 'And who made you Little Miss Fix It?'

Well, that was a question I couldn't answer until I wrote this book.

1. A Cardboard Box

My first major memory isn't really my own but you could say it has coloured my entire life. It belongs to my cousin Debbie. She spent a lot of time at my house when we were very small. According to Debbie, we were really close in the early years. But it all changed long before any good memories could attach themselves permanently to me.

Debbie: '*Do you remember bouncing on your mum and dad's bed? You must have been four or five. We were bouncing so high we could see a cardboard box on top of the wardrobe. We got it down and when we opened it we found photographs and letters and pieces of paper we didn't understand. Then Auntie Susie [my mother] came in and she went mad. And I remember seeing that look in her eyes and thinking, God, she's just like my mum . . .*'

My mother threw Debbie out of the house then and there, and though she couldn't have been more than five or six, my mum didn't even watch her walk down the street and round the corner to where she lived. Then later that evening, Debbie says, our mothers, the two sisters, had a massive row on the front doorstep of Debbie's house. '*Susie shouted at Mum because she was having an affair with a married man then my mum shouted back, "Well, you sold your f—ing kids for a divorce." The door slammed and Mum came upstairs and punched the living daylights out of me. I was told never to go round to your house again, I wasn't to have anything to do with you, and soon after that day I pretty much decided I hated you.*'

As far as I was concerned Debbie turned from my playmate, cousin, friend into someone I feared. She had to hate me or she'd get hit again, and very soon I started to loathe her back. She says now she hated herself for all the horrid things she did to me, but she was just re-directing her own fear and pain. We were kids, trying to survive a storm that wasn't of our making. A secret storm at that. We never spoke afterwards – in fact, I went out of my way to avoid her. I'd try to find other routes home after school because I was scared she'd beat me up.

Without Debbie's friendship, I was very lonely so I relied on my pet dog, Sally, for company – I'd named her after my great-aunt Connie's dog and walked everywhere with her, pouring out my heart. I truly believed she could understand every word. I was an only child and both my parents worked – Mum for the local council, and Dad put in long hours as a welder – so, broadly, growing up in Hertford during the sixties and seventies was boring and lonely. It wasn't a bad childhood, but it wasn't exceptionally happy either. Sounds horrible to say that about my family life, but that's what it was.

My memories of early childhood are fragmentary and mundane. I walked to school on my own, so the lollipop lady is vivid in my mind, with her yellow coat and zebra-striped pole commanding the traffic to stop. I can remember once standing outside my grandparents' house with an umbrella, poking holes into fresh deep snow, and my mother saying, 'Don't do that, you'll hurt yourself.' I continued, and the next thing I knew the umbrella point had gone through my boot and blood speckled the white snow.

My one strong memory of that time is of being at home in Hertford with Mum, who was in such pain she couldn't stand up. She asked me to go to our neighbour's house and get her to call the doctor. Down the path I went to the house next door with my message. No one had a phone in those days, so the neighbour had to go down the road to the callbox. The doctor came and Mum was taken to hospital. She had her appendix removed. I don't remember being told what an important part I'd played, helping my mum, but I felt I had. I was three years old and liked the feeling of being important to my mum. Life quickly returned to normal and I don't remember feeling important to my mother again.

I can't recall doing anything with just my parents. Dad wasn't around very much. When he came home from work, he'd go straight off for a bath, then often to the pub. I'd ask him where he was going and his answer was always the same: 'To see a man about a dog.' I didn't buy that, and wanted to know what he was going to do that was more important than staying at home with me. I invented Samantha Piglet, and he went along with it – yes, he was going to see Samantha Piglet. She became my enemy and I hated her. I never went to him with questions or problems. Recently, when I asked Dad what he remembered of me as a child, he had just one story to tell: apparently I used to hang off the handle of the lawnmower while he cut the grass.

Without doubt the nicest childhood memories I have are all to do with my beloved grandparents. I was exceptionally close to my dad's mother, Edna May. She was a true lady, always impeccably dressed, and I never heard a bad word come out of her mouth. She was kind and generous about everyone – even when I didn't want her to be. My grandfather, Tom Henry Failes, treasured her. He was always making romantic gestures, even when they were in their seventies. If he'd been away working, or just out for the morning, he'd always come back with a little something: a bear attached to a chocolate heart, or flowers, perhaps. My nan would tut, roll her eyes and call him silly, but I know she loved it.

Tea at my grandparents' house meant a china teapot, cups and saucers, and cake on a pretty plate. We went to them nearly every Sunday, and often on outings with them to historic homes or gardens, the model village or, as a special treat, the beach at Brancaster, in Norfolk. We often went camping with them too, which meant that holidays, thanks to their presence, were peaceful, happy and enjoyable.

I always thought my grandparents were unbelievably rich. For one thing, they had a detached house. My grandfather had been a financial director at GK Lincoln Electrics, having worked his way up, and by the time I came along they had a lovely home in a hamlet called Bulls Green, near Bramfield, Hertford. It overlooked quiet countryside, and they had a big garden, which I loved. It was picture perfect, right down to the robin on the spade, the strawberries Granddad grew and the blossom-heavy apple and plum trees. I would walk with him down to the village shop and he would show me the birds' nests – I'm sure that's where my love of the outdoors comes from: I need to see green when I look out of my windows. It makes me feel safe.

The other reason I decided they must be rich was because of Cresta. You've got to go back a few years to remember this, but it was a drink with a bear on the front of the bottle. In the advert the bear said, 'It's frothy, man,' and there were lots of different flavours – cream soda, raspberry, cola, orange, blueberry, bubblegum, you name it. On Sundays beside the tea-tray there would be another filled with Cresta bottles, one of every flavour, and I could choose whichever I liked. They must be rich, I thought, if they can afford all those.

On the journey home I would watch the moon and talk to it as it followed me, then go to my room, look at it out of the window and tell it I'd got back safely. But I don't think home was where I wanted to be. I used to run away quite often, even when I was at primary school. I'd pack a bag and pedal off to my nan's. It would take me about three hours. Then my nan would put me and my bicycle into the car and Granddad would drive me home. They never asked why I'd run away and they never let me stay. They might buy me a bar of chocolate for the journey home, but that was all.

What was I running away from? I didn't really know. The loneliness probably. There wasn't much life in our house. There was very little laughter, and if there was love, I don't remember it. Neither Mum nor Dad was a cuddly kind of person. No, all life, laughter and love had been thrown into the bottom of a brown cardboard box and put on top of a wardrobe out of harm's way. Or so my mother hoped. After Debbie and I had found it, the box was moved. But I spent a lot of time in that house on my own so I looked for it everywhere. Even in places that were out of reach – like a cupboard in the eaves above the bed, which is where I finally found it. I snooped a lot, and over the years, I came across things in that box I didn't understand at first, and pieces of paper I couldn't read. It was a perfect puzzle for a bored little girl with an over-active imagination and it kept me guessing. Who was the slim lady in the photograph? Who were the two little boys she was with? Who was drinking Coca-Cola out of a bottle on a beach – and why was his photograph hidden above my mother's bed?

I couldn't ask any questions. In my house, as a child, I was very much seen and not heard. I was deeply envious of a girl at school called Marion who had a big family. Not only did she have a twin, Michael, she had older brothers, which I longed for. She had long blonde hair and I thought she was beautiful. She always had friends back at her house after school, but I couldn't do that because my mum wasn't there to watch us. My house was empty after school, empty and cold, but there was always something going on at Marion's. When I visited there were always lots of people around the table. At our house we'd sit down and eat together but it wasn't the same: it was quiet.

Sundays were particularly important to Dad. He'd go to the pub and be back at three o'clock for Sunday lunch. He was very strict about table manners and could be fairly sharp which made me nervous and eager to please, though he never raised his hand to me. Looking back, I can see why he was like that. His brother, Peter, was privately educated but my dad had preferred to stay at the local school. He used to say he hadn't been bright enough but I think it's possible he is dyslexic.

When he left, Dad started as an apprentice welder and worked his way up his trade, standing on his own two feet and never asking my grandparents for financial help. It made him a proud, reserved man, and the only way he knew how to deal with me was to treat me as if I was a boy.

Unfortunately for him, I wanted to be a ballerina. From the age of four, I loved ballet. I loved the music and disappearing into dance. My first teacher was a tall lady called Jean Clough. She was quite tough but I loved her. She saw potential in me and gave me solos in the school shows. I practised happily for hours – I wanted to be perfect in case one day my parents came to watch.

The only time I rushed home after school was on Thursdays to see *The Little House on the Prairie*. I wanted to live there, with all those children, running through that field of corn. Actually, I wanted to marry Michael Landon, blue dungarees and all. I've always said to my girlfriends, 'Have more than one child, if you can.' To me, it seems unfair just to have one: otherwise on the bus it's always Mum and Dad on one seat, then you on your own. Same in the car. I know everyone says brothers and sisters fight all the time but I wanted siblings to break the monotony, the silence, the intense boredom. I even invented a witch to make life a little more exciting. She lived in the toilet and if I wasn't in bed after flushing it by the count of four she'd get me. But I was the one doing the counting.

I had some fairly hideous jobs around the house. On Sundays I scraped and cleaned the whelks and cockles, and scrubbed and peeled the potatoes. Worst of all, I had to take the net curtains for their annual wash at the launderette. I'd literally heave because they were so yellow and smelt so disgusting – my dad smoked heavily then. I'd run over to the launderette, put the curtains into the machine, then run out again so no one saw me. I've no idea why I was so embarrassed by it – I didn't get that from my parents. My impression was that my parents weren't particularly house-proud and I was conscious of how uncared for it felt, especially compared to my nan's where everything was pretty, matching and in its place.

But at least I had Sally, and to this day I love dogs. When I was ten years old I came home from school and Sally wasn't at the black wrought-iron gate that Dad had made. She was always there – she seemed to have a sixth sense for when I was coming home. I knew something was wrong. I walked into the back garden calling her but still she didn't come. I went into the kitchen, where my uncle was putting in central heating. He told me my dog had been put down that morning. I was devastated. No one had warned me. Later I found out that Sally had had liver failure, but I resented my parents for not telling me and not giving me the chance to say goodbye.

Maybe that was why I set fire to the garage, though I can't remember thinking that at the time, or maybe I wanted my mum's attention. All I know is that I did it on purpose. I knew where the matches were – I knew where everything was in that house, even Mum and Dad's naughty 8mm cine films. How did I know they were naughty? Because I watched them. I worked out how to put the reels on the camera and project the image on the back of their bedroom door. Anyway, that day I had a lot of time on my hands, which was probably why I came up with the idea of starting a fire. I took the matches through the back door to the garage, where Dad had a workbench with bits and pieces on it and, I'm sure, a dangerous collection of flammable items. I found some rags and put them on the bench with some twigs from the garden and struck the match. The rags started smouldering, the twigs crackled a bit, then flared up. I didn't feel good about it, but I didn't put it out. In fact I went back a couple of times to check it was cooking nicely.

Luckily by then we'd had a phone put in so when the flames got big enough, I got scared and rang my mum. I told her there was a fire in the garage. She sent Grandma Jessop over to put it out. So my plan had failed. Nothing much had been damaged except that the fabric on a garden chair had melted. I told Grandma I'd been playing with matches and, strangely, Mum didn't beat me for this, even though her own mother was telling her I should be locked up. Instead I was hit for crimes that had been committed shortly before I was born – but I didn't know that when I was being chased up the stairs by my enraged mother with a slipper in her hand. Then I did what most children do: I blamed myself, told no one and tried hard to be better, quieter and hopefully disappear altogether.

I excelled in one thing: ballet. Eventually Jean Clough recommended I try for ballet school and I auditioned for a couple. I chose the Legat School of Ballet, which was a boarding-school in Crowborough. I was eleven and had no worries about leaving home. In fact, I couldn't wait. I'd be dancing all day and I was sure I'd make lots of friends.

However, it wasn't quite what I'd imagined. As soon as I got there I hated it. The school was a creepy old monastery. Each room was like a cell, with just enough room for a bed and a chair. On the first night, a girl said, 'There are four monks buried in that wall down there . . .' She pointed. 'There's one there, one there, one there . . . What's your name? . . . Right, Sheryl Failes, you're there. Right between two of the dead monks.'

The next morning I had to get up at six to do yoga. When we took our showers, the pipes were so old the water came out brown. The dining room was freezing.

The others were incredibly confident but I felt out of my depth. I was good at ballet, but they were good at singing and acting too. They had big personalities, and were used to making a noise and getting noticed. I was quiet, easily embarrassed, and sounded like a foghorn when I sang.

My nan had two sisters, Connie and Irene, and my great-aunt Irene lived down the road, so during my first and second terms I kept running away. She always sent me back with a box of mints, but she did tell my nan and father every time I turned up on her doorstep. One day near the end of the second term I must have appeared particularly despondent because Auntie Irene rang my nan, and she put pressure on my dad. My parents came to the school and, unseen by me, watched me through a window. Dad told me afterwards it was like watching a different child and he immediately said, 'Get her out of there.'

The headmaster told him I had the makings of a prima ballerina, so Dad asked if I could stay on as a day pupil. We went to a nearby village and looked in the window of an estate agency. Dad offered to move house, but I felt I wasn't nearly good enough. I left the school. For years I had daydreamed about being a ballerina, but after just two terms I returned home.

I was glad to leave the ballet school, but I've always regretted it too. I think I was embarrassed because I'd made a big move to a private arts school and it hadn't worked. Even though I'd only been there for two terms I felt like I no longer fitted in so to survive being back at a state school I went the other way and also gave up my beloved ballet. It took me a while to settle into the Simon Balle School. New start, new friends. But it was there that I discovered I was good at sport – swimming, netball, basketball, running. I did the lot and finally started to make friends.

I spent so much time imagining a different life. A perfect life. Inevitably, nothing could live up to my childish fantasy, and it wasn't just ballet school that was a disappointment. There was a woman who lived a few doors up the road. She was so glamorous, always so smart, in red suits, matching high-heeled shoes and a mac cinched in at the waist. Her hair was long, dark and wavy and her makeup was always immaculate. I watched her walk past our house to the bus stop every morning on her way to work, imagining her day, her life, and decided she was everything I wanted to be. One day we got on the bus together. I followed her upstairs, where she sat down and started to smoke. It completely shattered my illusion. She was so pristine, and the cigarette made her look ugly. I've always loved Grace Kelly, who was to me, like my grandmother, the epitome of elegance. I have never read a biography of her because I don't want to discover that she was like the woman on the bus. I want her to stay as perfect as she is in my mind. And that, I suppose, is my Achilles heel: I'm forever searching for an imagined perfect life.

*

To relieve the boredom of life at home and earn some money, I started working in a sweet shop on Saturdays and Sundays. I was fourteen and soon added two paper rounds. One was in the local hospital where, as well as delivering the papers, I ran a sideline. The old boys in their beds would ask me to get them fags from the shop. I did a roaring trade, and I found I liked earning money. I used to save up and buy something special every few weeks at the market on Saturday. It was always the five-pound T-shirt, never the two-for-one deal. I have my nan to thank for my fashion consciousness.

Then everything changed: I fell in love. As was often the case, I was at home on my own, staring out of the window at what was going on in the street. I often saw this blond guy walking to the shops with his dog, a golden retriever who was never on a lead. Plus he had a skateboard. One day, on my way home, I saw him with a boy who went to my school. We smiled at each other. The next day the boy at my school said, 'Ray Walkom wants to go out with you.'

As I didn't know the blond guy's name, I didn't know who he was talking about. I was with my friend, who nudged me. 'He's the boy with the dog,' she said. 'Go on, say yes.' So I did. Ridiculous, really. We were now going out with each other and we hadn't even spoken!

Soon after, Ray rang me to invite me to a party his sister was having at the community centre on the estate. He picked me up and walked me there. From that moment, we were glued together, best buds. Finally I had someone to love who loved me back. We were always at my house or his house, but usually mine because there we could be on our own. Ray and I would talk for hours and hours at the dining-room table in my house. He'd ride his bike with me sitting across the handlebars. We went camping with his parents at Mumbles in Wales. They were very happy times, and I could escape the monotony of home. If he'd said, 'Lie down in the road, the bus won't touch you', I'd have done it because I trusted him. When he was old enough, he got a blue Ford Cortina with a horn that played a tune and he'd play it every time he went past the sweet shop I continued to work in on Saturdays.

I can distinctly remember the first time he tried to tell me he loved me. He took ages building up to it, 'I've got something to tell you . . . Well, there's a song about it . . .' He started humming 'Love Is In The Air'. Then he told me he loved me. It was the first time anyone had ever said that to me. Even for young love's dream, we were exceptionally close. I told him everything – well, nearly everything: I didn't mention Mum's stinging 'wet hand', or the slipper, or her rages when she chased me up the stairs and pulled my hair, but I did tell him about the cardboard box.

I think having a proper boyfriend must have made me stronger, because one day I found the courage to ask my mum about the elegant slim lady in the photograph I'd found in the box. It intrigued me: she was carrying a boy in one arm and holding another boy's hand. They were standing in front of an American car and smiling. To my amazement Mum told me the elegant lady was her, and the boys were some children she used to look after in the States. I was astonished. My mother was nothing like the woman in the photograph. She was no longer slim or elegant – in fact she was unrecognizable as the same person.

I told her I'd seen another picture, of a boy drinking Coca-Cola on a beach: was he the same boy who was holding her hand? She confirmed that he was but she said nothing else.

I suspected there was more to it because some of the documents in the box had mentioned marriage and showed my mother's name, Cecilia Susan Jessop, and another name, Gaylord Bradford. I asked my eldest cousin Michelle about it but she couldn't shed any light. It wasn't until a year later, when I was fifteen, standing with my back to my mum, peeling potatoes at the kitchen sink, that she suddenly announced, 'I've got something to tell you. You have two brothers.' I guess it had got back to her that I'd been asking questions and she'd realized she had no option but to tell me. I think she would have preferred it to stay a secret, squirrelled away in a cardboard box.

'What do you mean?'

'I had two children.'

'What? Where do they live?'

'In America.'

I couldn't believe it. I'd always wanted an older brother. Now I had two and she'd kept them from me! I was livid. I told her I hated her. How could she do that to me? I had two brothers and I hadn't been able to grow up with them. I was furious, curious, upset and ecstatic all at the same time. I bombarded my mother with questions. She answered very few, but gradually a story emerged. She had met and married an American soldier who was posted to Britain after the war. His name was Gaylord Bradford, but everyone called him Brad. I was told that he drank and beat her up, so she left America with their two children and returned to England. But he wanted the boys back and, for reasons that I have never understood, she sent them to him.

I was horrified. What sort of woman sends her own children away? The only excuse I was offered was that things had been different back then. She had been living at home with her own single mum, earning very little money working in a pub, sharing a room with the boys. It had seemed that their father could offer them a better life in America. A drinker? A wife-beater? Would they really have had a better life? Then I discovered that Dad and Mum had started going out, that Dad had met the boys and so had my nan. I was told that the boys had started calling him 'Dad', but then my mum's sister, Mary, Debbie's mum, had told them that their real father was in America. The next time my dad tried to tell Gaylord Junior to do something, he refused, saying, 'You're not my dad.' My father had been prepared to bring them up as his own but now that changed, and Mum blamed Mary because she had to give them up. That was what she told me at the time, anyway, and no matter how many questions I had, I felt I could never ask them, but they never left me. They still haven't. What I do know is that all this happened because she was pregnant again – with me.

I was very angry and confused about it, especially when I found out they'd known about me all along. I got their address from the letters their stepmother had sent to mum shortly after the boys had been put on a flight back to the US. Luckily for me, fifteen years on they hadn't moved. I wrote to my brothers, introducing myself, in the hope that one day we would meet. When an envelope arrived from the States I was ecstatic and delved into a world of American football, graduations, proms – a whole lifetime in a jiffy bag. I poured over the pictures and imagined the time they would become real. They were two huge strapping men – *my* strapping brothers. But America was such a long way away. Nowadays it's easy to fly there but then it wasn't like that. I started to think I'd never meet them. In the meantime, at least I still had Ray. Our relationship had become even more intense, and when I was sixteen I lost my virginity to him. It wasn't like it is in romantic novels, or even in those juicy 8mm cine films, it was more like . . . 'Was that it?' I don't really remember the sex, but I remember the companionship. And it was nice.

One evening we were fiddling and fumbling on the sofa in my house, the two of us stripped to our underwear, when suddenly the front door opened. My dad had come home early from work. He went bananas. When I think about it my parents were lucky I hadn't lost it at the age of ten – I could have been getting up to anything in that house and they wouldn't have known about it. But Dad was a strong father figure, even if he was absent a lot of the time. I was never allowed to wear a short skirt. Once, jumping off the bus, I split my skirt right up the back. Dad looked me up and down. 'That the only way you can get a boy, is it?' I've always been aware of not looking tarty. Even in my twenties it wasn't allowed. I remember ironing a heavily Bananarama-influenced outfit, my makeup and hair already done. Then I walked past Dad and he did an Indian war whoop.

Anyway, that afternoon Ray and I grabbed our clothes, ran into the kitchen and realized too late that we had each other's jeans on. Dad never said a word, but I ran to my room and Ray went home. When Mum came home Dad told her, and she came upstairs to say she was disappointed in me. Then the two sets of parents got together and decided to stop us seeing each other. Banished to our teenage bedrooms, we weren't allowed even to speak to one another. As a protest, we both stopped eating.

Bravely Ray came to the house and stood under the window whistling. I opened the window and saw he'd written 'I love you' on the wall. He called up but it never crossed my mind to go down to him. My parents had said I couldn't see him, so I didn't. Thankfully, they soon relented, and the star-crossed lovers were back in one another's arms. I relied on him for friendship, love and, above all, trust.

I guess I put all of my eggs in Ray's basket. He left school that summer and started at plumbing college. A year later when I left, I started doing bits of modelling locally so Mum and Dad suggested I attend a two-week course at the London School of Modelling to boost my confidence. But the city scared me, and I was out of my depth again. I heard the word 'dyke' for the first time and made myself look stupid by not knowing what it meant. The school signed me to their agency. When they suggested to me that my name, Sheryl Failes, wasn't going to cut it I reinvented myself as Rikki Balmain, a mix of my dad and granddad's name. I wanted to do catwalk work but I wasn't getting any because I was a meagre five foot seven and in those days you had to be at least five nine and preferably five ten – it was Kate Moss who changed that. Then, when the first photographer spotted my pointy canines, he said, 'She's OK if you're shooting *Dracula*,' which told me I probably wasn't going to pull off a career as a model, there being few *Dracula*-themed shoots on offer.

Why did I attempt to go into modelling? It wasn't because I thought I was pretty. In fact, I'd found the course overwhelming. One day one of the relief managers at the sweet shop I worked in said to me, 'You're so pretty.'

'No, I'm not,' I replied.

'Yes, you are. Doesn't your dad tell you you're pretty?'

'No. I'd get a big head.'

'There's a big difference between getting a big head and receiving a compliment.'

That was news to me. Nan told me I was beautiful, but all nans say that sort of thing.

After I'd dropped modelling, I started working for Trust House Forte. I desperately wanted to be independent, to move out of my parents' home and in with Ray. We both worked hard to save enough money to rent a place together. I did shifts, and the late one was from three p.m. to eleven. When I got home, Ray would often be with my mum, waiting for me. One evening I came in and his car wasn't outside the house. That wasn't unusual, but I had a funny feeling that something wasn't right. I took Ben, the German shepherd that Ray and I had brought together, put him into the passenger seat of my ancient rusty yellow Austin 1100 with brown fluffy seats which had been given to me for my eighteenth – I called it the Mustard Pot – and drove to his parents' house. His car wasn't there, so I drove on to turn round in a nearby cul-de-sac which is where I saw his pale blue Cortina parked. But Ray was nowhere to be seen.

I started worrying that someone had beaten him up at the pub he'd started going to, the White Hart. I went to his mum's house. She presumed he was in bed but when we went upstairs he wasn't there. Suddenly I said, 'He's with someone else.' She denied it – there was no way, he adored me too much – but I just knew he was. I drove back down the cul-de-sac, stopped where his car was parked and hit the hooter. Nothing happened so I went home.

After a while Mum shouted, 'Ray's just pulled up.'

I ran downstairs and opened the kitchen door because he always came through the back gate. I said, 'You've been with someone else, haven't you?' He said yes. Right then my world shattered. Just shattered. I was yelling and screaming. My mum ran down. 'What on earth's going on?'

'He's slept with someone else!'

She turned to him. 'Is this true?'

'Yes.'

'Get out.'

He refused. 'Not until Sheryl tells me to leave.'

I was hysterical. Devastation isn't the word. He was every-thing to me but I told him to leave. He was crying and pleading, but finally he left. I went back upstairs and, for the first time in my life, I asked Mum if I could get into bed with her. My dad was doing contract work in Germany so we were on our own. I was in pieces, crying, saying over and over, 'I love you,' to my mum, but she never said it back to me. She never has. My world was totally shattered – Ray, Mum, my missing brothers. The whole empty meaninglessness broke me.

At seven the next morning I was back at work. I hadn't slept. My manageress, Hazel, took one look at me and asked me what was wrong. More tears. She tried to send me home but I wouldn't go. Then a big bouquet of flowers arrived from Ray, but I didn't even put them in a vase. When I got home he was waiting. I refused to let him in. Over the next few weeks he wrote letters. He said he was sorry, that he loved me so much. Everyone told me he loved me. And I wanted so much to believe him that I saw him so that he could explain himself. Gradually a story emerged. He told me that all he'd done was kiss some girl down at the pub. I suspected he wasn't telling me everything but I gave in. I loved him, he was my absolute everything and as far as I knew, he was the only person who really loved me, so I took him back, but I don't think I ever forgave him.

Even though we decided to buy a flat and get married, I grilled him for months. I asked him over and over again for all the details and, of course, found holes in the story. Then I'd go on and on again until he said, 'OK, I'll tell you the truth. She wasn't a young girl ...' It turned out she was older, a mum, and then that it had happened more than once. It was the continual stories that hurt me most. In hindsight I can't really blame him: he'd never been with anyone but me and an older woman was offering herself on a plate. It was just that my expectations were so phenomenally high. After four years I'd let my guard down and allowed myself to believe that I was worth loving. But Ray's infidelity confirmed my worst fears: I *wasn't* worth loving after all. Then again, I had a whole family in America who were waiting to meet me.

Before Ray's infidelity, Gaylord had invited the whole family to his wedding. He was to marry a girl called Renee. I was desperate to go, but Dad wouldn't let me, even though he was away working in Germany. I was angry and upset. I didn't understand how scary it might have been for Dad to know that his wife and daughter were disappearing to America. I might have understood it if he'd talked to me, but he never mentioned it. I just wasn't allowed to go and that was that, so my mother went to America to see my brothers, on her own. When Mum got back, all she said was that Renee was lovely, but she didn't stay in contact with her sons, which was another thing I couldn't understand.

After the Ray debacle I didn't want to work shifts any more and began to consider a career outside the hotel business. A friend of Ray's mum offered me work experience in her estate agency on my days off, just filing and that sort of thing. Her name was

Margaret and she would take me home for lunch with her on the days I helped out. She was a brilliant mother and I became quite close to her. By now, Ray and I had set a date for our wedding, which was not far away, and I had the dress, but suddenly, over lunch one day, I blurted out, 'I don't want to get married – I don't think I'm doing the right thing.'

Margaret wouldn't let me forget what I'd said, although only I knew how hurt I was by Ray's infidelity. I had been using the wedding plans to cover up the cracks in our relationship. It wasn't so much that he had messed around but that it had taken me so long to get the truth out of him. I made a big decision. I signed the flat over to him, took just under half of our savings and went to America to find my brothers.

2. Twenty-one Frozen Burgers

I landed in Los Angeles full of unbridled expectation, buzzing with excitement and nerves, but no one was at the airport to pick me up. I was supposed to be staying with my brother David and his wife, Nancy, who was pregnant. I was terribly disappointed not to see them standing at the barrier – and it was scary. I had to leave my luggage with someone while I rang them to find out where they were. It turned out they were expecting me to get to San Diego from LA and they told me to get on another flight or a train. I'd had no idea how far away San Diego was, and in the end they came to get me.

My first impressions on seeing David were that he was tall, handsome, and just like a big brother should be, and that he looked just like my mother. I watched him get out of the car and walk towards me and tried to take in the enormity of the moment. Here was my brother. A real, live brother. We hugged, and I wanted to envelop him, tell him his sister was finally here, the one he'd been waiting all his life to see – Oh, no! That was my little fantasy.

We went back to their house, talking all the way because we had a lifetime's worth of catching up to do. Later my older brother, Gaylord, turned up. He was completely gorgeous. He looked like Magnum with a great big moustache. We hit it off immediately. I learnt that his marriage to Renee had failed and he was now a single parent to my niece, Julia. Though he had custody of her, she lived with his dad, Brad, and stepmother, Pat. The next day we went to meet them at their beautiful ranch in El Cajon overlooking the Mexican mountains.

I was a bit nervous about meeting Brad. All I knew of him was that he had been a drinker who beat up my mum, but he was very pleasant to me. He'd married Pat after my mother left him. She was Scottish and had been working in the States as a nanny. A born-again Christian, she had taken on the boys and brought them up as her own. Now she was doing the same for Renee and Gaylord's eighteen-month-old daughter. For this and many other reasons I thought Pat was amazing.

David and Nancy welcomed me into their home, but I was aware that it was not the best time for me to be there, with Nancy pregnant. I was sleeping on the pull-down sofa in their lounge, which must have felt very intrusive to them. Luckily Pat and Brad invited me to go and stay with them instead, which suited everyone, so off I went to their ranch. Brad was a teetotaller now and pretty much kept himself to himself. Pat would make him a jug of iced tea and he'd watch TV in his bedroom. She had to go food shopping every day because he'd only give her a daily allowance even though he'd obviously done well for himself.

Pat and I got on brilliantly but there was a complication. She and Brad had a daughter. Her name was Vicki and neither of us was very impressed with the other. We were half-sisters to the same brothers, with nothing and everything in common. When she came over we circled one another, snarling quietly, neither knowing what to make of the other. I was jealous of her because she had grown up with my brothers, and she was jealous of me because she'd had to put up with them through her childhood while I slipped in as an adult, the prodigal sister returned.

It was soon clear to me that my mother's decision to send her sons back to the States had had an impact on everyone. Gaylord was wonderful but he had survived the trauma by putting Mum on a pedestal. I was so shocked – to me, she was anywhere but on a pedestal. He honestly believed his life would have been better if she'd brought him up. Pat had cared for all the kids and made the ranch a home – but Gaylord didn't want to hear that he hadn't missed out on a great mum.

I settled in pretty quickly, but California was very different from Hertford, and I was often reminded of the protected life I'd led in England. I met a woman one day when she came to visit Julia. Her beauty was undeniable but there was something wrong with her nose. Pat told me it was the side-effects of cocaine. Cocaine? What was that? Pat explained that it was a drug, but I couldn't understand how a drug could do that to her nose. Surely drugs were pills, or something you smoked. Pat told me what cocaine was and how you took it and it shocked me.

I was having a great time getting to know my brothers and had no intention of going home. Unfortunately US Immigration felt differently. I had overstayed my three-month visa, so Gaylord and I went to San Diego to plead for an extension. We got it and planned a trip to Big Bear Lake with Julia. We had a great time even though there were a few hairy moments when Gaylord, a diabetic, forgot to take his insulin. I enjoyed looking after Julia so when Pat and Brad decided to spend a weekend in Las Vegas I offered to take care of her so that they could have some time alone, which they'd never had before.

On the night they left for Vegas Vicki came over with her husband, Scott. I knew Gaylord didn't like him because he'd told me he was bad news. Julia was tucked up in bed and asleep. Somehow the evening ended in a fight between Scott and Gaylord, who was quite big. He said, 'Scott, don't hit me. I'm not going to hit you back, because if I do I'll kill you.' Scott hit him again and again, but Gaylord stuck to his word. That was when I learnt that in America you dialled 911 for the emergency services, not 999. Vicki was hysterical and begging Scott to stop, but he wouldn't. In the end the police and an ambulance arrived. Gaylord had a broken nose, but Scott got away without a scratch. Julia was still fast asleep in her bedroom.

Just after the ambulance had left with Gaylord in it, Pat rang and asked me if everything was OK. I said yes. They were a long way away and there was nothing they could have done about it and, anyway, it was all over. When they came back and found out about the fight they were so angry I hadn't told them the truth that they gave Gaylord enough money to put the two of us up in a hotel. A week later I still felt unwelcome so, after six life-changing months, I flew home.

All my childhood I had dreamt of having a different kind of family, with older brothers. Now this alternative family had become real. But real life is very different from an imagined one, and I had been a little shocked to discover that my American family was as flawed as any other. Having said that, when I left California I intended to go back, move in with Gaylord and get a job. So, as soon as I got home, I began plotting my return.

In America I'd learnt how independent I was. I'd been travelling on my own, then helping with Julia, and I'd gained confidence in myself. So now when my mother told me what to do, it rankled. I couldn't wait to get back to my brothers. Our relationship was completely independent of her and, more than that, I knew how they felt about having been abandoned, especially Gaylord. As far as I was concerned she had no right to tell me anything. There was only one thing for it: I would work hard and save my money for a one-way ticket to LA.

I got back in touch with Margaret, to whom I'd blurted out that I didn't want to marry Ray. She'd written to me while I was in the States warning me not to come home too soon. Apparently, Ray's family were angry that I'd ditched him just before the wedding and run off. I had clearly been black-listed, even though I hadn't left him out of pocket.

Margaret offered me a job as a trainee negotiator in her and Ron's estate agency. I liked the work – and socially things were looking up, thanks to my new-found confidence. I met a great guy called Mark Roe – I still know him well – when I was walking my dog, Ben, past the pub one evening. He invited me to join him and his friends for a drink. At the same time he introduced me to the notion of a group of friends hanging out together – I was nineteen, but this was a novelty. I traded in the car I had at the time, a Chevette, for a rebellious purple Capri automatic 1.1 with black stripes, and started to live a little.

It was while I was working for Margaret and Ron that I met Colin Kyle. He was a right Jack-the-lad, very flash, and drove a Triumph Stag. First time he took me out he said, 'Shall I come round with the roof up or down?' Frankly, I should have known then. He wore pale blue jeans, no socks, white loafers and a pink T-shirt – I thought, my dad's going to go mad. We went out but it was never serious: he had had loads of other girl-friends who weren't as naïve as I was. Colin would go out one evening and not come back till the next, but it didn't really bother me because I was hell-bent on getting back to America. We lasted about a year, by which time I was fed up with Colin and the property business.

I stopped working for Margaret and Ron and got a job in Shenley for an investment holdings company. It was a bit of a trip for me in my Capri, but I loved it. I was a receptionist in the most glamorous place I'd ever stepped into. Shenley Manor was a beautiful old building, whose reception area was bigger than my house. There was a helipad at the back and the boss had a sunken bath in his office. I just loved the reception desk. I loved being smart. I loved wearing heels. I had become the woman in the elegant suit I had watched on the bus as a child. I was in my element, watching the expensive cars pull up and welcoming in the well-heeled. The boss never went shopping: the shops came to him. Boxes and rails would disappear up the stairs to his office. It was a whole new world.

I was soon promoted to PR to the chairman, dealing more with corporate entertainment than the press. Basically, my job was to invite people to the amazing events we put on. It was the best job in the world. The company had a box at Brands Hatch, a box at Tottenham on the halfway line, a box at Ascot and another at Newmarket. Then my boss's son asked me out. He was a couple of years older than I was and his name was David. When he took me home to meet his mum, Maggie, I immediately adored her. She was the mum I wanted to be like if I ever had kids. Like my nan, she loved her boys and did everything for them, and like Pat, she made a home and was always there. She was glamorous and good fun, too. I idolized her and we got on really well.

After I'd been going out with David for a year he said he wanted us to get married. He bought me a ring and a house for us in North Weald. It was off-the-scale money – we took helicopters everywhere and started going to the races, incredible restaurants, Ronnie Scott's and on holiday to Marbella. For the first time, I knew what it was like to live the high life. And I loved it.

Then something happened.

On the Saturday of our engagement dinner at Ronnie Scott's we were summoned to David's father's office. I was a bit taken aback but when he said, 'Jump,' we jumped. I was worried he was unhappy with my work but that wasn't it. He said that when I had been at the house the previous weekend, I hadn't said goodbye to him properly. I apologized and told him it hadn't been intentional, but that didn't convince him. Apparently his other son's page-three girlfriend always made a fuss of him when they left. She was particularly gorgeous but, in my view, she was always kissing his arse, and I told him so. He got angry with me and raised his voice. All the while David stood by and never said a word.

After a year and a half, our relationship ended. David wasn't going to go against his father, and I wasn't the type to forgive a betrayal too readily. I handed in my resignation.

To nurse my wounds, I sold the Metro Turbo that David had given me, and went to a quiet area of Ibiza for a week with my friend Cheryl. It was the first time I'd been away with a girlfriend, and it was just what the doctor had ordered. We went clubbing once, but it wasn't really my thing. Mainly we focused on getting brown and sunbathed topless. Not that I had anything to roast: I was as flat as a pancake then.

We came back in time for Hertford Carnival. We thought we looked great because we were so brown, and pranced around showing off our tans. I bumped into Colin – I'd seen him once since our break-up when I was with David. He'd told me he'd spotted me driving one of David's family cars and had heard who I was going out with. 'It's all right for you, off in heli-copters, but I've crashed my car and I have to drive a Nissan Micra,' he'd said. At the carnival I told him I had sadly split up with David, and that my plan was to go back to America. He asked whether he could write to me there so I gave him the address.

At last I had enough money to buy a ticket to LA. One of the benefits of going out with David was that I'd managed to save all my earnings. He was incredibly generous and I'd never had to pay for anything. I told my parents I'd soon be off again.

A few days later I came home from work to find a letter on the dining-room table with my name on it. It was from my mother, and it was pages long. It said she didn't think I should be going to the States – 'I know I complain about the mess, but it's a mess I like to have around. Your career is here.' To me, it was too little, too late. I wasn't seeking her approval any more.

Mum and Dad took me to the airport to see me off properly this time. Dad took a step towards me to hug me goodbye, gulped, and suddenly he was running the other way. I asked Mum what I'd done wrong. 'Nothing,' she said. 'He's just worried you're not going to come back.'

As soon as she said that I burst into tears. After I'd gone through Passport Control I rushed to the nearest Ladies to try to calm down. But I couldn't. My father cared – did that mean he loved me? Two ladies outside the cubicle saw the state I was in and asked if I was okay. I couldn't speak. 'Have you left your boyfriend?'

Eventually I got the words out to reply. 'No, it's my dad . . . I didn't think he loved me, but he does. He's so upset – he thinks I'm not coming back.'

From that moment, my relationship with my dad changed. It had taken twenty years, but finally I knew he loved me and from then on I felt more confident with him. That was a huge moment in my life.

It was wonderful to be back on American soil but I was soon to get another mighty shock. Nearly two years had passed since I'd seen my brothers and Gaylord had changed beyond recognition – I walked past him in the airport. When he called my name, I turned and saw a frail, thin, gaunt man in front of me. I was too shocked to say anything.

A lot had happened to the family while I'd been at home. Scott had shown his true colours and he was in prison for a number of hideously violent crimes. Renee had disappeared, and David and Nancy had separated. However, every cloud has a silver lining, and mine was Vicki. Gaylord was living in a small rented apartment so he took me back to stay with Pat and Brad, who were, as ever, scooping up the kids. Vicki would drop her daughter Trisha at the ranch each day before she went to work at a bank. Between Julia and Trisha, Pat and I were kept pretty busy and I loved it. At the end of the day, Vicki would come to collect Trisha and we would talk. Once we started, we never stopped, and became firm friends – no, sisters.

She and I got on brilliantly. We'd go out and have the biggest blast. I hired a Chrysler Sebring convertible – it was the bee's knees, that car, and so were we when we were in it. I'd got it so wrong: all these years I'd been wanting a brother when actually it was a sister I'd been waiting for! Everyone said I looked like the Californian and she the English rose, with her fair skin and jet-black curly hair. I absolutely loved that girl. It was probably the best time in my life, I just remember laughing with her a lot.

When Vicki had cousins over from Scotland, we went out

with them one evening to a club she thought was cool. We were having fun and the manager came over to talk to us, he offered us a gold card so we could go back there whenever we wanted to. Vicki was blown away. Then some guy sent over cocktails. They were thick and creamy and delicious, and the barman told us they were Screaming Orgasms – we'd never heard of them before, and fell off our stools in hysterics. Then I said, 'Come on, let's dance.'

Suddenly Vicki stopped laughing. 'We can't dance together! Do you dance with your girlfriends in England?'

'Yeah – always.'

She was, like, 'No way! Everyone will think we're lesbians.'

So no dancing but at least we were allowed to go shopping together.

On the way home in my convertible we got pulled over by the police. I reassured Vicki that my British accent would get us out of trouble and promptly started talking like the Queen. They asked for my licence so I handed over my big green piece of paper.

'What's this? This isn't a licence!' They asked me if I'd had a drink. 'Well, we had a couple of Screaming Orgasms earlier.' Vicki was creasing up in the back. They asked me where I was going, so I told them we were a bit hungry. Did I know which way I should head? I pointed vaguely, and they offered to escort us to Taco Bell. Vicki laughed about that for years.

Since Vicki had got rid of Scott, she had met a new man called Tony Pota, who single-handedly renewed my faith in the opposite sex. He was Italian American, a landscape gardener with a nice house and a lovely temperament. They were living together – so happily that I began to believe that the elusive happy ending might even be possible for me. Colin had been writing to me since I'd arrived and sometimes went into work really early so he could call me. He even sent me flowers and taped messages with love songs. Might Colin be my Tony Pota? He certainly looked good on paper.

Pat asked me what I was doing in California when it was obvious that this boy back home really loved me and, as far as she was concerned, all the local bums were on drugs.

I listened to Pat, and seeing Vicki's happiness made me understand that I still hankered to be married and settled. I was secretly hoping that David would ring me to say sorry for letting his dad talk to me as he had, but he never did, and I suppose Colin started to seem like a plausible option. I wrote to Dad and said, 'I know you don't like Colin, but I'm going to come home and give it a go with him.' And I did just that.

I got a job as PA to the chairman of Ripmax Models – not the fashion kind, the remote-control variety – and when Colin asked me to marry him I said yes. No fireworks, no romance, no love's young dream – I'd had that, and it hadn't done me any favours – but it was a way out of home. And he was never anything but lovely to me. When I was married to him, he always looked after me, although he wasn't very good with money and always spent more than he had. He was a chancer, he was ambitious and he had aspirations, but I thought we'd be OK.

We got married in April 1986. Two weeks before the big day I'd discovered I was pregnant. I'd never consciously wanted children – I'd never had any contact with them until I met Julia – but I was pleased. We went on honeymoon in Thailand and when I got back I continued working at Ripmax Models until the baby was due. Married life was lovely. I said to my nan, 'This is the happiest I've ever been,' and I believed I meant it.

Bianca was born by Caesarean section and, ecstatic, I named her after my nan – Bianca Jade Edna May – although Nan didn't know that until the christening. When she heard the vicar say the baby's full name, Granddad had to hold her because he thought she was going to collapse. Bianca was a gorgeous, easy baby. I was in hospital for three weeks with painful complications but when we got home Colin proved to be a great dad. I had some role models to emulate in parenting now: my nan, Pat and Maggie, all of whom were women who had made a home in which everyone felt safe and welcome. That was what I set out to do. I knew who I didn't want to be like.

But appearances can be deceiving. To outsiders we were quite a glamorous couple: we had a lovely lifestyle and we could afford things many others could not. But we were also mortgaged to the hilt, not that I knew it at the time: Colin would pick up the post on the way to work, and I didn't know anything about our finances or try to find out. That was Colin's department. He told me we could afford this, that and the other, and I had no reason to doubt him. I thought we must be doing OK because one day he announced that he wanted to start up a company. He needed capital to do that. My parents were selling their house and they said they would downsize and lend Colin twenty thousand pounds to put into his new business, which they did.

Because I was married and not living with them, I'd become closer to them. Colin and I always looked after them – we took them out for meals and on holidays, and I guess they saw that money as an investment for me and my family. It was a very generous gesture.

Gradually, though, as Bianca grew into a toddler, I started to question how I felt about Colin, but I didn't want to know the answer. He said to me once, 'Did you really mean what you said to your nan, that you're the happiest you've ever been?' I could tell he was pleased that I was happy but I couldn't seem to hold on to that feeling. Colin would always say, 'I love you,' but as time went on I found it harder and harder to say it back. I wasn't sure of anything any more. Had I married him for the right reasons? What did I really like about him? He never went out on his own so I had no reason not to trust him. But something was slipping away from me.

I'd believed it when I'd told him I loved him before we got married, but as the chemistry between us waned so, it felt, did the love. He'd done nothing wrong, I just 'fell out of love' with him. I put that in inverted commas because now, looking back, I know that all he ever had been was a convenient way for me to escape my home. I'm not sure that I ever really loved him.

The lack of passion bothered me. I was so turned off, I thought I'd gone the other way. I disappeared into misleading romance novels, which made it hard for me to go on pretending to myself that I was madly in love. What I felt for Colin was nearer friendship. I was relieved when I read a sexy scene and started to feel a bit fruity. After that, on several occasions I had a word with myself and planned a sexy night at home, but when Colin walked through the door I'd go numb. I'd lie in bed hoping he wouldn't touch me. I must have knocked his confidence and I think what I really wanted him to do was grab me and make love to me. I wanted something big to happen. I wanted to feel how those women in the books felt. Ravished. Excited. Passionate. Loved.

We went away for Valentine's night – he'd booked a room in a nice hotel and arranged for Bianca to be looked after. After a few glasses of champagne he plucked up enough courage to kiss me. I willed myself to feel something, but it didn't work, so I did my wifely duty, and afterwards I lay there thinking, I really, really didn't want it to be like that. I cried silently in the dark, hoping Colin wouldn't notice. It was a very lonely and disconcerting place to be.

A while later I developed some dry patches on my arm and finally went to the doctor about them.

'Could you be pregnant?' he asked.

'No way – we've only had sex once in about eighteen months.'

'It only takes once!'

I was staggered. I couldn't be. I confessed there and then: 'I can't have another child. I want to leave my husband.' I hadn't fully admitted this to myself so it surprised me when I blurted it out – but it was true.

When the test came back positive I went to see the doctor again. I thought looking after two would be impossible on my own.

He said, 'But what difference will two make?'

We talked for a long time about all my options. Sexless marriages were not uncommon, I learnt, but I didn't want that for the rest of my life. Having deliberated briefly, I knew what I had to do. Keep the baby and give my marriage another go.

Mason was born on 6 October 1989, and when he was four weeks old we moved to Hoddesdon and bought a big house called Maplewood in a development called The Lynch set round a lake. There was a recession on so we got a good deal. I went round the show house and told the estate agent it was amazing but I didn't think we could afford it. He said, 'Well, if you don't put in an offer you won't know.'

I relayed this to Colin and we put in an offer we thought we could afford, which was accepted. With a new house, and a beautiful new baby, my family was complete. Maybe everything was going to work out.

Within months I knew I was kidding myself. I tried desperately to feel for Colin what he said he felt for me, but you can't manufacture love. Friends would say, 'What if you never find it? You look so happy together.' And it was true: we never rowed, we did 'look' happy together. But I wasn't happy because I was living a lie. It wasn't everything that I wanted. If you read enough books you come to believe that excitement is possible. I didn't love Colin nearly as much as I'd loved Ray. I suspected I would never love anyone else like that but I also knew I didn't want to live the rest of my life without the chance of finding passionate love.

And then something happened that gave me the courage to tell him. After twenty-five years together, my parents announced they were separating. They were going to sell their smaller house and get a place each. Dad didn't want a mortgage so he was looking for a studio flat, and Mum was happy to get a mortgage and buy a one-bedroom place. I admitted to them how unhappy I was and that I didn't want to wait until I was their age to divorce. Dad was worried that I was unsettled

31

because they were splitting up, but Mum already knew things weren't great because when I'd told her I was pregnant she'd said it was a bloody stupid thing to do in the circumstances. She should know.

For a few months Colin and I talked about the state of our marriage but didn't do anything concrete about it. We both knew it was over – it was just a question of timing: I was worried about telling my nan, there was all the stuff with Mum and Dad going on, and of course we had the children to think about, particularly Bianca, who was very close to Colin.

One night a group of us went out for a Chinese and Colin sat next to a woman called Mandy Dorney, who was there with her husband Mark. Colin was whispering into her ear and I knew he was telling her about us. Mark got drunk, went outside and slept in their car, and she got very giggly. I knew immediately that something was going to happen between her and Colin. I wasn't jealous – in fact, I was pleased. I had my out.

So Mum and Dad and Colin and I split. Bizarrely, for a short time, Dad and Colin shared a rented property while every-one sorted out the house sales. Dad was concerned because when Colin had the kids over they were allowed to do whatever they liked, so he told me to have a word with Colin. Dad had always been strict and he didn't like Bianca and Mason being out of control. But that's often the way with separated parents. Who wants to be the disciplinarian rather than the fun parent?

As soon as Colin moved out things began to change. He told me the children and I had to vacate our home because he couldn't afford the mortgage and he wanted to rent it out. We would have to move into something cheaper. I believed he was still thinking about the children – he had Bianca's school fees to worry about – so I agreed.

My lawyer said, 'Whatever you do, don't move out of the house.' But I didn't think it was going to help my kids to live in a house we couldn't afford, so I ignored his advice and left it. Colin said he was going to rent us a house in Hertford and found a place for £150 a month. It was pretty terrible – Dad wasn't impressed – but we painted the walls to cover the mould and moved in. At least we had somewhere to live, and Colin seemed to be supporting the kids and dealing with the split.

Then the landlord, who happened to be an old acquaintance from my estate-agency days, told me he'd sold the house we were renting, but as a favour to me, we could go on living there until the sale completed. It turned out that Colin had rented it on a month-by-month basis – it had remained on the market.

Meanwhile he'd found a family to cover the mortgage on our house in The Lynch. I don't know how they managed that because they couldn't afford electricity and everything was key-operated. The house soon fell into disrepair – there was even a broken window at the back. When I was told I had to leave the place we were renting I had nowhere to go to. At the same time Colin stopped giving me money for the kids. Very quickly the whole situation deteriorated badly, and the day came when I found myself sitting in the garden of the rented house, all packed up with nowhere to go. I couldn't afford a hotel and Mum and Dad no longer had a house.

Then I had a call from an old neighbour of mine. She told me our home in The Lynch was empty: the family renting it had done a runner. I rang my solicitor, who told me to get in there immediately and not to leave until I'd changed the locks. I had to break into my own house because when I contacted the letting office for the keys they wouldn't hand them over – they worked from an office above his.

I had been in contact with social services for a while, and I'd been told that if I could find somewhere to rent with the kids, they would pick up the bill. They also told me that if I'd stayed at The Lynch they would have taken over the mortgage. Now I was back at home they did. It was then that I discovered we were mortgaged to the hilt and always had been. A staggering

£2,000 a month was needed to cover the payments. We had never been able to afford that house.

After that, things went downhill even faster. Bianca, Mason and I had to live on sixty-three pounds a week income support. I took on any part-time job I could find: leaflet-dropping, which I could do while Bianca was at school and Mason in the pram, and bar work in the evenings, while Mum or Dad babysat. At weekends I looked after a show home, and again Mum and Dad helped out with the kids – it was sweet, actually: even though they'd split, they did it together.

Bianca was taken out of her school. I didn't discover this until the school sent me a letter during the holidays. She was placed in the only school that would take her at the last minute: a poor-performing state school that no one wanted their kids to go to. She went from learning French to cutting pictures out of a catalogue and sticking them into an exercise book.

After that, Colin and I communicated through his accountant. At my lowest points I rang her because I didn't have enough money to feed the children. She told me that he had left three weeks' worth of food for the children in the garage. True to his word he had kindly left twenty-one individually boxed portions of frozen burgers and chips.

At least I still had a car, a blue Escort Cabriolet. I'd moved on from stripes and fluffy bits: this car had a phone in it. A huge one. Colin kept asking to have the car back, but I needed it to get Bianca to school.

Although things were tough for me, Bianca was still having a lovely time when she saw her dad. They went on special trips to the zoo, parks, and he bought her a beloved talking teddy bear. Meanwhile I had no money to spare and was always conscious of running out. My parents helped when they could, but they were still owed the £20,000 they had lent Colin. They never got a penny of it back.

Soon afterwards, Colin declared himself bankrupt. Then he opened an estate agency called Mason's. I told him to his face that a sign over a door wouldn't make up for his son not having enough food. I didn't regret leaving him, but I do regret the effect it had on the children. It might have been my fault that our marriage collapsed, but it certainly wasn't *theirs*. When I suggested splitting up I never believed for a second that it would end as painfully as it did. I am truly sorry for the trauma the children went through, especially Bianca, more so because I know how common it is for children to be caught up in the crossfire. However angry the adults might feel, this shouldn't be the case. Everybody suffered.

I was in a desperate situation. But unbeknownst to me a tearful knight in a Tottenham Hotspur strip was on his way to Hoddesdon.

3. Pants on Fire

One evening in 1990 I went with a friend called Wendy to a special shopping evening at a local children's boutique. Mum had agreed to babysit. On the way back we decided to go for a drink in a new bar in Hoddesdon. When we walked in Mark Dorney was at the bar with another couple of guys. They sweetly offered us a glass of champagne. I hadn't been out for so long, it made a lovely change from sitting at home watching TV – so when I was offered a refill, I said yes.

A group of people in a corner were making a right racket – someone was standing on the table. Someone mentioned they were Tottenham players. But that was lost on me. I never watched football, didn't know any teams, and Colin wasn't much of a fan. Mason was only ten months old, too young to be showing an interest in the beautiful game.

The Tottenham crowd got louder and louder. Someone at the bar said, 'Look, there's Gazza.'

I said, 'Who?' I must have been one of the few people who didn't know who he was. The 1990 World Cup had passed me by – I was too busy being evicted with two small kids to settle down in front of the telly with a cold beer to watch it. I know now that it is generally agreed that Paul Gascoigne, as he was known before that World Cup, played better than any Englishman had in the past twenty years. He slipped, got up and went on playing. He got round defences that seemed impenetrable. The Geordie boy wowed the crowd, and Bobby Robson was congratulated for taking on a relatively unknown player. He seemed to be everywhere on the pitch, all the time, giving England hope that they might finally win the mighty prize. That year he'd made the front page of the newspapers for having cried his eyes out at the 1990 semi-final between England and Germany.

'Gazza' went to the toilet a few times and was bumping into everything. People were asking him for his autograph and when he next walked past me, he said, 'What about you? Do you want me to sign something?'

'It's OK, thanks. My boy's too young and my daughter isn't into football.'

'What about you? Do you want one?'

'No, you're all right, thanks.' Who does he think he is? I wondered. The next time he went to the toilet he bumped into me semi on purpose. Then he came up to me, took my hand, pressed a scrap of paper into the palm and said, 'There's my number. Give me a call, leave me yours.' He was pissed but, then, they all were.

When he'd left me I looked at the paper. It said 'Gazza' on one side and 'Paul Gascoigne' on the other. I've often thought about that. Gazza on one side, Paul Gascoigne on the other: it's pretty much all you need to know about what happened next. I told myself I didn't know who he was, but I didn't throw the piece of paper away. If some hideous drunken oaf had bumped into me and my girlfriend in a bar, held my hand in their sweaty paw and forced their number into my hand, I would have scrunched it up and put it in the ashtray. But I didn't. I put it into my bag and kept it.

We left the pub and got into my car, laughing. I'd had a great night. I really shouldn't have been driving, even though it was just round the corner and while I was turning round in the church car park as a joke we punched in the numbers on my giant car phone. Paul was still in the pub and wouldn't pick up. We listened to it ring, and then it went to answerphone. There wasn't a message, or his voice, it just suddenly beeped. Wendy shouted my number into the phone and only when she had bellowed the last digit down the line did I end the call.

The next day I felt very embarrassed and very hungover, turned my phone off and tried to forget what I'd done. I didn't want him to think I was the sort of woman to call up any man. I didn't do that kind of thing normally. And, anyway, I had enough on my plate to worry about.

Three weeks later my mum was completing on her new flat and I had offered to give her a hand moving stuff in. In the car, I turned my phone on – it had been switched off all that time – and it rang almost immediately.

'Oh, my God,' said a voice with a Geordie accent, 'you are the hardest woman in the world to get hold of.'

I nearly died. It couldn't possibly be ... But it was. Paul started chatting away as if we were old mates. Despite my shock and acute embarrassment, he was easy to talk to. Mason was making noises in the back, which Paul could hear. 'Is that your baby?'

'Yeah, he's just turned one. I've split from my husband but I'm not divorced. I've also got a four-year-old daughter.' That would put him off, I thought.

'I like a challenge,' he said, then told me he loved kids. Later he told me he'd tried my number every day for three weeks. I was very flattered. We chatted for a while, and I remember I laughed a lot, he had a funny way of putting things.

'When can you come out? I can do any time, any night – I never go anywhere. I just have to see you. I can get my driver to pick you up ...'

A driver to pick me up? I wasn't sure. But he wasn't going to take no for an answer.

'You think I'm going to let you go after waiting to speak to you for three weeks?'

After talking it over with a friend, I agreed to meet him. What harm could a drink do? I let his driver pick me up from a pub that was near his house because at that point I didn't want him to know where I lived. I was nervous because it was a first date, not because I was about to have dinner with Paul Gascoigne the footballer. I honestly didn't know what a big deal the 'Gazza' thing had become.

We went to collect him from some television studio. He came out smiling, in high spirits, and immediately started laying on the charm. Compliments first, then a bit of piss-taking. 'You're more beautiful than I remembered,' he said, gazing into my eyes, 'you're gorgeous,' and then he was taking the mickey. 'You're far too beautiful to be a woman.' My dad takes the piss a lot, it's a language I understand, but I wasn't so sure of the compliment. He certainly made me laugh, though.

He took me to the Swallow International Hotel on the Brompton Road, near Harrods, where he had a suite. As soon as we sat down he went straight into all these tricks with matches and napkins and making things disappear. We drank Laurent Perrier rosé champagne and had something to eat. I loved it – he was so funny, the food was amazing and everything was great. He asked me to stay the night, but I had responsibilities and had to get home. Even if I'd wanted to stay, I couldn't. He insisted on driving me back to the pub where his driver had picked me up.

In the pub car park he leant across to me and we shared the first of some seriously magical kisses. It was like somebody had set fire to me. One kiss stirred everything up. Emotions, feelings and the rest ... I was so relieved everything was still working because I'd begun to wonder. He got very excited which got a bit much for me and I tried to get out of the car, but he said, quite openly, that he didn't mind coming in the car. That was all very new to me. I'd gone from feeling dead down below, laying my hopes on the stuff of romantic novels, and suddenly here was this red-blooded lusty man just bursting for me. That 'wow' feeling I'd been searching for landed in my lap. My pants were on fire, and I was thinking, Oh, my God, what now?

From that evening he rang me a lot. He'd invite me places but often I couldn't go. Once he rang me when I was on my way out to the theatre. He asked me who I was going with.

I told him it wasn't a date, just an old boss who'd remained a friend and had a spare ticket. Immediately Paul told me not to go. *He* wanted to take me to the theatre. I was so flattered: how lovely it was that he didn't want me going with anyone else because he really, really liked me. He was in Newcastle, at the Dunston working men's club with his dad, and called at regular intervals throughout the early part of the evening from the payphone. 'I'm getting obsessed with you,' he said. 'I get like this – I've got to talk to you all the time.'

I was happy he was missing me so much, and happy to be so important to someone that he wanted to talk to me all the time. He had unleashed something in me that I wanted more of. I was happy, too, that he wanted me as much as I wanted him. 'I've told my dad you're going out and I don't want you to, and he thinks you shouldn't go either. I just want to talk to you.' So guess what? I didn't go to the theatre that night.

After our second date, I didn't make it home. We went back to his house in Clyde Road, Dobbs Weir. It had a pillared door, but it wasn't grand or large – nothing like the footballers' homes you see in *Hello!* today, but the wages weren't the same either. It lacked a woman's touch, but the man was clearly house-proud. On one side of the sitting-room fireplace there was a big porcelain tiger with a Fry's Turkish Delight in its mouth, and another prowled by the window. The kitchen was in a bit of a state. A radiator hung off the wall, there were holes in the cabinets and a door off its hinge.

He told me an ex-girlfriend had been hard but mad. He said she'd taken a knife to him, that she'd punched him, that they'd had big fights. He admitted he'd been very jealous of her and made her change her clothes if he didn't think they were appropriate. I didn't think anything of it. He told me she was a bit unstable, and I believed him: here was a man who gave me a coaster when he handed me a drink – why would he pull a door off a cupboard?

After he'd given me a tour of the house, he led me back to the sitting room, pulled me on to the lime-green sofa and started kissing me. It was amazing, obliterating, passionate, and more than I'd ever dreamt of. I also felt totally vindicated: passion did exist and was worth holding out for. I had been right to leave Colin and end my marriage. I had been right not to settle for a half-life. When sex is that good, you want more. It's the kind of sex that blots out anything else.

After our third date he bought me a box of Roses chocolates and put a single cross on the tag. One kiss. 'I've only put that kiss on so you can't sell the tag.' I had no idea what he meant, but I knew there'd been a few kiss-and-tell stories about him in the papers.

After that we fell into a pattern. We'd go out for something to eat, then back to his house or, more often, to one of the two hotels he flitted between, either the Swallow International in London or the one in Waltham Abbey. After that first time we rarely went to his house – in fact, he never seemed to be there, always preferring a hotel.

The hotels were fun for me, new and exciting: I was a single mother of two on income support so it was hard to turn down a night of wild passion in a five-star hotel with a couple of bottles of champagne. Sometimes we'd arrive at the room and there'd be empty Laurent Perrier bottles outside awaiting collection. But that was just Paul, his lifestyle. He was earning a lot of money from sponsorship deals, had his photo taken everywhere, had been voted Sports Personality of the Year and had even planted a tree. The pièce de résistance was probably reaching number two in the charts with 'Fog On The Tyne'. 'Gazza' was a household name.

I was only seeing him every now and then so when I heard rumours I began to wonder. A story was printed about Paul being out with a 'mystery woman' with whom he had been seen eating chicken wings. He called me and said she was his sister. I wasn't convinced. By now people were 'helpfully' telling me that the guy I was seeing was also seeing other girls. He could be very persuasive: he called again and told me to watch the news. There he was at the unveiling of his statue in Madame Tussaud's. Live on telly he dismissed the mystery woman as his sister. It was hard not to believe him.

But sometimes even an act like that couldn't get him out of trouble. The bottom line was that I knew I wasn't the only girl he had on the go. One day curiosity got the better of me and I had a look in the bag he guarded so carefully. I had no right to do that, but I did it anyway. During my childhood I'd become a pretty good snooper – it was the only way I ever managed to get to the truth of anything. I was looking for evidence that he couldn't be trusted. And I found it. He had a big leather folder that contained the business cards people gave him, and signed photographs of girls like Daniella Westbrook, and Donna the Dart from *The Golden Shot*. I'd find short, vulgar poems too. Once I confronted him and he laughed – he thought it was funny that I'd gone through his stuff. It wasn't, though. It was terrible of me to do it and I was stupid not to act on what I'd known I'd find.

'I can't help it if they're sending things to me. It's not me, it's them. I don't want to know,' he'd say.

'But why would you keep it?' I'd ask. As usual he'd laugh it off. It didn't mean anything.

But if that was so, why did he keep stashing those things and why did I keep snooping? Once I found a picture of a girl from a Nivea ad and he told me she was trying to contact him. Months later I was shocked to discover it had been the other way round. Another time we bumped into a famous TV presenter. Immediately Paul ignored me and flirted with her, kisses all round, hugs and chat, then afterwards he bragged about how she had begged him for sex. I know now that that was nonsense and much more likely the other way round. Anyway, Paul would never have lasted to the begging stage. He'd have said yes immediately.

One minute I was everything, the next nothing. The phone would go quiet for more than a few days and I would begin to worry. When he called I would try not to sound relieved. After a while I started playing him at his own game: when he called, I wouldn't pick up the phone or return his call. Then the dynamics would change: suddenly the phone would be ringing off the hook and he would leave messages, desperate to talk to me, full of apologies and excuses.

After a while, when he'd suffered enough, I would relent. When I called him back he'd insist in his charismatic way that he'd just been too busy to make contact. Things had calmed down and he was really looking forward to seeing me again, the sooner the better. Suddenly, seeing me was the only thing that mattered to him. He *was* busy, I couldn't argue with that. He was also very convincing.

Colin and I were still tussling over Bianca. Whenever she went to see him he would tell her what a great time she'd have if she lived with him. He said he wanted both children, but I was never convinced that he did. And I would never have agreed to him having custody of them, which he well knew. Once when Bianca returned from staying with him she'd cut off a great chunk of her hair. I was in hospital having my wisdom teeth out and she came to see me after my operation. The first thing I noticed were these tufts sticking up. I asked where her dad had been when she'd done it. 'I don't know,' she replied. She revealed there was often a woman called Jill in the house. I knew he'd been seeing lots of girls since we'd split up – and good luck to him, I didn't mind – but if there was going to be a girlfriend who would be around the kids, I wanted to meet her. Colin arranged for this to happen and I liked her. But she wasn't around for long because things between Colin and Mandy were getting more serious. I'd been right that evening in the Chinese restaurant.

In the meantime, Paul was being incredibly generous. He was

interested in the predicament I was in, living off sixty-three pounds a week must have seemed laughable to him. His life was so different, but I think he knew what it was like to have so little, because he started turning up with bags of Marks and Spencer's food for us. For that I will always be grateful.

A couple of months after I'd met Paul, Maggie, my near-miss mother-in-law, called. She knew I'd left my husband, and her son, my ex-fiancé David, had also separated and wanted to get back in touch. He started calling me again. I didn't see him immediately, just chatted on the phone, and he didn't push it. He was a gentleman and I think he realized he had some ground to make up with me because he hadn't stood up to his dad that day. But it was clear he was interested in making up that ground.

We met up for dinner and I went through a rather odd patch. On the one hand there was this polite, groomed gentleman who wanted more but was holding back, and on the other, there was this fast-talking footballer who didn't know how to hold back and gave only what he wanted when he wanted to and nothing more. I had no sex with David, and mind-blowingly brilliant, can't-get-enough-of-it sex with Paul. At last I had met the man in the novels I'd read: Paul was offering all the passion and the romantic gestures that meant so much to me. I liked David, but I found it harder and harder to accept his invitations to dinner and kept cancelling on him. So one day, lying on the floor in my bedroom, I told him over the phone that I was sorry but I had feelings for someone else.

Mad, mad, mad. Here was a good man offering me everything. He'd take on the children, he could support us all, and I would have been able to remove Bianca from that terrible school. David was stable. He was safe. I knew he loved me and he was one person I trusted. But I didn't feel for him what I now felt for Paul, weak at the knees with butterflies in my stomach. He said, 'Is it Paul Gascoigne?' His dad had a box on the centre line of Tottenham, so I guess he'd heard something.

I told him it was and immediately added that I had no idea whether it would go anywhere, or even continue in the sporadic form it had taken so far, but while I was consumed with thoughts of Paul, there was no room for anyone else.

I was really falling for Paul and found it increasingly difficult to accept that he was seeing other women. By now I knew I wasn't the only one in his life: there were too many 'mystery women' for him to pass off as his sister. He was having a brilliant season playing for Spurs, taking, or some say 'dragging', them to the FA Cup Final by scoring what is now a famous free kick in the semi-final against Arsenal. He was Gazza the football god – and I was a single mother on benefit from Hertford. You do the maths. I'm not stupid: I knew I was lining myself up to be shattered again, and even more so now because I wanted desperately to be the only one and not one of many, although that was pretty unlikely. In the past year he had put food on my table, helped me out with transport and played with my kids more than their own father had. He'd become a hero to me. Not Gazza. Paul. A lovely guy who made my heart sing and set my pants on fire. But he wasn't mine. Far from it.

However, Paul hadn't been playing football since his danger-ous challenge on Gary Charles in the FA Cup Final in July. He would have been sent off, but was carried off on a stretcher. He was still recovering from three operations on his cruciate ligament, one of which was filmed. Not playing meant no training so Paul had probably been partying quite hard that autumn, which sort of explained his irregular calls and long absences.

It was easy for him to live the high life: he had the money for it and plenty of people to do it with him. In fact, his knee's recovery was set back by an injury from a stunt he pulled at a nightclub. I wasn't with him but I visited him in hospital. He had bought me two tickets for the ballet and asked me to pop in on the way home. I left Mum in the car, went up to his room and sensed that I wasn't the only girl who'd been in. I was embarrassed asking for him at the nurses' station . . . There goes another mug. He was in bed with his leg in traction, but that didn't stop him wanting sex. A little light relief. I got on to the bed and lay next to him but I wasn't going to do anything – I was worried the nurses would come in. It was only a short visit because my mum was downstairs, but a quickie would have done him.

I was so in love with him, and so scared of getting hurt that for the half-term break in October 1991 I decided to back off. My parents, bless them, paid for me and the kids to go with them and my grandparents to Mallorca on holiday. We had a lovely time and I began to get a little perspective. For about a year I had been at Paul's beck and call – cancelling that theatre trip had been just the beginning – and had gone through a lot of hurt and disappointment. While I was away in Mallorca I was unreachable. I *couldn't* pick up the phone and I *couldn't* call him back. I believed I was protecting myself. I was also testing Paul. I knew what he was like during the few hours or days when I didn't pick up the phone.

When I got home I looked at the answerphone. It was chock-a-block with messages. It rewound for ages then finally started to play.

'Pick up, it's Gazza.'

'Call me back.'

'Where are you?'

Then he got stroppy and threatened to come to the house to talk to me. 'This is the last message.' Then another and another and another. I listened to them all with growing excitement. It was going to be OK. He did like me after all. I finally called him back and told him I'd been away. He was quite upset. He said he'd hated not being able to get in touch with me. I didn't tell him I didn't want to see him any more if he kept going out with other girls because I had too much pride for that, so I tried to be blasé. You're busy, well, I'm busy too. He didn't want me to be busy without him any more. But he was allowed to do as he liked.

On 29 October 1991 it was Bianca's fifth birthday and we had a party at home with an entertainer. It was nearly a year after I'd met Paul. Colin was invited, Mum and Dad were there, friends, neighbours and my grandparents. Suddenly my dad pulled me into the dining room. 'Why is Paul Gascoigne leaving messages on your answerphone?' I told him to ignore it. 'But he's saying if you don't pick up he's going to come round.' I told him it was a bluff.

When everyone had finally left, except my parents who were helping me clear up, the doorbell rang. Dad went to answer it. He came to fetch me. 'I thought you said he wouldn't turn up.'

Paul was standing on the doorstep. I don't know why but his toe was bandaged and he told me he shouldn't have been behind a steering-wheel. Somehow he'd driven someone's car round. He said, 'I want to talk to you.'

I told my dad I was just nipping out and we went and sat in the car. He started crying. 'I can't do this,' he said. All I could think was how much I must mean to him for him to be in tears. 'I can't live without speaking to you.'

I felt bold enough to tell him I didn't want to be one of many. I told him I was falling for him and I was afraid of being hurt.

'I've sacrificed my leg driving round here. That's how important you are to me. I want you to be my girlfriend.'

It was a pivotal moment. He knew he had to calm down. His love of the night-life was jeopardizing his career, but football meant everything to him and I guess he needed an anchor. So we became proper girlfriend and boyfriend and the dancing on tables stopped. At least, it did when I was around. From then on he started living a very ordinary life with us at home, doing physio and trying to get back into shape.

After we'd had that conversation in the car, did I walk back into the house and announce I was going out with Paul Gascoigne like it was a big thing? If I'd been going out with Pierce Brosnan I might have done. But no, not Paul. His superstar football status didn't mean to me what it meant to others. It never did. It only ever got in the way. I didn't see it as the very big thing everybody else did, though Paul swears that the first time Bianca saw him, she said, 'Mum, what's Gazza doing in our house?' All I knew was that I'd met a man who fired me up and he said he felt the same about me. I loved his unfailing attention when he was with me, always clasping my hand and holding me close. I had fallen for his eyes, his curly lashes, his crooked smile, his wicked sense of humour, his devilment and, weirdly, the back of his neck. Was I important to him? Had he meant what he'd said? I wanted to believe he had. So I did. Simple, really. We were a couple, I was going to be 'happy ever after' and that was that. Fantastic.

4. Who's the Daddy?

Paul was a hero in many different ways. I no longer had the car, so Bianca had to do this long walk up an extremely steep hill to get to school. It was fine for me – I was trying to get rid of the baby weight and pushing Mason up it worked wonders – but it was exhausting for a four-year-old. Then my dad moved in with me. He could walk to work from where we lived along the canal, which meant I could use his car. But then Paul lent me his black Mercedes, top of the range. It was a bit embarrassing because everyone knew it was his. Then he bought me a white Fiesta from a fellow player's girlfriend.

He never moved in, but he was with us all the time. Mason worshipped him, they became great mates, and when he said, 'Dada,' he meant Paul. For a while everything was perfect. Then one of the neighbours told us that a guy was sitting in a van with the windows blacked out and occasionally winding one down to stick his lens out. It was too late. He had snapped Paul coming to and leaving our house. It made the papers. Why was I surprised? Paul had always rung me when he'd been caught with a girl to tell me it was nothing, she was his sister, a friend, the press were bastards and had set him up – a different version of the same lie. I waited for the denial. But this time he set them straight. Yes, Paul Gascoigne and a nearly divorced mother of two living on benefits were now an item. After that it seemed as though the whole world was looking at me.

The press descended on our doorstep, or so it felt to me. The Lynch was a perfect setting for them: they could sit by the lake and wait for me to leave the house. They left a right mess – pizza boxes, discarded coffee cups, chocolate wrappers. People complained because they couldn't get in or out of the cul-de-sac. Only days after Paul had made his announcement about me, I was due to go to a christening. My dad thought I was mad to go but there was no way I could let my friends Jill and Kevin Lake down. It was my godson's brother's christening.

'How are you planning to get there?' he asked.

'I'm just going to go outside and get into the car.' But Dad had bad knees at the time and was worried he'd get wound up, be unable to control his temper and go for them with his stick. As soon as I stepped out of my house they went bananas. I remember the pictures – I had curly hair and looked really startled. I'd thought I could just walk out, be snapped a few times, then drive off. I hadn't expected to be completely over-whelmed. But there was a pay-off. There was no more skulking around with Paul. Now he took me everywhere with him. Out and proud. We could go wherever we wanted together with whoever we wanted. It was often Linda Lusardi and her husband Terry Bailey, or Terry and Kim Harvey.

Whenever we went out Paul was always up to no good, always messing about, but it was mostly cheeky rather than anything else. One of our regular haunts was Mr Chow, in Knightsbridge, and he often clowned around in there, doing shots with everyone. He always had to be the one sailing closest to the wind. We had a barbecue one afternoon and Paul turned up with a chocolate liqueur and plied us with it. I was ill, but he liked it because it tasted like milkshake. I remember him saying, 'Why doesn't alcohol taste like Coca-Cola?' If it did he could have drunk it faster.

One day we were sitting at home, watching TV and eating ice-cream. All of a sudden Paul screamed, jumped up and shouted, 'Sheryl, help me!' He ran into the kitchen and threw his ice-cream into the sink. He was gasping for air, sobbing and screaming – terrified. I tried to hold him – I had no idea what was going on. Eventually he went dead quiet. I asked him what was wrong, but all he could say was that he was having a bad turn. It happened when he was happy and all was well. Suddenly he'd panic that it was going to end. A question hung over his head: what would happen to him when he was dead? I realized he had a terrible fear of everything ending. Death terrified him.

I'd begun to notice he also twitched a lot. His head and shoulders were always twitching and at some point he started clearing his throat too, very noisily. It was almost like a retch but deep in his throat. When I heard that noise from the loo, I thought it was more of the same, but then I started to suspect Paul was making himself sick. One evening at The Lynch, it was confirmed. After we'd eaten a big Chinese takeaway, I saw seaweed floating in the toilet bowl. Finally he confessed that he'd been bulimic for some time and it had wreaked havoc on his digestive system, so he'd started taking laxatives as well. The bulimia ruined his teeth and up till very recently he'd often have sores on his knuckles from ramming his hand down his throat as it got harder and harder to cause the reflex needed to vomit. I felt sorry for him and naturally wondered what it was all about. But he rarely spoke about his family or childhood, so I had no idea what the source of his anxiety was.

After he'd had a bad turn he'd calm down eventually and we'd just hug on the sofa. During one of those long cuddles *Ghost* was on the television and we watched it together – it was shortly before he moved to Italy to play for Lazio, and the theme tune 'Unchained Melody' by the Righteous Brothers became our song. If we were out and there was a pianist, he'd ask them to play it.

In the New Year he took me to meet his family. It was a Sunday and we'd been out the night before. I got up, did my hair and felt I looked all right, but I was only wearing jeans. He looked me up and down. 'You going like that?' he said. Immediately I was apologetic. Did I look a mess? What should I wear? He said, 'You're going to meet my family.' Clearly I didn't look nice enough for his family, so I changed. It hurt me. My hair – long, loose curls – looked the same as it had the night before. But obviously something was different. He was very stressed. There was a big hoo-ha about getting there – the train times didn't work – so I suggested flying, but he didn't want to do that. We ended up driving all the way to Newcastle. It wasn't a relaxed journey. I was nervous about meeting them: I knew they'd been introduced to some of his other girls and I wanted them to be pleased that he'd chosen me over them. I wanted so much to be accepted.

I had met his sister Anna before – she'd been living at his house while rehearsing for a big audition in *Phantom of the Opera* the previous year. Whenever Paul spoke to her I was desperate to know whether she'd got the part but he shut me up. I felt stupid for asking, as if I was intruding.

That first time we went to Dunston together Paul's family had a new St Bernard puppy. Paul went outside to pose with it for the photographers who had found out somehow that we were in Newcastle. When he came back he went off with his brother, Carl, and I was left with Carol, his mum, and his other sister, Lindsay. I wish I could say we fell into easy chat, but we didn't. Conversation didn't flow, but the drinks did, and that made it easier all round.

Later on we went to the Dunston Excelsior, the working men's club, where his dad spent most of his time. Women weren't allowed in the bar. There was a women's room, not nearly as nice as the men's area – torn linoleum, plastic tables, a dartboard, that sort of thing. There was a lot of 'soft southerner' talk but I tried hard not to it let it get to me. I laughed it off, determined that if I couldn't beat them, I'd join them in whatever they suggested, darts, dominoes, you name it. Paul was sending drinks from the men's to the women's bar, where Carol, the other wives and I sat. I was drinking Cinzano and Paul would send triples, but I knew that however strong it was, I had to match them drink for drink. I couldn't be the soft southerner. Paul had told me already that his family were hard so all night long we were knocking back the booze. How I managed not to be ill, I'll never know.

Back at Carol's house we put on the karaoke until eventually everyone stumbled off to bed and I thought I'd done all right: earlier in the bar Carol had said to her mate that I wasn't stuck up and appeared to be one of them.

In the morning I saw that the bed was covered with dog hair and up the wallpaper there was a splatter of something I suspected might be dried-up vomit. The weekend had been a baptism of fire. We'd had a good time, though, and I'd survived.

Mostly in that first year everything was pretty wonderful between Paul and me. We were in the clutch of passionate new love, and nothing else seemed to matter. And if it did, it was surmountable. A couple of moments when he became very aggressive took the sheen off, but I always found a way to dismiss them. Once we were in the Swallow at Waltham Abbey with Anna and her boyfriend John-Paul and she mentioned that someone had written to Paul, wanting to meet him. She claimed it was Seal, the singer. I piped up and told Paul he'd really like Seal's music. Immediately he turned on me: 'How do *you* know what I'd like?' I felt stupid, tried to laugh it off and pretend it hadn't hurt. But it had. It had also jarred my confidence. Why wouldn't I know what he liked? Wasn't I the love of his life? The woman of his dreams? Didn't he tell me things he'd never told anyone else? That was what he was saying to me.

But such moments were rare. Paul carried on being generous. He'd buy things for the kids that I couldn't afford, and I never had to pay for anything when we went out. He bought us food regularly, and made my life much more comfortable. But I couldn't stop the house slipping into negative equity and I knew repossession was looming. At some point I was going to be homeless again.

Fairly early in 1992, there was talk of Paul moving to Italy. I didn't want him to go – the kids and I were used to having him around – but he finally passed a fitness test, Lazio signed him for £5.5 million and he was poised to leave Tottenham. He rang my friend Wendy and told her he was thinking of asking me and the kids to move to Italy with him, but he didn't mention it to me. I would have gone at the drop of a hat. Paul and Mason were almost inseparable. Mason was now at the tricky age of two and often didn't go to see Colin at weekends. He was still a baby in many ways and there was so much paraphernalia to cart about. Anyway, he was much more used to Paul than he was to Colin. Bianca, though, was older and she loved her daddy, which meant everything was much harder on her. Watching home videos of that time you can seen how Colin treasured Bianca. She really was his gorgeous little girl.

I was worried about her. I knew Colin spoilt her but I never stood in the way of her relationship with him. Bianca was taken to places I couldn't afford to take her to and given things I couldn't afford to buy. It got so bad that she would say, 'I hate you and I want to live with my dad. He says we're going to have the best time together, just me and him.' By this time, though, Mandy had left her husband for Colin and set up home with him, along with her son Rhys. For six months I had a terrible time with Bianca as things deteriorated. She'd visit her dad, then have huge tantrums when he brought her home. She'd try to get away from me and back to him, while he'd stand at the door and watch. I was at my wit's end about how to deal with it.

I'm sure Colin became more difficult in his dealings with me because Paul was in my life. He cited Paul in the divorce proceedings, but I had Paul's name removed from the papers because he hadn't broken up my marriage. I'd done that. All by myself.

In his way Paul was supportive, I loved him completely and utterly and we were happy together. One afternoon my home phone rang and when I answered it a girl's voice said, 'Is that Sheryl? Can you get a message to Paul?' I told her I wasn't seeing him until much later. It didn't seem to bother her. 'Tell him that Tracey's had her baby, seven pounds five ounces, and they're both doing fine.' When I mentioned it to Paul later he laughed. He said it was probably one of a couple of girls he and a team mate who regularly stayed over knew, messing around. He referred to one as Scar-face. I chose not to make anything of it and, like him, to laugh it off. But it niggled at me.

And then something happened that would affect my relationship with Paul for ever and always.

Paul was taking his whole family on holiday to Florida and he asked me to come with them. Everyone was going, Lindsay and her boyfriend Darren, Anna and John-Paul, Carl, their mum and dad and his oldest friend Jimmy 'Five Bellies'. There were nine of them, and I made the numbers up to a nice round ten. Mum and Dad said they would look after Mason and Bianca, which I felt guilty about. How could I go to Disney World in Florida without them? Hopefully we'd go together some other time. As usual Paul was difficult to refuse so I left them with their grandparents and went with a stuffed bag. I'd packed my entire wardrobe because I wanted to look good in front of Paul's family. I was still desperate to make a good impression and for them to like me.

From the very beginning they were frosty, but I didn't know why. I thought my visit to Newcastle had gone OK. But maybe I was just another girl taken to Dunston never to be seen again – all right for a visit but not for a holiday.

After we had breakfast, we set out, I thought, to experience Disney World. Instead we headed towards the Epcot Center but before we got to see any of it, they'd found The Rose and Crown English pub. During our time there we visited most of the bars in the Epcot Centre and Universal. I had to make a quick shift in my mind from what I'd expected to what was going on. In a minority of one I had no choice but to go along with their plans but I was disappointed not to be spending more time on the rides.

Each evening we'd meet up in the hotel bars. One evening I was getting ready and Paul said he couldn't stand waiting for the hairdryer so he told me to meet him there. By the time I got down everyone had already had a few drinks. They'd been sitting over a few cocktails discussing me. Unfortunately the press had been listening and had written it all down. The next day Paul rang his friend Micky Falcus to find out what was in the papers. Micky told him there was loads and Paul relayed it to me. It was horrible to be on the receiving end of that hurtful press. 'Sheryl left to walk two paces behind ...', which was obviously my fault for not holding his hand. 'Family moan in the bar about how long it takes her to get ready ...' I agreed with them there – it did take me a lot longer to get ready then than it does now, but I'd tried the casual jeans look and it hadn't gone down very well. I always felt I had to dress up for Paul – for him and the press, if I'm honest. Seeing myself looking terrible in photos did my confidence no good at all. Paul's disapproving sideways glances weren't helping either.

Each family member had a charge card on Paul's bill that meant they could get extras and go shopping within the hotel retail outlets. The manager called to ask Paul to extend the credit to cover their expenditure. Despite not having stood up for me in front of them, he now wanted me to go through the itemized bill to mark up what was being spent. He was effing and blinding. Too many phone calls, too much room service, too many extras – he started getting very agitated, and to be honest I felt sorry for him. It was a huge financial responsibility.

The following night out everyone was even more pissed than usual, and we bumped into Fred and Yvonne, a couple from Hoddesdon who ran a video shop we used. They joined us and the drinks carried on flowing. Jimmy was particularly drunk because he'd been told to down all sorts of shots. At the end of the night Fred and Yvonne had to help us get him to his room. Jimmy, practically out of it, forgot to pick up his bum-bag, which contained his room keys, park passes and money, so I grabbed it and followed everyone down the long corridor. I told Paul I had it and straight away Paul went into one: 'Why did you pick that up? You want to shag Jimmy? Then go and shag him! Why the f— did you pick it up?' I froze, then panicked, what did he mean? What was he talking about? I told him I picked it up because Jimmy had left it behind but it didn't matter what I said, it bounced straight off him.

As he and I made our way to our room he began swearing and calling me names. F—ing cow. Bitch. Slag. Next thing I knew his hands were round my neck and he had me bent backwards over the minstrel's gallery, shouting in my face. I kept trying to tell him I'd picked it up because Jimmy had forgotten it. He wasn't listening, just went on screaming at me.

Suddenly he had me by the hair and literally dragged me down the corridor to Jimmy's room. It was almost like a cartoon with my feet scrabbling to stay on the floor to stop my hair from being ripped from my head. Paul had me by the hair with one hand and hammered on the door with the other. Carl opened it. I was cowering and crying – covered with red marks, shocked and in pain.

'Sheryl's got Jimmy's bum-bag – go on, there's your boyfriend, give it to him!'

Carl said, 'I don't know why she's got it,' and closed the door. Next thing I was yanked by the hair again back along the corridor all the way to our room. Inside, Paul went mad. He pushed me up against the wardrobe, the wall, the door, all the while shouting accusations and insults in my face. Suddenly there was a knock at the door. It was Security and Paul had to let me go to open it. I heard him say we'd had a bit of an argument. Then he got annoyed because the bloke wouldn't go away. I was on the floor, huddled in a ball, and he said, 'You all right, Sheryl? Tell him you're all right – tell him. You OK or not?'

There was a pause. In the end life comes down to seconds. I made a decision. I said, 'Yes, I'm fine.' The security guy left and I thought, Oh, hell, I'm in real trouble now – but suddenly Paul switched. Just like that. In the blink of an eye.

'Oh, my God, what have I done? I promised my dad I'd never get like this over a girl again. I'm so sorry ... Oh, my God, oh, my God ...' He was sitting on the end of the bed, rocking backwards and forwards.

I was in a state of complete shock. No boyfriend had ever laid a finger on me before in that way. What do you do? The sensible thing is to get the hell out and never, ever, go back. But I didn't do that. And it wasn't the first time I'd had my hair pulled or been hit by someone who supposedly loved me.

He cried and cried and cried, while I lay there, shattered. He told me he'd sworn to his father he wouldn't get like this over a girl again. That was the second time he'd said it and I still didn't fully understand what he meant. I don't remember comforting him, but I don't remember berating him either.

In the morning I got up, got dressed again and went down-stairs. No one spoke to me. Not a word. I knew they all knew. Carl must have told them. I thought, Wow, they must really hate me. Look what I made him do. I made him so angry. I went to lie on the little beach by the hotel's lake, feeling so isolated. So alone. It was a feeling I knew well. He was accepted by my family, but I almost always felt left out when his family were around. It was them and me from the beginning, never us.

A couple of days later we went to the mall and Paul insisted on buying me a ring and a watch. He didn't say why, just that he wanted to buy something for me. I didn't want anything but he was adamant. It came, though, with a caveat. 'Don't tell my family. We'll leave them in the safe.' He was probably trying to make amends, but the jewellery meant nothing to me, especially since I had to hide it. I remember more fondly a walk along the beach. It was one of the few times we were on our own. We sat on some swings and he serenaded me with an Elvis song 'Wooden Heart'. Funny he should know that one off by heart.

Despite these moments of generosity and tenderness, I just wanted to get away, get home, get back to my kids. Insanely, I was angrier with his family than I was with him, for slagging me off and not doing anything to stop him or even just finding out whether I was OK. That they'd said nothing focused my fury and maybe my fear.

I've always said I didn't know what domestic violence was. As far as I was concerned, what had happened at Disney World had been a one-off. What else would I do? I had survived love, pain and loneliness for years so, on one level, it wasn't that big a deal. He had told me it would never happen again, I chose to believe him and locked the truth of what had happened away. I didn't tell anyone when I got home and in a way it became my guilty secret. That was the only way we could be in love again. Then he asked me to move to Italy with him.

I looked at my options. Single mother living off the state in social housing, or moving to Italy to a house with a swimming-pool and a man who loved me? You tell me which one you'd choose. He'd hit me but he'd sworn he'd never do it again. He'd also pay for the kids' education. As long as I didn't think about what had happened in Florida, it was a no-brainer. So I made the big decision for the kids and I to move to Italy to be with Paul.

Mason and Paul had bonded. They were very close and enjoyed each other's company, a lovely thing for me to see. All Paul ever had to do was love my kids the way I did and I'd be his. However, I knew I was going to have a big problem with Bianca. Paul was there when I told her. He was great, actually, very responsible and supportive. I hadn't had much of that. One of the loneliest things about being a single parent is that when your kids are naughty or run into difficulties, there's no one to stick up for them except you. We sat Bianca down and told her that in Italy she could have whatever she wanted.

There would be a swimming-pool and she could have a pony, anything. Nothing worked. She was adamant. She did not want to go to Italy. She wanted to stay with her father.

Paul had to leave for the pre-season training and we agreed I would join him later. We spoke on the phone a lot and I remember him telling me how scared he was during those first few weeks in Italy on his own. He claimed he didn't like the fuss they made of him. He didn't like the attention. And training was tough. They took it a lot more seriously than they did in England. He told me it was too much for him and, more importantly, that everything would be OK when I got there. He just needed me. Mason and I, sometimes with Bianca, would go over for weekends and stay at the Hilton in Rome where Paul was living temporarily.

When he was training, Mason and I would go down to the pool and hang out there. One weekend a little girl took a shine to him and they started swimming together, so I got talking to her glamorous mother. Swimming or no swimming, her red lipstick was still on. When she got out of the pool she'd change into a dry swimsuit. She was a typically well-turned-out Italian lady, and despite her pidgin English and my non-existent Italian, Bettina and I struck up a friendship. She knew Paul, as did a lot of the other girls who went regularly to the pool. I always wondered how well they knew him. One weekend Bettina told me there had been something of an upset. A busty girl had been playing ping-pong and Paul had thrown her into the pool. An older woman had complained about his rowdy behaviour, swearing in Italian.

Later that day, I asked Paul about this story and he was very cloak-and-dagger. At first he said it was nothing, but then he got irate.

After that I had an uneasy feeling that everyone knew what he'd been up to except me. Some regulars used the hotel as a fitness club, and he was always very friendly towards them. I started trying to piece all the bits together in my mind, but

I heard so many conflicting stories that I could never quite get a handle on it. Was Paul, as ever, just 'having a laugh', or was there more beneath the surface that I didn't know about? Still, my doubts weren't strong enough to stop me moving to Italy.

First, though, I had to resolve the ongoing furore with Bianca.

It was soon after I got back from Rome that Colin brought Bianca home one Sunday evening and she refused to get out of the car. It was a particularly bad tantrum. She wanted to live with her daddy and her daddy wanted her to live with him. I called Wendy in tears, and she suggested I call Colin's bluff. We were fairly sure that he didn't really want her and I was certain that Mandy didn't – she already had a child – but with the move imminent I felt I was left with no alternative than to agree to Bianca's demands to stay in England with her father.

Colin picked her up from me a few days before Mason and I were due to move to Rome permanently. Afterwards when I rang, she was usually too busy having fun to come to the phone, and I'd hear her giggling with Rhys in the background. It was humiliating, depressing and heart-wrenching. If I did speak to her I'd ask her whether she was sure she didn't want to come with Mason and me. But she was adamant that she was staying with Daddy. Wendy stood at my side and helped me not to backtrack. She said, 'Make him the ogre, or she'll make you the ogre for taking her away from the perfect life she imagines she'll have with just her and her dad.'

I knew she was right, but inside I was terrified. I believe I knew in my heart that it wouldn't work out with Colin and Mandy. Mandy had her own child and I doubted Colin could carry on giving in to a five-year-old's every whim, but I had to let Bianca find that out for herself. It was risky, though. I moved to Italy with Mason and, in doing so, committed what I believed was the worst possible sin. I deserted my child.

*

Five days later my dad rang me. He'd had Colin on the phone. Apparently Rhys's doctor had said it was too upsetting for him to have Bianca living with them. He was very attached to his toy goblins and trolls and one day when he wasn't looking Bianca had thrown one over the fence. They'd spent two days making 'Wanted' posters for the missing goblin, and all the time she'd known where it was. Things weren't all *Little House on the Prairie* for her there.

'We've got to pull together to help Bianca,' he told my dad.

'No,' said Dad. 'Not we. Sheryl will. I'm coming to get Bianca.'

I flew from Rome to Heathrow, met Mum, Dad and Bianca at Heathrow, then flew straight back with Bianca. She was very quiet. All she ever said was that she hated Mandy and she hated Rhys. She never said she hated her dad. I was worried about her – and I was just as worried about whether it would be too much for Paul to have me and both children in Italy when he wasn't settling in well. I was right to be concerned.

5. Big-headed Blonde Bitch

We arrived in Italy in the summer of 1992, and Paul's first game for Lazio was on 17 August. While Mason and I had been coming over for weekends we had had someone to assist us with the language, finding a house and locating the best school. Her name was Jane Nottage and she was Paul's PA in Italy. From the start he told me he couldn't stand her. As soon as I arrived he told me she wound him up. He moaned that every time he went training she was there, bugging him. When she called the house, he made me answer the phone and refused to speak to her or to do anything she asked him to do. But he didn't show any of that to her. As far as she was concerned, they were best buds. I know that because she wrote a whole book about it in which she described him as her brother. The way he talked about her to me made it seem as if he couldn't be in the same room as her. He wanted me to keep her away from him. I spoke to his agent and his accountant, Mel Stein and Len Lazarus, because he was so pissed off with her. They said Paul needed her so he had to try to get on with her, and they wouldn't get rid of her.

They were right: we did need her, and through her we found a house. The landlord was called Mr Quadrocci, which means 'four eyes' in Italian. It was the beginning of my happy-ever-after. We moved in, and Jane 'busied herself', as Paul would say, with sorting us out. I couldn't have done it – I didn't speak Italian, had no contacts, and I was trying to settle the kids. But when Paul got back from training he'd work himself into such a rage because she'd been at the ground or at our house again and things went flying – a plate, then a table, and once even the fridge. He kept all the bottles of spirits on top of it and the whole lot went across the room. His anger scared me. Cautiously I would try to calm him, keep out of his way and pick up the pieces, anything to stop him from getting angrier. But it didn't matter what I did, I couldn't stem that anger.

I doubt that any of his rages were to do with Jane, or any other of the reasons he flung at me. I think they were more to do with the extreme pressure he was under at Lazio. In Italy it was a completely different ballgame. Literally. They'd train in the morning, have lunch together, then train in the afternoon. Every Friday night, even if it was a home match, the management took the players away so they could be together. And every other weekend they'd go to away matches, not get home until Sunday and then it was back to training again. Paul wasn't used to it, and after sixteen months out of football, he wasn't fit enough.

The focus of his temper soon moved away from Jane. He once had a go at me for having brought Bianca to join us. He reminded me that we'd moved out with just the one child and two was too much. But he'd known from the beginning it was always my intention for Bianca to be with us. The night before the children started school, my mum and dad were there and Paul was away. Just before I sat the kids down for tea he rang me up and said he wanted the kids to change their surname to Failes, my maiden name, from Kyle, which was Colin's. When I tried to say it was too late to do that to Bianca – she was starting at a new school the following day – he dug his heels in. As ever, this seemed to have come out of the blue but I wonder now if someone in his family had been having a dig.

'Do it or go.'

'But what am I going to say to her, Paul?' .

'I don't care. I'm telling you now, I'm not having a Kyle under my roof. I'm paying for her, I'm bringing her up, so I'm not having that bastard's name in my house.'

He was angry. I wanted to keep the peace, Paul had moved on from the furniture, to taking his anger out on me, so I sat down with Bianca to ask her to change her name. She was in her pyjamas, and ready for bed. She looked so vulnerable, and there I was, after everything she'd gone through, telling her that her name wasn't Bianca Kyle any more, it was Bianca Failes. I explained that it was easier if we all had the same name.

'But I don't know how to spell it, Mum.'

We all tried to teach her ways to remember it. Frog. Apple. Igloo ... It was really hard for her and, in any case, she didn't want to learn how to spell her new surname. But Paul had made his feelings clear. And that was that. He said, 'Jump.' I said, 'How high?' I wasn't strong enough to say, 'Shut up, you silly bugger,' or call his bluff.

The next morning I went to the school early to explain that Bianca's name had changed. They seemed fine about it and were happy to put the new one on the text books. But the old name had already been written in some and Bianca had to painstakingly change it herself.

Sadly I didn't see it at the time but this was the first example of the subtle tightening of Paul's control over me and it continued. He told me I couldn't talk to people in England on the phone because it was too expensive. But he was out of the house a lot. I didn't have friends in Italy and I didn't speak the language, so I often called people at home. He started asking me how long I'd been on the phone. He sometimes came home at lunchtime for a break, and then he'd be angry about the state of the house. We didn't have a cleaner and I had the two kids running about, but if the house wasn't spotless when he walked in all hell would break loose. There were lots of trees and the doors were always open, but if the leaves had blown in, he'd flip. He'd call me names and hurl abuse at me. 'F—ing winding me up', 'Bitch', and 'It'd be all right if there was one thing you could do.'

I reacted by trying to please him and keep the house immaculate. Perhaps unsurprisingly, I'm still like that now. Mess makes me jittery, and I'm rarely without the Hoover in my hand. But whatever I did it was never enough. There was always something to set him off.

Every time Paul went to the club for the Friday night pre-game gathering, the security guards came to check that I was in. Where would I have gone? I didn't know anyone. On his away-match weekends, I wasn't allowed to go to England either. He said he couldn't afford for me to go home all the time. 'I'm not made of money,' he'd say. I wasn't allowed to go anywhere or do anything. I was completely isolated. I was told many times how lucky I was to have him. Once when we were in a five-star restaurant I told him not to gob into his napkin. He told me to remember where I'd come from. 'You were pushing a pram when I met you.' He always threw that one at me. I was supposed to feel fortunate and grateful, which in a sense I did.

The verbal abuse soon became physical. First it was just pushing. Then he started to grab my arms. Next he'd shove me up against the wall. I often had a sore forehead because he'd press his to mine while he shouted in my face. Soon I was being pushed on to the floor and pinned down. He'd lift my head and slam it against the tiles. Always the back of the head. Never the face.

The first time it happened in Italy, I couldn't believe it. I'd honestly thought what had taken place in Florida had been a one-off. Within a few weeks, to varying degrees, the violence had become a daily occurrence.

Once my parents and grandparents and Paul's family came to stay at the same time. Paul and I went to the supermarket to get some extra chairs, and as we were walking along the promenade to the shops, a couple of girls came over and said, 'Hi,' in Italian. Like all the other fans, they would just start talking to 'Gazza' and ignore whoever he was with. This time, though, it was like he knew them. Back in the car, before we'd pulled away, I asked him if he did. Immediately, and with force, he slapped me around the back of the head. While I was trying to work out what had happened, he grabbed my hair and bashed the side of my face against the steering-wheel, then the other side against the window. I tried to speak. 'I didn't mean anything, I was just asking.'

He launched into a tirade of fury. 'Who do you think you are, telling me what I can and can't do? You big-headed blonde bitch – good thing you've got looks because you've got nothing else going for you. Do you think you're the best-looking fanny in the world? Do you?'

Do you think you're the best-looking fanny in the world? I must have heard that a thousand times. But his favourite, and mine, was big-headed blonde bitch. I wanted to call this book *Big-headed Blonde Bitch* but, sadly, the publishers thought it would put readers off. Between you and me, though, that's what it's called in my mind.

Just as quickly he stopped bouncing me off car parts and started the engine. And then he switched. 'You've got to forgive me now. Now. You've got to forgive me before we go home. Forgive me!'

It's hard to forgive someone when your ears are ringing and your head's throbbing. But the thing that had hurt me most were his words: *Good thing you've got looks because you've got nothing else going for you.* Normally he didn't ask my forgiveness but, then, normally my mum, dad and grandparents weren't waiting for us at home. And probably for that reason, I said, 'Paul, you can't keep doing this to me.' He responded by driving faster, straight past the house. I remember thinking, Idiot, you should have kept your mouth shut.

There were lots of sharp bends and he was looking at me, shouting, 'Tell me now – say you love me now! Forgive me right now! Say you love me!'

It's nearly impossible to say those words to someone when they've just bashed your head against a window. I couldn't say it. 'Say you love me, say you forgive me, say you love me.' He was driving like a lunatic around the cliffs, crossing the central reservation to the other side of the road, then veering back. It was terrifying. 'Say you love me. Go on, say it – say it!'

So, finally, I said it. 'I love you.'

'No, you don't, you're just saying that, you don't mean it. You're just saying that. You don't mean it – you don't!'

He was driving faster and faster and more and more erratically. Now I really started to panic. I said it with feeling, desperate for him to stop. 'Yes, I do, I love you. I love you!' I was pleading with him. 'Let's just go back now. We won't talk about it any more. They'll be getting worried. It's fine, it's fine, no problem.'

He was going fast downhill, straight towards a cliff on the other side of the road, shouting, 'If you don't love me, I'll end it now! We'll go together, right now!'

I started screaming, 'I love you! I love you! Please stop! I love you! I forgive you!'

It will surprise no one who has been in this situation that he slammed his foot on the brake and stopped the car at the last minute. For such a self-destructive man, it's amazing how long he's managed to stay alive.

So we sat there. I just wanted to get the hell out of that car. I hated him and I hated myself more, but underneath there was the sense of relief that I was beginning to recognize came after a big attack. Relief because he would make more of an effort to be nice to me, for a couple of days, at least.

After a while, Paul started the car, turned it round and drove home. As we pulled up at the house he told me to cover the marks. My ears were bleeding as he'd yanked the earrings out of my lobes, so I pulled my hair down over them. With them hidden, no one would know what had just happened. Funny how someone in a fit of rage, over which they have no control, can restrict the blows to places no one will see.

We got out of the car and suddenly Paul was charming again. I was filled with relief that the attack was over, I was back at home, safe. I disappeared to the bathroom to check my ears, did my best to stop the bleeding then busied myself in the kitchen while he played fabulous host.

I saw him turn like that many, many times while we were in Italy. One minute fury, then all smiles and Gazza the clown was back. He'd do mad, exciting things, like driving the car up to the pool and getting everyone to jump off it into the water. He'd get the music blaring and have everyone dancing around the pool. He could create as much fun as he could havoc. I would bury the fury and bitter, bitter disappointment, and tell myself it would all be okay in the end.

After that incident in the car, things escalated. The abuse was no longer confined to the house. In a restaurant he'd be twisting the skin on my thigh while I was giving a waiter my order. If we were ever in a group and I laughed, I'd get a pinch or a twist. I let him get away with it, but so did people who could see what was going on. Once when I came back to the house with my nose bleeding a babysitter was there. She didn't say anything.

When we travelled he started doing it on flights. He'd spit in my face, shout at me, head-butt me. No one tried to help me because he was Gazza, which made him a god. I refuse to fly Air Italia now. He'd always drink loads before a flight and take lots of tablets because he was so frightened of flying – Paul is scared of everything – and then, of course, an excuse would arise. I was talking or I wasn't talking, I was ignoring him, embarrassed by him, bored with him. I learnt very quickly not to pick up a magazine. He hated me reading, absolutely hated it. 'You're so f—ing rude, how dare you? I'm here with you and you're f—ing reading.' Quick gob in the face to keep me in my place.

By then I was aware that I was in a cycle of violence, but domestic violence? That had never entered my brain. It was either a beating or a pinch, a slap, a nudge and push that accompanied constant verbal abuse. But every incident appeared to have a plausible explanation. Stresses at the club. Bad press. Good press. No press. Too much press. The mess. The way I looked. The kids.

He was tough on Bianca and Mason, and Mason particularly. That was hard for me. At the weekend he'd demand that I lie in bed with him. I couldn't go to get the children up. He did that, while I had to wait for him to come back to bed. He set up the garage so that it was filled with toys, games, videos, fruit machines, cars. You name it, they had it. He'd take them down and tell them, 'Mum and Dad are going to have a lie-in,' then lock the garage door and come back up. All I wanted was to get it over with and get them out of the garage.

When it came to Paul and the kids, everything was a double-edged sword. His locking them into a garage sums it up, really. He could be good fun with them, and there were some genuinely nice times: he would attach Mason's toy car or his tractor to the back of his motorbike and pull him along in the garden, which Mason loved. They played guitar together, and messed around in the car. He did silly things with both of them, and he was very generous towards them. He provided them with everything. There was a stunning children's clothes shop called La Cicogna – he spent a fortune on dressing the kids.

But he was always pushing the boundaries and then it would become uncomfortable. He would dunk Mason under water and hold him there for a bit too long, throw him a bit too high, fight a bit too aggressively. I would have to break up the 'play fight', and then be made to seem the bad guy – 'Oh, Mum's made us stop.' There was always a slight sense of danger, like in a horror movie – the scene looks happy but the music tells you otherwise. I had that music playing pretty constantly in my head.

Italy was a strange dichotomy. I lurched from being hit to doing lovely things outside in the sunshine with the kids. We had a great lifestyle – the sunshine, the pool, the hospitality. Every Sunday when Paul wasn't at an away match we'd go out for a big family lunch. Paul always wanted to be out of the house by about twelve so there was a scramble to get ready after the kids had been let out of the garage. I never attributed Paul's urgency to his needing a drink. I never made that link. But I'm fairly sure now that that was what drove him to get out.

It was boring for the kids going out for long meals but at least in Italy everyone brought their children so the staff were used to them and there was usually another family for Bianca and Mason to play with. We became regulars in a few places where they knew that Mason would always fall asleep after lunch. They'd give us a table big enough for two chairs to be put together and he'd lie down and drop off. Mason could fall asleep anywhere. In some restaurants he had his own deck-chair.

But if Bianca and Mason went off to play in the restaurant garden, I was never allowed to go with them or keep an eye on them. Paul needed me by his side all the time. He'd always have a hand on my leg, an arm round my shoulders, some physical contact. They went on their own, but the restaurants were often down country lanes and I usually felt they were safe. If I wanted to go and watch them Paul would start off again. 'What? You embarrassed people will see us alone? You worried what people will think?' It was always easier to relent. But it wasn't very clever.

On Mason's third birthday, 9 October 1992, Paul got electric cars for the kids to drive round the garden. He went over the top – Christmas, birthdays, Valentine's, all those big days, he made a big deal of them. He lavished me with gifts, often after an attack but always on the big anniversaries, which were huge occasions, for the kids as well as me.

The children went to St George's, Bianca was in the primary school and Mason went to the nursery there. Bianca enjoyed it and made friends with the Spanish ambassador's daughter. I wasn't allowed to hang around the school gates making new friends. Paul hated me talking to the other mums, hated the idea that I was doing the school run. In fact, pick-up and drop-off were a nightmare because he timed them. In the morning I wasn't allowed to have a shower or brush my teeth. Why would I want to – unless there was someone down there I fancied shagging? It was easier just to go along with him, so I'd rush out with the children, looking dishevelled, just to try to keep the peace for them. Paul stayed at home while I dropped them off, and if I was a little bit late back, I got the third degree. Who had I been talking to? Some dads had been there, hadn't they?

One day there was terrible traffic and Bianca, Mason and I had to sit in the car hardly moving. I was thinking, Oh, God, oh, God, hurry up. I wasn't worried about the kids being late for school but about getting home before Paul went off to training. Suddenly I saw his car coming down the middle of the road between the two lines of stationary traffic. He saw us, turned round and came back up the middle. Pulling up alongside me, he shouted, 'What are you doing?'

What did it look like I was doing? We were stuck in traffic. So I told him, 'We're stuck in traffic.' Satisfied, he said he'd see me at home and left. He'd been trying to catch me out. Just because he'd have been off flirting with the mothers he'd assumed I'd be doing the same with the fathers.

It was three months since we'd moved from England. You'd think I must have been wondering whether my decision to join Paul in Italy had been a good one. You'd think by now I must have realized that this wasn't deep passion, the stuff of novels, true love, but I hadn't. I was too busy keeping myself and the kids intact. And Christmas was round the corner: we'd be flying back to England for the holidays.

Actually, it was lovely to be in Rome around that time of year. We'd go off as a family to the Hotel Hassler and Paul and I would drink champagne with crushed strawberries. These were beautiful, stolen moments. I loved walking down the

Spanish Steps, and just being in Italy's capital – it's a very lively, romantic city. There was a pet store and the kids always wanted to go into it. Once Paul took them shopping for my Christmas present. They came back with a puppy – two days before we were due to fly home to England. It was so cute, called Cappuccino, but we couldn't keep her. Without a second's thought Paul handed her to one of our bodyguards, Augusto, and asked him to look after her over the holidays. He and the other bodyguard we had were part of the Mondialpol Security Police and we knew them well. Augusto's wife would often come over to make pizza or spaghetti with Bianca and Mason. Luckily she and Augusto had two kids and they loved having Cappuccino. By the time we got back they were so attached to her that they kept her.

Paul's family would never leave Newcastle at Christmas because his dad wanted to be near the Dunston working men's club so we stayed in a hotel and all my family came. There were lots of presents, Paul being his usual generous self. Because my parents were around he was on his best behaviour, so in the new year I went back to Italy with him. If I thought about leaving him, I don't remember it – I was easily lulled into a false sense of security. And, let's be honest, the bar was pretty low where my sense of security was concerned. In any case, if I'd stayed in England I would have had nowhere to go, and I thought I was with a man who loved me. Yes, I felt surplus to requirements, yes, he hurt me, yes, he sometimes ignored me, but he'd taken me and my kids on and looked after us. What was there not to love? He said he loved my children as much as I did, and that was enough for me.

But the beatings and the verbal abuse continued. The days were pretty similar: wake up, no shower, rush to school, back to bed, then he'd go to training and I would get the house immaculate, tidy the kids' stuff away, shower, and get ready to go out with him for lunch if he was coming back. I was frazzled, trying to keep my wits about me. I just wanted to get through the day without an incident, and when there was one, I kept my mouth shut.

I only ever responded once. Paul had me pinned up against the wall in the villa, doing the usual biting and head-butting, and suddenly I brought my knee up hard. I nearly went over the balcony that time so I never did it again. Not a slap. Nothing. I was so busy trying to survive that I never sat down and wondered what was really going on.

His family came out to stay, and kept saying, 'He's so good with Mason and Bianca, when are you going to give him a kid of his own?'

I remember telling his mum, 'He's not mature enough to look after one. When he grows up, maybe.'

So she said, 'It's okay for him to look after your kids but not a child of his own?'

A salient point. I couldn't tell her he was beating me all the time, and that bringing another child into that environment was madness.

Having his family around helped me understand a little better the dynamics between him and his parents. Once his dad came to stay with one of his mates. He really is hard work: he barely ever says a word and it's impossible to know what he's thinking. Paul was always telling me that his family were the closest ever, that they were the best thing since sliced bread, but it didn't seem like that to me. One evening I asked him to ask his dad to stop throwing his cigarette ends down the toilet because they weren't flushing. Forget it – there was no way he'd say that to his dad. But if they were that close, why couldn't he? But Paul refused and I knew better than to push him. He often shouted at Mason, 'I wouldn't have spoken to my dad like that!' I think that shows fear, not closeness.

I quickly found out that Paul had assumed financial responsibility for his family as soon as he started earning money. He had bought houses for them all. He'd bought cars and insured them for his sisters, his brother and his dad. One day in Italy his mum was in the kitchen with us and she asked Paul for six thousand pounds because his younger sister, Lindsay, wanted to change the kitchen in the house she'd been given after his mum had moved into another. She was about eighteen. I could see Paul getting wound up about it and thought, Please don't wind him up because I'll get it in the neck. He said to his mum, 'She's got a free house, I've bought her a car, what more does she want?'

'I'm sure you want to see this family out on the streets,' his mother replied. Just like that. He was cut to the quick, and I felt so sorry for him.

I was stunned when I realized I had missed my period, despite being on the pill. A pregnancy test was positive. I phoned Wendy. 'Oh, my God, I wish I could be there to see the look on his face when you tell him. He'll be so excited.' But I felt uneasy. Then again he'd been saying he wanted kids and how much he loved them . . . I went to pick him up from the training ground to tell him the news.

When he appeared I got out of the car with a pillow stuck up my jumper. 'What? What you doing that for? Oh. Oh, right.' He got into the car.

That was that. Nothing more was said. Within two weeks I'd started bleeding heavily. I called my doctor to ask him whether I was miscarrying. He told me it sounded like I was and wanted to know whether I was sure about my period dates in order to ascertain whether I needed a D&C. I always knew when my periods were because they were such a big annoyance to Paul – not that it stopped him, but it didn't suit him. It's not surprising I got pregnant.

Not long afterwards one of his sisters had a miscarriage and, having said nothing to me when I miscarried, he started sobbing. I understand now that an abuser hates it when you're pregnant because you have something that they can't have.

That's why the violence often escalates, or sometimes begins, during a pregnancy. And why so many women miscarry. It's all about control. I know that now.

6. Rag Doll

By now I wasn't allowed to use the phone, or meet anyone's eye, let alone strike up a conversation. I was the busy little big-headed blonde bitch, who deserved nothing, was worth nothing and had been nothing until Paul came along. And when he was around there were constant put-downs and insults and almost daily violence. He must have known he wasn't being the perfect gentleman: the bodyguards were checking up on me. Also, he had started taking my passport to work with him and sometimes the kids' too. If it had been particularly bad the night before, he would send a bodyguard back to the house with a message: 'He really wants you to come and meet him for lunch.' I'd say I wasn't going. 'No, no, he's really sorry, he wants to meet you for lunch. If you go for lunch he'll give you back your passport. Just hear what he has to say.' So I'd go and lose any power I thought I might have had and promise to forgive and forget. I felt disgusting, humiliated and utterly alone. Since that first little look from Paul, criticizing my appearance, he had been chip, chip, chipping away at my confidence. There was very little left of me.

In October Wendy and John came out to Italy for their wedding anniversary, I was so looking forward to seeing them. I was probably a bit nervous too. They landed at Ciampino airport so I went to pick them up even though Paul had made it clear he didn't want me to. When Wendy came through the gate her jaw dropped. 'You look terrible. What's going on?'

I was thin, I had spots all along my jawline, and I obviously wasn't hiding the stress as well as I'd thought I was.

The moment Wendy saw Paul she said, 'What have you done to my friend?'

'What do you mean?'

'She's dead.'

'Don't be daft.'

But Wendy stuck with it. 'No, no, her body's there but her eyes are dead. Where's she gone?'

The next night we all went out to dinner. Paul was being a bit leery and cutting, which was unusual since we were with other people and on the whole he only showed his vicious side when we were on our own. He criticized how I looked, which shocked Wendy.

Paul had bought an over-the-top black-lacquer bed for the house in Italy, which rotated so that you could angle it towards the telly that came up out of a matching stand. It also had a telephone built into it, but it was faulty and you could over-hear conversations elsewhere in the house. I had heard him on the phone to his sister discussing her imminent wedding. I had decided not to go because one of Paul's ex-girlfriends would be there – a girl called Sarah. It had been during that uncomfortable period before Paul and I had become 'exclusive' (if we ever did) that he had gone out with Sarah. Anna had invited her, which felt like a two fingers to me, and was cross that now I was telling her, apparently, whom she could invite. I wasn't, but Sarah made me feel awkward, and I didn't want to have to watch the family all over her and ignoring me. I heard Anna say to Paul, 'Well, you're walking down with the chief bridesmaid and she was your girlfriend, too,' to which he replied, 'Yeah, but she doesn't know that.' I wasn't bothered about the chief bridesmaid, she had been with Paul long before me. Anna called me and said Paul wouldn't have a nice time if I wasn't there, which I thought was unlikely.

The wedding was planned for 14 November, four days before Paul was due to play at an England match against Turkey at Wembley. He had returned home to start training at Burnham Beeches so I decided to surprise him and go with him to the wedding. Paul had been saying how much he wanted me there and I thought that, after all, maybe I was being paranoid. Graham Taylor, the manager at the time, had said Paul could take time off to go to the wedding so I planned to meet him on the Friday night. I arrived at Wendy's with a suitcase full of possible outfits and we spent a fun couple of hours catching up and looking at clothes.

Paul arrived with the coach Lawrie McMenemy, having had a couple of whiskies with Graham. That should have rung warning bells. I went to get my stuff from the spare room and told him the good news that I'd decided to come to the wedding, if he still wanted me to. He started shouting at me, and Wendy came in. 'Not in my house, Paul. The babies are asleep and John's not here.' Embarrassed, I tried to usher him out – I didn't want a scene.

He'd obviously never wanted me to come to the wedding because when we arrived at Dobbs Weir he went ballistic. That attack went on for hours – and I mean hours. I spent what felt like the whole night running away from him, tearing around the house to avoid the blows. Paul pulled chunks of hair out of my head and I remember seeing it hanging off my black jacket. He kicked me, punched me, bit me and threw me on the floor over and over and over again. Eventually I escaped to the smallest bedroom, locked myself in and curled up on the bed. He kicked the whole door off its hinges. It only stopped when he felt blood on his hand. It was on my face: as he'd swiped the sides of my head he'd caught my earrings and ripped them out of my ears again.

Years later I went to see Beechy Colclough, the famous addiction therapist, to help Paul. He asked me if Paul could have killed me at any time. He would only accept a yes or no answer. I sat there for about an hour before I finally realized that I had to say yes. The night before Anna's wedding, during that prolonged attack, I could have died.

I was saved by the bell. At five in the morning Linda Lusardi and Terry Bailey arrived in a limo to collect Paul. He looked at me and said, 'I'll call you later.' Then he walked down the stairs and opened the door. 'Hiya! How you doing! Yeah, great, let's go . . .'

I was a mess. The house was a mess. I couldn't move. Much later that afternoon I called Wendy.

'Hi,' she said. 'Are you having a nice time?'

'I'm still here.'

'Whatever's the matter?'

She came over. I hadn't moved. My hair was still hanging in chunks off the jacket. It was a beautiful black jacket with white piping and hearts for pockets. Years later I gave it to a friend, and every time I saw her in it, I shuddered. I could only see it with clumps of my hair on it that Paul had pulled out of my head. Wendy told me we had to get a doctor and I had to come to her house. I was so embarrassed. So, so embarrassed. She helped me clean up. I couldn't sit. Everywhere hurt.

He called Wendy's house that night. Pissed, of course. He told Wendy he was having a terrible time, how awful he felt about what he'd done. I think he was blaming the whiskies he'd had with Graham Taylor – 'It wasn't me, it was the drink. Tell her I love her – tell her it'll never happen again. Tell her I'll never drink whisky again. Tell her I'm missing her – tell her I can't enjoy myself until I know she's all right. Tell her, tell her . . .' I couldn't speak to him.

The next day, all over the papers, there were pictures of him dancing on the tables, dancing with this girl, that girl – so much for the terrible time he was having. They also criticized me for my outfit! A journalist wrote it was disgusting for me to wear a miniskirt to a wedding. And I wasn't even there. I was trying to make sense of the worst beating of my life. While he was dancing on tables, I was trying to tidy the house and avoid my reflection in the mirrors on the walls. Wendy was worried I'd broken something so on Monday I called a doctor and my injuries are in my records.

On the Sunday my dad came for lunch at Wendy's. I could still barely move because of the pain. I'd covered most of the marks but I couldn't hide everything. When Dad asked me why I was in pain, I told him that Paul had attacked me. He didn't believe me. I asked Wendy to tell him what state the house and I had been in when she'd arrived, which she did.

'You mean she's not exaggerating?'

Paul kept ringing Wendy's house, drunk, throughout the day. She told him that we had told my father about what he'd done. Then Dad spoke to him and said if he ever touched me again he'd break both his legs. Paul blamed it on the whisky and said he knew he shouldn't have done it. He said to Wendy he was sorry about what he'd done to her mate. I didn't speak to him myself but by match day, later that week, I felt concerned for how Paul was feeling, and was worried about how he would play. I went to Wembley to watch the match and listened to the wild cheering around me. I felt hollow inside.

With his promises that it would never happen again ringing in my ears, I returned to Italy.

When we got back to Italy Paul was determined to show me what I meant to him. He told me the violence only happened because he loved me so much and was scared of losing me. I let myself believe everything he was saying, but the lull was short-lived. Nothing I could do was good enough and everything set him off. And then it got worse. Paul asked some of his family and friends to come and stay.

They all moved in. Paul demonstrated very effectively that he had no respect for me. He was rude to me all the time, belittled me in their company and would take them out, sometimes all night, and never let me know where he was. Were they a buffer that he used to protect himself from what he did? The whole dynamic had changed. I was in the way. I was ignored. I was the underdog. Do you want lunch? Are you coming home? 'Nah – we've all eaten.' Everything he said to me was filled with disdain.

One day I got him on his own and asked him if he wanted me to leave. I asked him! 'Just tell me. I don't know what you want me to do.' I don't think his behaviour could have made it clearer, but I was still trying to get his approval, to win back his love. It was futile.

The villa didn't feel like home any more. The kids would ask me where Dad was: he didn't show up for tea after school, he was never at home. Mason would cling to him when he was there, which annoyed him and gave him the excuse he needed to go out again. It was a horrible time. I don't know which was worse, being hit or being ignored. I'm sure the kids were discombobulated – I was: I'd had the shit beaten out of me, the man who said I was his everything could barely look at me, yet I still didn't want to leave.

Wendy and John had been planning to come out for their son's birthday but I told Wendy I wasn't sure whether I would still be there – Paul had made his feelings clear. We went ahead with the plans anyway, and, of course, I was still there when they came.

One evening we'd been out for dinner. When we got back I went upstairs while Wendy and John popped outside for a cigarette. Paul came into the bedroom. I can't remember what I'd done this time – got out of the car first, left the table before he was ready, looked at the waiter, it didn't matter: he'd find some excuse to lay into me. I knew that Wendy and John would hear the odd thump from our room upstairs but I tried to keep quiet because if I made a noise it would renew his fury – 'Yeah, that's right, go on, get everyone involved, go on, anything to get away from me . . .' He'd never done it with people so close. Did he want to get caught that night or was he just trying to make me leave?

He yanked my hair, pulled my ears, kneed me and bit my face – he did that a lot if he was somewhere where he couldn't swing his arms. When he head-butted me, it wasn't like in the movies when they swing their head at you, much more little jabs or constant pressure against my head. Did it hurt? I can't remember the pain during an attack, only the soreness afterwards, the tender skin, the headaches. During it I was simply thinking, Let this be the end, let's get this over with so it can stop. But I wasn't doing a very good job of getting it to stop that night because suddenly he had me out on the balcony and pushed me backwards. In the process he dislodged a flowerpot, which crashed on to the porch below where Wendy and John were smoking in silence, listening.

That stopped him long enough for me to run away. I got as far as the bathroom, which wasn't nearly far enough, and huddled on the floor. Paul came in and closed the door behind him. Suddenly Wendy was banging on it. The flying flowerpot had galvanized her into action. 'Sheryl, are you in there? Are you all right?'

The usual response from Paul: 'Tell her you're all right. Go on, tell her!'

Me – 'Yeah, yeah . . .' Same old bollocks.

But Wendy wasn't a bodyguard and she wasn't frightened of Paul. 'No, I want to see you.' She barged in, took one look at me cowering behind the toilet cistern and said, 'What the hell is going on?' She picked me up and took me downstairs, leaving John, who had joined us, to talk to Paul.

There, she begged me to come home. It wasn't right what he'd done and I had to leave. This time I agreed, but I had nowhere to go. It wasn't because I wanted to go but because Paul didn't want me to stay. If he hadn't kicked me out, I would have stayed. How long would I have taken it? Until I was dead? I suppose I have to be grateful that he had the decency to tell me to go before he killed me.

Trouble is, I had nowhere to live. I rang my dad and told him that Paul had finally told me he didn't want us there any more. It was decided by everyone that Anna and John-Paul, who were staying at Paul's house in Dobbs Weir, would come out to Italy, and the children and I would move in there until we found somewhere of our own. I packed my bags and then we all went out for lunch – Paul, Wendy, John, me, the children, his cousin and mates around a long table as if it were a totally normal day. I left the restaurant a few minutes before Wendy and John, caught a flight and, after seven months of hell, flew back to England.

By the time I got to Paul's house, Anna had left. I put the bags down, tired and depressed, went into the kitchen and found it empty. There was nothing in the fridge, no cutlery in the drawer, and nothing on the shelves, not even a kettle. Bianca called from upstairs that the doors were locked. Stunned, I walked from room to room, trying each door. Anna had locked the dining room, the main bedroom with the en-suite, the room she'd been staying in, and left open the small bedroom, whose door Paul had kicked in, a spare double room and a bathroom. The lounge had been stripped of paintings and ornaments.

Dad called Paul. 'What the hell is going on? Your sister is treating my daughter like a thief. Why are you doing this to her?'

As usual he made out that he knew nothing about it, that he hadn't had any part in it. Dad said, 'We're going to have something to eat and when I get back I want the keys to the other rooms to be here.' And they were. Anna had pushed them through the letterbox.

Within days, Paul was calling me at Dobbs Weir. When I didn't pick up, he sent his agent and accountant, Mel Stein and Len Lazarus, round. It was then that I told them how Paul had behaved while I was in Italy. And however much I loved him, and I did, and however much I wanted to believe he loved me, I wasn't in a hurry to go back. They said Paul resorted to violence because it was the only way he could beat me in an argument: he'd never win with words. To me, that was no excuse and, any-way, we weren't having arguments. He would just go into a rage and hit me. I never argued: I only tried to appease. However, they managed to convince me to meet Paul and hear him out.

I know that it wasn't up to Mel and Len to try and 'save me'

My beautiful, beautiful nan, with her two beloved boys – my dad Richard (left) and his brother Peter (right).

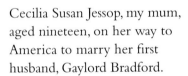

Cecilia Susan Jessop, my mum, aged nineteen, on her way to America to marry her first husband, Gaylord Bradford.

Me, Mum and Dad in Nanny and Granddad's garden in Bulls Green.

Another Sunday at Bulls Green.

Unable to walk, being supported by my wonderful nan, as I always was for the rest of her life.

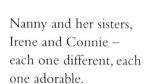

Nanny and her sisters, Irene and Connie – each one different, each one adorable.

The most elegant couple in the world, my nan and granddad.

Me aged four, a 'natural blonde'.

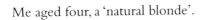

Mum, Dad and Ben, Christmas in Windsor Drive.

The cardboard-box photos that
changed everything.

No. 1

No. 2

No. 3

No. 4

My first attempt at modelling, aged fifteen.

Photo taken for the local newspaper in Hertford.

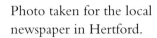

Another picture for the local newspaper.

The first photo sent to me of my big brother Gaylord.

We had this family photo taken on my first trip to meet my brothers.

My sis Vicki with Gaylord and his daughter Julia.

Pat, a wonderful 'mom' to Gaylord, David and Gaylord's daughter Julia.

Gaylord, Mum and David's reunion after eighteen years apart.

My one and only beautiful daughter Bianca.

Mason and my dad, two peas in a pod.

Dad and Bianca in the Seychelles.

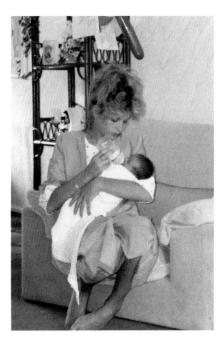

After an emergency section and three long weeks in hospital I finally came home with my precious daughter.

And then there were three.

Three going through a western phase.

Paul and me in Rome – our first interview with the *News of the World*.

The villa in Rome that Paul and I chose to call our home.

Mason and Paul in our garden in Rome on one of Paul's many toys.

Bianca, Mason and Paul having fun in our garden in Rome, 1992.

Paul, Mason and Bianca enjoying a bubble bath at Paul's house in Dobbs Weir.

On a family day out at a theme park: Mason, my mum, Bianca, Granddad, Nanny and my dad.

Paul joins us for Christmas Eve at the Belfry, 2001.

Me and Mason in Rome – we would go into the city centre for *gelati* some afternoons.

Boys and their toys – Paul and Mason in our garden in Rome.

Bianca and Mason in the kitchen in Rome on Bianca's first day at St George's School.

The love of Mason's life.

Mason's third birthday in Rome – Paul 'showing' him how to use his presents.

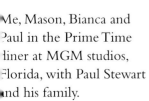

Me, Mason, Bianca and Paul in the Prime Time Diner at MGM studios, Florida, with Paul Stewart and his family.

We took the children
to EuroDisney.

Mason's third birthday – Italian cakes
take a little getting used to.

We came home for Christmas at Sopwell House with Mum,
Dad and my fabulous grandparents.

A special birthday treat for a very special lady: dinner with Raymond Blanc at Le Manoir aux Quat'Saisons.

Picking up Mason from school in Rome, looking 'Paul Perfect' on our way to lunch.

Me, Mum and Dad on our way into Stadio Olimpico to support Paul.

Buon Natale – Paul and I going out for dinner in our groovy Italian bespoke suits.

Paul in his element with the resident musicians of
Sabatini's, our favourite restaurant in Rome.

EuroDisney, 1992:
Mason was petrified
of the Captain Hook.

On a romantic break
in Monaco – this is my
favourite picture of Paul.

A 1997 fashion faux pas in
Sandy Lane, Barbados.

Love's young dream, 1991.

Our whole lives ahead of us.

Is this the last time I was the real me – with Paul?

Opening Christmas presents one year later.

from Paul. The truth is that no one can be convinced of anything unless they're prepared to be. I see that now. I thought they were so canny, getting me to go back to him, making out I was the only one who could keep him straight, keep him playing football – but I was the canny one. They were 'making' me do something I wanted to do in the first place, but couldn't admit to. So I agreed.

Mel and Len arranged for us to go to the Lygon Arms Hotel, a stunning place in a romantic setting in the Cotswolds. I was looking forward to seeing Paul again. I'd been on my own for a month, his pleas for me to come back had sounded urgent, and away from Italy, I was able to tell myself that perhaps it hadn't been that bad. Paul made me a proposition. He said it had got too much for him with me and the kids being there. He had gone from being a single lad to being a dad and he couldn't handle it. But he still wanted to see me: he loved me, I could come out to Italy at weekends, we could be a couple. He wanted us to stay together but live apart.

I listened, and felt immense relief. Maybe it would be all right after all. I was happy it wasn't over. It was going to be me and him against the world again. I would have the good times without the bad. His proposition suited me. I wouldn't let him become that woman on the bus: I wasn't prepared to admit my fantasy life was truly flawed. When he told me we were still special, I wanted to be transported back to when we'd first fallen in love, when what we'd had was unique, worth holding on to, a fiercer, deeper love than anyone had ever had. He never said sorry for hitting me, but he said to Wendy he was sorry about what he'd done to me because he'd let the pressure get to him. I let myself accept that. It was technically true: he had gone from single lad to dad, so it was almost my fault!

He *was* under pressure, of that I'm certain. Playing for Lazio was very hard for him. He came off the pitch forty-five minutes after his first game and was nowhere close to being worth the £5.5 million they'd paid for him. In fact, his performance was so disappointing that by January he had been dropped from the team. He was on the bench. Only Graham Taylor, as England manager, kept playing him, but England duty is not regular and wasn't enough to keep him occupied. I'm sure that was why his friends were in Italy and he was on the lash. When asked on Italian television what he thought of being dropped, he burped loudly. The fans loved it; the club fined him.

Despite the stunt, I know he must have been angry about being dropped and desperate at being unable to play football. No wonder he found a substitute to kick. This wasn't about me and the kids, it was about his career. My departure from Italy did not cure his concentration and fitness issues, or stop him drinking. In fact, in the three seasons he was at Lazio, Paul played in only forty-one matches. Moving to Italy had been a big mistake. For all of us.

So it was decided. The children and I would stay in England; Paul and I would see each other at weekends and for holidays. My dad, still on the case, said I needed somewhere of my own to live: Dobbs Weir was only temporary. He told Paul, 'You took her to Italy, then you kicked her out, and now you want her at weekends! You've got to help her.'

Mel and Len arranged for Paul and me to do a story that would earn me some money of my own. It was a nice getting-back-together story after speculation that had run in the tabloids about me leaving the villa. While I was in Italy Colin, my ex-husband, had sold a story about us to the press for £10,000. In it he claimed I had kept the children from him and he had been in a dire financial situation. I know that was the amount because when I bumped into Mark Dorney, Mandy's ex, in the street he told me that they'd gone to Cyprus on the money.

The story had included photographs of the children as babies. Back in the early days the press would never use photos of the kids, they were too respectful, but after we came back from Italy it was a free-for-all. I always believed that was because Colin had put photographs of the children into the public domain, which was where they stayed. There were journalists now wherever we went.

Hot on the heels of our reunion at the Lygon Arms, Mel and Len set up the interview with the *News of the World* for the extraordinary sum of £160,000. At the beginning of March 1993, I met Rebekah Wade, a features editor on the magazine, and flew out to Italy with her to do an interview and photos – funnily enough, there was a photographer at the airport, getting the scoop that we were back together again.

We took photographs up on a mountain where we used to go for ice-cream with the kids and admire the stunning views of Rome, then took some more in the city at a hotel where Grace Kelly had once stayed, and did the interview with a sort of *Mr and Mrs* quiz. Yes, it had been difficult, but we'd sorted out our problems, we were in love, and I was looking forward to settling down to a happy, normal life. What did I know of a happy, normal life?

The piece came out on 14 March. Now when I look at the photos from that shoot I can see what Wendy had meant. I was thin, I looked terrible, and my eyes were devoid of expression. Paul gave me £100,000 and kept £60,000 for himself. With my share I bought a home for me and the kids. That money and that house were the beginning of my long journey out of my destructive relationship with Paul, but it came with a catch. Mum, Dad and I were made to sign our first gagging contract. It didn't cross my mind not to but the wording was interesting. We were not allowed to talk to the press or public about Paul's 'personal and commercial affairs and those of his family as it would cause grave commercial and professional harm'. In return Paul 'agrees and undertakes not to visit the home to be acquired by The Trust save at the specific invitation of SF and further agrees not to molest SF or either of her children or to damage or destroy the contents of the home. In the event of PG assaulting SF then SF shall be entitled to call upon the Trustees of The Trust.'

Rush Close was part of a new development in Stanstead Abbotts, near Ware in Hertfordshire, a detached house at the end of a cul-de-sac near a canal. It was the show home, and I bought it for cash, with all the furniture and the fake curtains that didn't close. Bianca was coming up for seven and Mason was four. They never went back to being Kyle and Paul remained 'Daddy'. I got Bianca into Roselands, a really good local state school, and Mason went to nursery. I was with Paul, but not with him. We were boyfriend and girlfriend, but not a real couple. We were exclusive – or, at least, he had exclusive rights over me. He told me I was the only one, but when he was in Italy, partying with his family – he had moved them there permanently – who knew what he was up to? The kids and I got used to flying out for weekends and making room for him when he came home.

Life in Rush Close was happy. In fact, Bianca would say she was the happiest she'd ever been and that was because Paul wasn't there. Mason missed him more. Things were better between Paul and me when he turned up because he would be looking forward to seeing us. The sex was romantic – sometimes we'd go away to hotels, sometimes we'd cuddle on the sofa, like old times.

We went back to the villa in Rome for part of the summer holidays. By now he'd moved to a different one and had started spending huge amounts of money on things like kit cars and motorbikes. Paul suggested we went to Disney World in Florida – actually, he said to Mason, 'I want to take us all to Disney but Mum won't let me.' I was hounded and begged until I relented, and off we went. It was a lovely, happy holiday. Mason had always wanted to go, but Bianca wasn't so sure: she'd go in the hope that Paul would be nice to her. Disney is a hard thing for any child to turn down, but on all the subsequent occasions we went, however good Bianca was, she couldn't be good enough. On the plane to Florida, Paul and I would sit in two adjoining seats, with Mason and Bianca behind us, and always in first class – Paul thought you were less likely to die in a crash in first class. I had to be next to him. He'd let the kids buy stuff out of the in-flight magazine – watches, pens, anything. Once he bought them both watches, but he was pissed and when he woke up he'd forgotten and shouted at them.

Paul loves Disney, and usually our trips, which were arranged to paper over the cracks, were incident-free, Paul on best behaviour, being nice to the children, and I was his special girl again. But not always. On one of the many occasions we stayed at the Grand Floridian, the footballer Paul Stewart and his family were there. Paul had lived with him when he was at Tottenham. One evening, all the children were at the kids' club while we went out for dinner, and Paul Stewart was telling jokes. I made the mistake of laughing. Paul turned on me and pressed his head right up to mine: 'You wouldn't have laughed if I'd told that joke.'

The Stewarts said nothing and we all left the restaurant. As we were heading to our rooms Paul went for me. I was hurled over the empty loungers, dragged over the terrace, along a covered walkway. 'Ha-ha, you were laughing. Wouldn't laugh at my jokes . . .' Push, shove, push until we got to the kids' club to pick them up, and then it stopped. We lurched through the rest of the year like that. Fights, bust-ups, reconciliation, holiday. Fights, bust-ups, reconciliation, holiday. On and on. Thankfully, Bianca, Mason and I had a roof over our heads and the children were happy at their schools.

If Paul was seeing other women, I didn't want to know. Once I went to Italy without the kids and spotted a piece of paper in the wastepaper basket with my name on it. I picked it up and John-Paul had written, 'Sheryl knows about the Lazio hostess.' Once again, snippets of secrets and half-truths. When I asked Paul he denied it and ridiculed me for 'going through the bins'. Then he got John-Paul to call me up and say it was just a wind-up. I knew it wasn't, but as long as I had friends and support in England, I could go on kidding myself.

When Paul was in Italy he still controlled me but he couldn't do it as effectively as he did when we were together. He'd ring me all the time, wanting to know where I was, but eventually I started to make friends, go out a bit and get stronger. I even had a party, which would have been unimaginable in Italy. It was all thanks to Rush Close and to Rebekah Wade, who had enabled me to buy it. One day I was invited to lunch with a lady called Anne to see a mural she'd had painted in her dining room. The evening before, Paul showed up unannounced. The next morning he asked me what I was doing that day. I told him I was going out for lunch. Well, my head bounced off the corner of the kitchen unit and he started hitting me. 'You shouldn't be doing anything when I've come all this way to see you.' But his visit hadn't been planned and I didn't want to cancel. I went flying, hit my head again and temporarily lost the vision in one eye.

Again, I was saved by the bell. This time Terry Bailey was on the doorstep holding a fishing rod.

Paul had seen him the previous night before he'd come to me and had made a plan to go fishing with him, which he'd forgotten about. Off he went. My immediate thought was to cancel my lunch, but I decided not to let him have his way. I sat through it with a pounding headache. In the afternoon, he left a message: 'Hey, love, do you want to go to the theatre tonight? Get tickets to whatever you want to see.' He knew I loved the theatre, so there was the hook – and I was just another stupid fish ready to bite. This time I promised myself I wouldn't reply. Then he suggested dinner with Linda and Terry.

Finally I spoke to him. 'No, I've got a headache.' Which I did.

'Oh, yeah? You just can't let anything go. You're living in the past – you just let it drag on, making it worse . . .'

And I thought, Well, he *is* trying to make up for it, and I *am* dragging it out, and I *am* making it worse. What was I going to do? Make it worse or better? I attempted to make it better. He never said, 'I'm sorry. Are you OK?' He just wanted to know it was over. Move on. Never again. Until the next time.

My parents and I went to Italy for my birthday. The celebrations did not last long. Paul, clearly wound up, told me that his boss, Cragnotti, wanted to see me in the morning. I asked him why. Wrong question. 'I don't know – you're probably shagging him. You want to shag him, don't you?' The usual rubbish. He banged me against the bedroom wall, head-butted me and split my lip. It was unusual for him to harm my face – I think his aim was off. The blows stopped when my mum, hearing the noise, knocked on the door. Later, he told me I had to go to the meeting because I'd embarrass him if I *didn't*. 'That's my boss. Don't you dare embarrass me by not going. Why do you have to be rude, you big-headed blonde bitch?'

I told him there was no way I was going, looking like I did – you can't cover a split lip with makeup. But he insisted. The following morning, there I sat. Cragnotti didn't say a word about my appearance. He offered me a job working for Lazio in London – it would make things easier for Paul if I took it. I was thinking, You have no idea! There is no way Paul would let me take a job like that. Now I'm fairly sure that when Paul wasn't playing well, he blamed me. I was the cause of his dip in fitness, his lack of concentration, his slowing down, even when I was only seeing him at weekends. No wonder they wanted me out of the way. I'd be busy in England, unable to show up at the drop of the hat and ruin his 'concentration'.

Another evening we were coming back from a restaurant and again he started on me. He wanted me to admit that I didn't love him. 'But I do love you, Paul.'

'No, you don't. Just admit it.' He pulled into a lay-by. I asked him to take us home. He said he'd wait all night. I got out of the car and started walking. He pulled up and told me to get into the car. I'd only do that if he carried on driving home, I said. I was so used to his pestering that I knew he'd go mad no matter what I said. Sure enough, he attacked me in the car as we pulled up to the house. I got out, ran into the garden and hid behind a tree. He went into the villa, thinking I was in there. I couldn't shout for help. I was scared. When he was in a rage his feet would slap on the tiles, and all I could hear was the shouting and his slapping feet. 'Shell, you're doing my f—ing head in! Stop f—ing winding me up.'

I stayed behind the tree for ages, listening, until at last he calmed down and I thought he'd fallen asleep. I came out from behind the tree and walked up the path. In the house, the lights were all on and the door was open. I went to the door. I don't know where he came from but suddenly he was there, in front of me. I ran through the hall, the lounge, the room with the pool table and got into the master bedroom. In his rage he picked up a metal swing seat and hurled it through a glass wall. That stopped him and he went away.

I picked myself up and went to the bathroom, but when I came out, he was there again. 'Look what you made me do! That's great! Everyone's going to know now and you love it, don't you, everyone knowing? Can't just forget it, can you?'

He grabbed my hair and dragged me back to the bathroom. 'Look what you've done!' In the bottom of the toilet bowl was my heart necklace. At one point he'd had me round the neck and it must have broken. Then, when I'd gone to the loo, it had fallen off. Because it was heavy it had sunk to the bottom and stayed there. Well, that was it. He shoved my head down the toilet. Such things don't hurt physically, but it *hurts* to think about it – I was so humiliated.

I felt like a rag doll when he threw me about. I wonder what it felt like to him? The next day he took my passport again. This time I had marks on my face and my hair was matted from being stuck in the toilet when one of Paul's bodyguards came to the villa to tell me Paul wanted to meet me for lunch. That time I told him categorically I was not going. 'You've seen what he does. None of you do anything – you all know what's going on.'

Looking back on it now I realize it wasn't their responsibility to stop it happening. It was mine and mine alone. And I didn't. They kept telling me how sorry he was, how he wanted to go to this place on the beach with me. Poor Paul had left training early he was so distraught, poor Paul couldn't concentrate. 'You have to go.' So, I cleaned myself up and they took me to this beach place.

Paul had booked a room in the hotel. 'I'm so sorry, it'll never happen again, I just love you so much, please forgive me ...' Same old, same old. We ended up in bed, then pretty soon afterwards we got up and went out to get a drink. Despite everything, the sex was still good. Or maybe because of it.

When he was injured, which was often, I'd fly out to help him. When he wasn't, we'd all go to watch him play. He always ensured we were made a fuss of when we arrived, that we were met and taken to a private room. Now I wonder if he was just keeping me out of the players' bar where those gorgeous hostesses were and the glamorous girlfriends who knew too much. Being ushered into private rooms sounds impressive, but it's actually pretty boring because you're in there by yourself, which was how he liked it.

Paul would want to go out and have a drink even if they'd lost. One night when his sister and her boyfriend were there we went to Sabatini. It was in a little piazza, there was a clock tower and cobbled streets. I loved that restaurant and it was one of the few places of which I have fond memories. When anyone came past, Paul would always do the same act: 'Can I have the time, please? You got the time?' and they'd always tell him what it was. He thought that was really funny because the big clock tower was right behind them. Paul loved lobster and one night when he ordered it he told the waiter he'd come and show him which one he wanted. He went to the tank and was pointing. 'I want that one, no, that one – that one,' he said, in his pidgin Italian. 'Not that one, that one.' He was being loud and everyone was laughing, Gazza the clown was in the building. 'You don't understand!' He dived headfirst into the lobster tank, and while upside down and underwater he pointed to the lobster with bubbles coming out of his mouth and shouted – 'I want that one!'

We spent a lot of the summer of 1993 in Rome. During that period Paul put on a lot of weight so he was probably drinking much more than I ever knew. It was getting harder to hide from the kids what was going on. Once when a friend had come to stay, we were all crammed into the car and my friend had to sit on Jimmy's knee in the front. Mason was on mine and Bianca was squeezed in on the other side of him. Paul started on at me, swearing and shouting and calling me names. My friend tried to intervene, told him to stop because the kids were in the car, which was more than the driver ever did, even though he too was a member of the Modialpol Security Police. All the times I was in Italy, they never did anything to help. Who was I going to call, the police? They were the police.

Things were particularly bad over the Christmas holidays. On Christmas Eve 1993 the whole family went to Hanbury Manor, a country-house hotel in Hertfordshire, where I saw a guy who was going out with my friend Debbie. I said hello to him. Paul came over and I thought, Uh-oh ... We went to the bar, and Paul was on good form, talking to everyone, but on the way home, before we got into the car, he started going on at me about the guy in the bar. Halfway home, he pulled up on the verge of the A10, and started going on about whether I'd slept with this guy – 'You went out with him, didn't you? Someone told me you did. Just tell me and we can go.'

I would have said anything to persuade him to drive home

so that I could get the kids out of the car and out of harm's way, but nothing worked. We sat in that lay-by for ages, with me trying to tell the kids they weren't going to miss Father Christmas. Later that evening Paul punched a hole in the wall. I hung a picture over it but the kids always knew it was there.

Next morning we were all looking at what Santa had brought and the kids were ecstatic – Paul had gone over the top again. Then I glimpsed a car on the driveway with a big bow on it. It was a BMW. How did I feel? Ecstatic? Excited? It meant nothing to me. Actually, it meant a lot – none of it good. I pretended I hadn't seen it and tried to plan how I'd react. He was trying to get me to look out of the window. When finally he succeeded, I couldn't muster any enthusiasm. I just couldn't. I told him it was too much. I'm sure he hated that. I wasn't grateful – I couldn't be bought. The car couldn't make up for the hitting because that was unjustifiable. And I was beginning to think that maybe I was worth more than a car.

We were back at Sabatini for New Year's Eve. It was the custom in Italy to set off firecrackers to mark the occasion. Paul put a knotted napkin on his head and dived under the table, shouting about bombs. Everyone was laughing except an American couple who had no idea who he was and just thought he was mad. Take away the football and you're left with a madman. I tried to explain to them that he could get away with it because he played football – which still made no sense to them. Once in Monte Carlo Paul made a major social faux-pas. In the restaurant of Fayed's hotel the sommeliers wear a wine ladle around their necks on a chain, an ornate cup that they use to taste the wine. Paul grabbed it and started swilling the wine around and spitting it out. He just about managed to get away with that too. He was always stripping naked, playing tricks and pulling stunts.

In Italy his football career was deteriorating. He was overweight and unfit. Then in January 1994 he broke a rib playing against Sampdoria. Around that time he was also held by police for allegedly punching a press photographer in Rome. Lazio suggested we go on holiday for some R and R. Paul, Bianca, Mason and I went to the Forte Village in Sardinia. It was a beautiful place and we were treated very well. It was out of season but one evening there was a dinner dance. The kids had been really good throughout the meal so when Mason wanted to dance I stood up with him. Paul said, 'What are you getting up for? You want men to look at you.' All the usual abuse started. But I was determined to dance with Mason and do the Mum bit on the dance floor. Paul got increasingly bad-tempered. especially when Mason fell asleep with his head on my lap. Then, of course, I had to carry him back to the room – 'Tied to the apron strings. He's not a baby, why can't he walk?' I knew he wasn't going to stop. I just prayed he'd fall asleep while I settled the kids in the connecting room. They were always in a connecting room, never with us because that would have got in the way of sex.

Paul didn't fall asleep. When I came in from the kids' room, he pushed me, then shoved me up against the wall. A lamp went flying and a mirror fell off its hook and smashed. 'Look what you've made me do.'

The next day we were in the limo on the way back to the airport when Bianca suddenly blurted out, 'Dad, you said you wouldn't be like that any more. You were horrible to Mum last night – I heard her crying and something smash.' I froze.

He turned to Bianca and said, 'You keep your f—ing mouth shut!'

I tried to intervene. 'Hang on a minute –'

'No! What goes on in this family stays in this family.' And that was the end of the discussion.

During term time I would visit Paul quite regularly but, more often than not, it would end badly. Later he told me he had manufactured those fights because it was easier for him that I left hating him rather than loving him. I thought he caused them so that he had an excuse to go off with someone else while I was back in England: he could say we weren't together at the time, because after an attack I would tell him it was over, go home and pull out the phone. Then he would ring my friend and neighbour, Ami, complaining he couldn't get hold of me. She would tell him to go away, but he would talk her round in circles and finally Jay, her husband, would take pity and come round to ask me to put my phone back on.

If Paul couldn't get hold of Ami, he'd call a local taxi firm and they would come to the house. The doorbell would ring in the middle of the night and a driver would be outside to tell me it was vital Paul spoke to me right away. The first few times I was so taken aback it worked. I thought maybe something really bad had happened. He often got his family to call too. Eventually I wised up, and the next time a taxi came round I thanked the driver, closed the door and went back to bed.

After my departure from Italy in 1993, I went back to him countless times and always with butterflies in my stomach. I looked forward to seeing him and expected the best, but almost always came home bruised in one way or another. They were the rag-doll years. I would say it was because I loved him, but that statement doesn't hold much water now. What sort of person loves someone who hurts them? I wanted Paul without the violence and the abuse. I wanted him as he'd been when he'd said he couldn't live without me, when I was more important than anything else, when I meant everything to him. That had been a tiny purple patch at the end of the summer of 1991. It wasn't a lot to go on, was it?

7. Kiss and Tell ...

One evening in March 1994 Paul and I went to dinner at Le Gavroche in London. At the end of the meal out came a cake with 'Will You Marry Me?' iced on it. I said yes because I wanted to believe it was possible to be in love passionately, happily, without the drama. I wanted my fairytale wedding and my fairytale life. I kept the bill. It came to £849.80, of which £738 was spent on wine. The cake was free.

I was happy to be engaged to Paul, but then something happened that put the wedding plans on hold. During the Easter holidays in 1994 the kids and I went to see him in Italy. His parents were there too. We were at the ground watching an unscheduled practice match when suddenly I heard a terrible yell from the other side of the pitch. Paul had always said, 'Shez, you'll know when I'm hurt because I'll stay down.' And, true to his word, whenever he went down during a match, he'd always get straight back up, look at me and give me a sign, but this time he stayed down and the screaming didn't stop. We watched as they carried him towards us. He was swearing his head off and his leg was hanging at an odd angle. The yelling was more from fear than pain. He was shouting at the guys for lifting him badly, carrying him the wrong way and jeopardizing everything.

I panicked and went straight into protective mode. I had no idea how you should carry an injured player and I had no idea what he'd done to himself, but that didn't stop me yelling at them too. I was so worried about him – he looked like a terrified, helpless little boy. I left my kids with his dad and went in the ambulance with him.

At the hospital there was chaos. I wasn't allowed to let them do anything to him. He only wanted his knee surgeon

Mr Browett – he didn't trust anyone else: 'Sheryl, don't let them touch my leg. Sheryl, don't let them do anything. Sheryl, Sheryl . . .'

Arrangements were made speedily to fly Paul home to England. But the press were speedier still. There were loads of journalists on the plane with us all taking photos, shouting questions. Somewhere there's a news clip in which you can hear Paul saying, 'Sheryl, they're driving me mad. Sheryl, tell 'em, tell 'em.' I had to stand up and tell them to leave him alone. I doubt I made any friends doing that. He was taken to the Princess Grace Hospital and I, of course, went too.

The children stayed in Italy with Paul's mum and dad. I hated leaving them – she rang to tell me, 'These kids can't do anything for themselves.'

Rebekah, who'd become a friend, arrived at the hospital and Paul was winding her up about some guy she was seeing, but I could tell it was forced jollity and I knew he was terrified. It was awful watching them take him away for an operation. I cried and cried after he went in. I was so worried because *he* was so worried – would they be able to fix it? When he finally came out of surgery he wouldn't let me leave the hospital. They put a mattress on the floor and I stayed there for four days and four nights, twenty-four hours a day, trying to keep him happy. It was an impossible task.

He was like a caged tiger and angry with everyone. The nurses weren't helping him, he said, they didn't know what they were doing, they were lying to him. I was exhausted. Eventually Mr Browett said I should go home for some rest. Paul told him I was all right where I was – 'You're all right, aren't you? Tell him.' So, as usual, I said I was fine. But by the evening he was so agitated that I knew he was going to blow up. Instead of begging me to help him, he was shouting and swearing at me and calling me all the names in his not very imaginative repertoire. I told him I was going.

'You're not going anywhere.'

I looked at him lying in the bed, his leg in traction, and realized he couldn't stop me. But he gave it a good try. He picked up his crutch and threw it hard at me. As usual his aim was good. I told him I'd see him in the morning.

Despite the hurtful words, as ever I found extenuating circumstances to excuse his behaviour. He *was* facing a year off the pitch and they were worried about his recovery. It didn't occur to me then that his worsening mood might relate to the need for a drink. Bottom line, I was concerned about him.

He couldn't play football for a year with his leg in plaster but he quickly found another outlet for his excess energy, fuelled nicely by there being no need to curb his alcohol intake. In England he didn't have to live by Lazio's strict rules: he wasn't training twice a day, and could go out on the town as much as he liked.

One day Rebekah rang to tell me a local Hoddesdon family were trying to sell a three-part story about Paul to the press. As soon as I heard the story, I knew who the family were: Dave and Karen Boare had children at the same school mine attended, lived in the road behind Paul and drank in Paul's local, the Fish and Eels. A few months ago Paul had gone in a limo to London with Dave and some other mates. They'd stripped Dave naked and locked him out of the limo. Paul used limos regularly so I got to know the company well, and their driver that night had told me some of what had gone on. He was always very nice to me. I don't think the owner was very impressed by what sometimes took place in the back of his cars when Paul was on his own and even less so when it was just the two of us.

I called the driver to find out if there was anything else I needed to know before the story was published. He told me that in fact they had *all* stripped off and they were seeing how far they could put their fingers up their backsides. Then Paul told Dave to get out of the limo, which, foolishly, he did even though it was obviously Paul's intention to leave him behind. I don't think they went far or for long.

The second instalment detailed how Paul wanted to run away with Dave's wife, Karen. Of course, this was news to me. In the interview Karen said that Paul had begged her to come away with him, told her he wished I was more like her, had kissed her, groped her boobs and had a good old fumble with her one evening after her husband had gone to bed.

The third story was about another girl who lived in Hoddesdon and was referred to as 'T'. Rebekah didn't have anything else to tell me and at the time I had no idea who T might be. When I challenged Paul he laughed it off: he had no idea what I was on about, he said. There was no girl in Hoddesdon called T. It was, as usual, all lies, bollocks. But the first two stories came out.

When he was confronted with the papers, Paul denied what Karen had said. 'I wasn't snogging Karen when Dave went to bed. I didn't do that. No way, she's a moose.' After that Karen was referred to as 'the trollop' by the school mums. Later, when I was trying to get Bianca into Presdales, a good secondary school, she ended up doing me an enormous favour. Bianca was offered a place at the less good school in Hoddesdon, and when I was asked why I couldn't accept it, I wrote to the school enclosing a copy of the kiss-and-tell article: it wouldn't be fair to Bianca to have to see that woman or her children every day. She got a place at Presdales.

One evening Paul and I were out at a small London restaurant, but our romantic evening was ruined because he was drinking a lot and was on a short fuse. Needing a break from his abusive comments and behaviour, I went to the Ladies. But that night he followed me in, shouting his head off, not caring who heard or saw. Was the booze making him careless, or, having got away with so much for so long, did he just not care? I know now that abuse rarely ceases just because you are in public. They simply find cannier ways to keep you in your place. Tables can be pushed painfully into stomachs; tablecloths provide the perfect cover for crushed toes, pinched thighs and kicked shins; and no one is ever any the wiser.

To make it up to me he took me to the Ritz in Paris, the highlights of which were seeing Linda Evangelista in the elevator, buying a beautiful Versace suit that Madonna modelled and booking in for a new pair of boobs. I'd been thinking about doing it for ages, perhaps no longer being totally flat-chested would help boost my confidence.

In May, to celebrate Paul's birthday, which we always made into a big occasion, we went to Sardinia. Jimmy 'Five Bellies', his girlfriend and his son were there, Lindsay and her boyfriend, me and the kids. One day Paul organized a boat trip to a deserted beach for a picnic and while we were there he told me to take my top off. I never went topless any more – I wasn't allowed to look at a man, so whipping out my new boobs was unthinkable. 'Go on! What's the point of having them if you're not going to show them off?'

I felt cheap, but I did what he told me to do. I always did. Next day there were photos of me topless everywhere. I was embarrassed but Paul found it hilarious.

That holiday was a disaster, if not for the usual reasons. Paul Merson, the Arsenal player, was there with his wife, Lorraine. He had just come out of rehab and was sober so it must have been their worst nightmare to see Paul and his entourage swagger on to the beach and start knocking back the beer.

On Paul's birthday, we went to the smart restaurant on the top floor of the hotel for dinner. We got dressed up to the nines and left the kids with a babysitter. I'd ordered a cake and the evening went really well. Later Paul spotted laser lights in the distance and said, 'Let's go clubbing.' No one seemed that keen but it was his birthday, so I piped up, 'If you want to go, we can go.' He was excited about the prospect of more drinks and more partying. For some reason, though, he started to work himself into a state. He didn't believe me when I said I'd go too. 'If you were with your mates you'd want to go, you'd be right there, but because it's me . . .' I was happy to go so I was almost laughing at him. I used to call him 'Mr Workyticket' when he was like that, but only in my head. I went back to our room to tell the babysitter we'd be out later than expected, then went into the bathroom to touch up my makeup.

When I came out Paul was in the blindest of rages. 'You stupid bitch, f—ing slag, big-headed blonde bitch, f—ing c—t, f—ing slag. You never want to go out with me!'

Immediately I was trying to calm him down, ready to do anything to stop it becoming physical. 'Don't be silly, we're going out. Come on, let's go.' The lead-up to being hit was always worse than the beating itself. While it was going on, I'd shut down and get through it. But while he was working himself up to it, calling me every name under the sun and telling me how f—ing useless I was, I could see myself panicking, trying desperately to appease him. Now I'm angry with myself for being so pathetic in taking all those insults, for not walking out, calling for help, making it stop. I'm angry with myself for putting up with it for years and years.

Paul got my face in his grip and shouted, 'You told the f—ing babysitter to go f—ing home, you f—ing stupid bitch.'

'No, I didn't.'

'Yes, you f—ing did! You never want to f—ing go out with me. You never want to f—ing kiss me. You never want to make love. You never want to hug me, do you, do you, do you? You don't, do you?'

On and on and on. He wasn't listening to anything I was saying. As far as he was concerned, I had let the babysitter go and that was that. I told him over and over again that I'd asked the babysitter to stay longer and was redoing my makeup but he went after me and beat me up again. It was a bad one. He often went for the hair at the side of my head and hurled me against a wall – if there wasn't a wall, he'd fling me at the floor, a chair, a table. Then he moved to my arms – I was always bruised at the top of my arms. I remember being somewhere hot with his mum and she kept telling me to take my cardigan off, but I couldn't because of the bruises. That night in Sardinia he started shaking me by my hair, then threw me over the coffee-table and chairs. Before I'd had a chance to catch my breath, he held me down and kneed me, shouting and swearing all the time.

Then, all of a sudden, he stopped. He told me to take the kids and get out. 'I hate the kids and I hate you. Take the f—ing kids and get the f— out. My life's been shit since I met you. Ask anyone, they'll tell you – they know what you're like.' He went to get the suitcases but then remembered he hadn't wanted them cluttering up the room. He called Lindsay, woke her up and asked for the suitcases. She told him Jimmy had them. So then he called Jimmy and he dutifully came down with them. I was curled up on one of the low chairs, and Jimmy asked if I was all right. Paul turned on him. 'F—ing hell, are *you* all right? Jimmy wants to know are *you* all right?' As if it was wrong that he should be asking after me. 'She paid the f—ing babysitter and told her to f—ing go!'

'Paul,' said Jimmy, 'you paid the babysitter, gave her a big tip and told her to leave.'

What did he do? Nothing. What did I do? Nothing. What did I think? Thank God he knows it wasn't me. Thank God Jimmy knows I haven't done anything wrong. Thank God they know it wasn't my fault. Jimmy left and Paul fell asleep.

The next morning I was on the beach digging a hole with Mason and I could hear Paul talking to Paul Merson. 'How's it, like, not drinking?'

Paul Merson came out with the usual post-rehab patter that I've heard a thousand times: 'One day at a time ... One more drink and I'll die.'

Paul said, 'I was pissed up last night, really went for Sheryl. It was a joke – I had a go at her about paying the babysitter, then Jimmy told me it was me.' Paul Merson didn't look like he found it the slightest bit funny. As for me, did I hate him? No, I hated myself. For taking it. Then I sat tight, kept quiet and counted down the days before I could go home. I never ended the relationship to his face. I'd just crawl back to the safety of Rush Close and refuse to speak to him.

To add insult to injury, Jane Nottage's book, *Paul Gascoigne – The Inside Story*, was serialized in the *Sunday Mirror*. In it she described Paul as her brother, best mate and great friend. She wrote that I was the problem, that I had tried to keep her and Paul apart, and blamed me for her getting the sack. I rang her in front of Paul and asked her why she'd written that. She said that that was what she'd been told. I made Paul tell her that that was far from the truth and that, in fact, I had protected her from Paul's rants. She also described a trip when Paul's parents came and I had cooked for everyone else but not given them any food. The day she was talking about, I had done spaghetti for whoever was at home, but they were out and not expected back. A tiny misinterpretation maybe, but they were starting to add up. The whole Jane Nottage debacle provided a perfect example of what we all had to deal with wherever Paul was concerned. I was being told one thing, Jane another, and all the while there were other people who were desperately trying to protect him, often because that was what they were paid to do. But at the time it just felt like endless stories coming out against me.

Not only was Paul hitting me black and blue, he was also letting me take the rap for his bad behaviour and, no doubt, saying worse behind my back. I was knocked sideways by the revelations in that book. I told him it was truly over.

After we'd had a big row, there was always a few days' grace, and then the phone would start to ring. When he knew for sure that I wouldn't answer he started writing, letters, poems, sometimes incoherent ramblings. I have so many cards, boxes and boxes of them, most of which are about how hard it was to be without me, how pig-headed and ignorant he'd been, how he'd never find anyone like me. He wrote that he told everyone how bad he'd been to me, how much he wished he'd married me and had more kids, and how hateful the idea of me with anyone else was. There was a lot about Mason, how desperate he was to stay in touch with him, but only if I was there, because otherwise he couldn't handle it. He wished he'd given me more space and said over and over how much he loved the three of us and that he ALWAYS would. I kept everything he sent to me, even the dried flowers that came with the cards.

When that didn't work Paul decided on another tactic. In July he did a story with the *Sun* in which he admitted to giving me a hard time, pushing me about and generally being a bit of a bastard. He was deeply ashamed of himself and wasn't ever going to do it again. But it was exactly that: a story. Most people took it as such. Some friends of mine even asked me why he'd do such an odd publicity stunt. I responded by insisting there would be no reconciliation.

By then I should have known myself better. Paul, still on a major offensive, offered me the villa in Italy and said I could go there with my girlfriends and our children. The morning we were due to fly I ordered a minibus and we were about to set off when a limo arrived. I didn't want it so I sent it away. But we had a good time in his villa and I was grateful to him.

By August my resolve had crumbled and I flew to Monaco with Paul for a 'trip of a lifetime'. I was going to the home of Grace Kelly, my heroine, and was completely overexcited. We stayed at L'Hermitage, overlooking the shimmering sea, staring at the fabulous boats and all the beautiful people. I got to be Paul's princess again. On our return Paul went back to Italy and mostly we remained apart. Mason went to see him from time to time, and Paul would dress him in a suit to match his own. They'd go to the Hotel Hassler and hang out together, which Paul knew made me happy.

In early 1995 we were back in Florida, and my mum and dad flew out to meet us (a fact we had to hide from his family because Paul was made to feel bad if he was on holiday with us and not them) and they stayed with the kids while Paul and I went to Sarasota to have some time on our own. We were on the beach when Paul pointed out a guy who was big in Scottish football. It was Walter Smith. The name meant nothing to me but it turned out that he was the manager of Rangers and was there with his wife, Ethel, and their kids. I was missing Bianca and Mason so Paul sent for them and my parents to come and join us.

Walter suggested we move to Glasgow and that Paul play for Rangers. I liked the way he included me and the children – I hadn't come across that in the football industry before. He clearly saw us as a family. Paul was excited at the prospect of joining such a big club and working under such a reputable manager. I was excited about him leaving Italy and all those bad memories, and about planning the move together, as a proper family. This was a major turning point: for the first time, I felt we were a team.

Over the next few months Walter had several meetings with Paul about moving to Glasgow, and stressed that we would be moving as a family. Finally we were going to be happy and settled. Paul told everyone he would give up the booze for his new club. We went away for a weekend to celebrate, just the two of us, in Sardinia, but on the first night we heard that Jimmy and Terry had been in a bad car accident. Jimmy had been driving when the car left the road and hit a tree. He had got out unhurt, but Terry had fractured his hip in five places, his liver was ruptured and he had injuries to his legs and back. I assumed we'd fly home, but Paul wanted to stay on holiday.

*

Before leaving Lazio we decided to take a holiday in Las Vegas and LA before flying home via Guernsey so Paul could get his financial affairs in order. I found out just before leaving that I'd come home from Sardinia with more than a sun tan. I was pregnant again. I was surprised since I was still on the pill. Then again with a sexual appetite as high as Paul's, it wasn't really that surprising. A pill can only do so much. I was pleased. It cemented everything. Paul loved me and we were moving to Scotland as a family. People had been telling me for years how much he loved kids, so I was prepared to forget his reaction to my earlier pregnancy. I was convinced he'd be pleased too. We went to the airport in the limo, and he was making lists of all the things we had to buy if he was going to move to Scotland. He was always making lists. We were almost at the airport.

He said, 'Right, what else?'

'You better put down a cot.'

There was a pause. 'Right, now if I get those speakers from Sony . . .'

It was just like last time.

'I'll have to put that in storage, move those, leave that . . .'

More silence.

'Did you hear what I said?'

'All right, all right.'

We pulled up at the airport and went into the Virgin lounge. I was desperate for him to say something – I wanted a reaction. An hour passed while we checked in and had a drink, but he said nothing. Finally I plucked up the courage to say, 'Paul, you not going to talk about it?'

'Why do you have to keep on? Why do you have to put me under pressure? Don't go on about it!'

We flew to Las Vegas first. I was tired, but all he wanted to do was stay up all night drinking and gambling. Fine, that's what you do in Vegas, but eventually I'd have to go to bed. He'd wave me off with barely a backward glance. The baby wasn't mentioned again.

We flew on to LA, where we were to stay at the Beverly Wilshire in a lovely suite. As my brothers were in San Diego I thought we could go and see them.

'I didn't come all this way to visit your family.'

'What about if I just ring them? Maybe they could come here? We could have tea.'

'No. What did you come here with me for if that's what you wanted to do?'

So that was that. I didn't see Gaylord, David or Vicki.

Paul spent the next two days on the phone buying his dad a car. He seemed to buy John seven or eight cars a year. John would sell whichever car he had been given, then phone Paul and say, 'I haven't got a car.' Paul just bought another. He never said no to John, ever.

Paul didn't want to do anything in LA, but if I tried to go down Rodeo Drive to have a look, I'd get the third degree. So it wasn't worth it. I stayed in the room watching TV while he sorted out his dad's car. Finally he agreed to go with me to Rodeo Drive. It was torture: he ogled every single woman we passed – not just a glance, a full-blown comedy mouth-open gawp.

When we passed a baby shop I said, 'I want to go in there.'

'What for?'

So we didn't go in. He went into Louis Vuitton and he spent thousands on luggage and other bags. We carried on walking and I thought, I'm going to regret it if I don't get this baby something from Rodeo Drive. I went back to the baby shop. Paul wouldn't come in. I bought a little bib.

Back on the street, a man stopped me, told me I was beautiful and asked me whether I was an actress. Then he gave me his card. It was a perfect LA moment, even better because I'd been feeling so down with Paul staring at all those women. Of course Paul took the card from me and ripped it up, but he couldn't take away that moment when I'd felt good about myself.

When we stopped for a drink he chatted up the waitress in

front of me. He was clearly doing anything he could to under-mine me.

The next night we went to the Polo Lounge, and when we walked in, there was the guy who'd given me the card. I tried to avoid him, but he came over and said, 'Don't forget, give me a call . . .' That night Paul didn't say a word.

We flew to Rome and while we were there we went to dinner at the Hotel Eden. He was being a bit narky and he was definitely drinking. For some reason we started to argue about Jane Nottage. I told him I still didn't understand how all that time he'd been rude about her she'd thought they were best friends. That book had really thrown me and I still needed to get to the bottom of who was double-crossing whom and how many more lies had been told. Instead of answering me, he started on about what I was and what I wasn't. Bitch, slag, money-grabbing, cow, tart . . . You're not the best-looking fanny in the world . . . Paul had given me a diamond tennis bracelet and I was wearing it that night. He started picking on my parents. 'Your mum and dad are nothing. They couldn't care less about you.' My hands were under the table and every time he said something horrible I snapped a diamond off my bracelet. Snap, snap, snap. For a brief moment I felt I had control over the sit-uation. What he said wasn't going over me, but it wasn't going through me either. It was my secret revenge, the only way I could fight back.

When we went back to the room and he'd shut the door, he said, 'You're getting rid of that f—ing baby. I don't want a slag like you having a baby of mine. You're getting that kid out of there because I don't want it turning out a poof like Mason. Always sitting on your lap. I tell you what, I'm going to make sure Anna comes with you because I don't trust you. Anna'll make sure you get rid of it.'

The next day I told him I wasn't going to Guernsey. 'Yes, you bloody are. You understand all this stuff, you're not f—ing off.'

So I went along with it but I promised myself that as soon as we got home it would be over.

When we arrived in Guernsey, Mel and Len turned up with a newspaper and showed an article to Paul. It said Piers Morgan and I were going out with each other and we were going to make music together. First I'd heard of it. Max Clifford mentioned it in his autobiography years later. Apparently Max was asked whether 'Gazza's Girl' was going out with Piers Morgan and he said, 'Yeah, they're going to make a record together, and she's going to play the flute and he's going to play the banjo ... or whatever.' Of course he was being sarcastic, but they printed it anyway.

Paul was not pleased. Not only was I pregnant but he had a piece of paper confirming that I was the lying, cheating slag he'd thought I was. That little piece of mud stuck, and it was rumoured for years that Regan was Piers Morgan's child. Paul used to throw it at me during rows.

Paul dropped me back at Rush Close and his parting words were 'I'll ring you in three days to make sure you've done it.' Then he went to Newcastle.

I went to see to my doctor and told him my predicament. He said I was in no fit state to make such a decision. I was clearly very upset, and as it was early days I had a little time to think about it. But I didn't. Paul was ringing back in three days. My doctor said he would speak to him. I think he knew what was going on. A year before there had been an incident on Bonfire Night in our cul-de-sac. Each year all the residents would put money towards the celebration and we'd open up the garages, have barbecues, serve food and let off fireworks over the river. Once, Paul had come with Terry and Linda. At some point, Linda had got Terry a hot dog. Later, when I was in one of the garages clearing up, Paul came up behind me and kicked me hard in the back of the leg. I stumbled, and he went into one. 'You don't f—ing love me, you didn't ask me if I wanted a f—ing hotdog.' Kick, kick, kick, kick. Then someone walked in and Paul stopped. I'm pretty sure it had been my doctor, who was a neighbour and now sat opposite me, telling me I had a choice.

I went home and thought, It's my choice. I love this man, we're moving to Scotland, we're a family, I'm keeping the baby. Why wouldn't I have his child? I wasn't going to abort a baby just because he told me to. I'd had a baby on my own before and I'd do it on my own again if I had to. In any case, I'd always considered myself a single parent. It was easier when Paul wasn't with me – having him around was almost like having another child to look after. But I still loved him and wanted the perfect happy family I'd hankered for all my life. Two days later I told the doctor I'd decided to keep the baby.

That was the end of my Scottish dream, but I felt OK about it.

A week later Paul finally called. 'Well, you done it?'

'No.'

'What do you mean you've not done it?'

He flipped. I'd never before refused to do what he said. He called me every name under the sun. I hung up on him. His sister Anna rang me and asked me why I was keeping it.

They'd all been telling me to have a baby, I reminded her, and I wasn't going to abort this one because he said so. End of story. Countless phone calls followed, many of them insulting, including one from an adviser of Paul's who said, 'Why are you keeping it? It's only a foetus.' Paul moved up to Scotland, taking his friend Cyril in my place. It seemed that it was finally over between us.

In the public eye, things weren't looking good for Paul. He played his first match for Rangers, a pre-season friendly against Celtic, and foolishly celebrated a goal by miming playing a flute, which is an Irish Protestant Loyalist symbol, in front of the predominantly Catholic Celtic fans. It did not go down well.

Paul has always read every paper each morning, devouring stories about himself, and was very aware of negative press.

Maybe he was feeling lonely and unsupported, I don't know, but he started ringing, saying how sorry he was he'd reacted that way. He sent letters, cards, flowers, then started coming down to visit, staying sober, keeping his behaviour in check. Other emissaries were sent with the same message. He loves you, he's sorry, this time he's learnt his lesson. It went on until I relented. By the time I was five months pregnant, I had forgiven him and taken him back. Once again, I thought he'd changed, that things would be different.

This chapter ends as it began, with a kiss-and-tell. One afternoon there was a knock on the door and a woman I knew vaguely was standing on my doorstop. Her name was Tricia Dolan. She had come to a birthday party I had given at Rush Close with Wendy. A little while afterwards Paul and I had bumped into her at a restaurant. She'd said hi, but Paul had stiffened. As soon as she'd been out of earshot, he'd said, 'You should watch what company you keep.' I didn't see her again, so when I got a card from her congratulating me on my pregnancy I thought it a bit odd. But there she was on my doorstep. She wanted to come in and talk to me, so we went through to the kitchen and I put the kettle on to make tea.

'Sheryl, I've got something to tell you. Remember when I saw you in the restaurant? Did Paul say anything?'

'No,' I lied. 'Why?'

Why indeed? She proceeded to tell me that she'd had a three-in-the-bed with Paul and Terry Bailey, Linda's soon-to-be-ex-husband. Suddenly her name struck me. Tricia, the initial T, Hoddesdon, Paul bristling – 'You want to watch what company you keep.'

'The reason I came to see you is that I've heard the Boares are trying to sell a story on me. If that's the case, I want to sell it first because I want to make the money.'

I decided that I wanted to know what had happened before

anyone went public. I sat there, five months pregnant, with goose-bumps all over my arms, and listened as she told me what had happened between her, Paul and Terry. All the time Paul, playing the devoted soon-to-be-dad, was ringing and the answerphone was picking up: 'Hi, darling, are you there?' 'I love you.' 'I'm worried about you.' 'Call me back.' Meanwhile I was asking this girl for details. I asked every question you can imagine. Sideways, backwards, anyways ... Who had done what to whom? I wanted to know it all before Paul told me it was lies.

She told me that Paul and she had been messing about, he was standing, one leg in plaster (so I worked out it was sometime in April 1994 after he'd broken his leg and we weren't seeing one another), touching her boobs and playing with himself. She didn't think he could have sex with a leg in plaster but when she came back into the room, Paul was lying naked on the bed, still playing with himself. They had sex. At that point, Terry came in; she wanted to stop but Paul told her to continue. Then, according to Tricia, Terry joined in.

Then I called Rebekah Wade. 'Remember T from Hoddesdon? I've got her in my front room and she wants to give you a story.' I gave Tricia Rebekah's number and she left. Then Paul rang again. 'Where have you been, darling?'

'I've just had a visitor, a friend of yours.'

'Oh, yeah? Who's that?'

'Tricia. She's just told me you had three in the bed.'

First he tried to say he didn't know her. 'You sure?' Then: 'Sheryl, it wasn't three in the bed, it was four! We used her like a whore.'

Tricia did the story with Rebekah, the photos, the poses, gave the sordid details to the great British public to digest over Sunday's eggs and bacon, but before the exclusive could hit the newsstands, another paper printed the story. It was front-page news. Gazza's three-in-a-bed romp. Paul was quick to retaliate. He went to Rebekah and gave her a better headline: 'Oh No It Wasn't, It Was Five.'

I'd got to the bottom of the story before Paul had a chance to weave his web of deceit and everyone was making money. Except me.

8. Mr and Mrs P. J. Workyticket

Paul set up a big birthday lunch for me at the luxury Danesfield House Hotel in Buckinghamshire and invited my whole family, including my grandparents. In front of them all, he went down on one knee and asked me to marry him for a second time. I said yes. Again. My nan cried – for happiness. Mason was delighted. Paul produced a stunning ring. But Bianca cried and ran out of the room. She said, 'I don't want you to marry *him*.' She tells me now she was willing me to say no. I tried to tell her it would be different this time. He'd promised he was never going to hurt me again, we were moving to Scotland as a family and there was a new baby on the way. She knew better than Paul that he wouldn't be able to keep his promise.

My third pregnancy, like the other two, was easy. Physically speaking. However, the change in Paul was undeniable. The bigger I got, the more he looked at me with disgust. Once during a row, Paul did actually hurt me, then said – 'something else for you to tell your mates' – which guaranteed that I didn't. I know now how very common it is that domestic violence escalates during pregnancy, it was like that with me. Paul never wanted to talk about names for the baby. He came to one scan with me when we found out the sex. He said, '*She* wants a boy.'

The radiographer said, 'I thought you'd want a boy,' but no, he wanted a girl. He didn't want another little boy getting close to me. Mason was too close already.

When I was about seven months pregnant, and feeling like a blimp, Paul and I went to Quaglino's for dinner with my neighbours Ami and Jay. Paul was down on one of his regular visits from Scotland and was still trying to make up to me for trying to force me to have an abortion. We had a few drinks at the bar first. He was downing champagne with Jay, and drinking a shot of espresso between glasses, a habit he'd picked up in Italy.

Eventually we walked down the sweeping staircase and were seated with our backs to a glass partition, facing away from the room. The tables were quite close and an American lady started talking to me about my pregnancy. She also made an offhand comment about Paul, implying that he wasn't behaving as an expectant father should towards his partner. Tanked up on alcohol and caffeine, Paul had been making cutting comments about my appearance. Then the waiter came over to us. 'Excuse me, Mr Gascoigne, a woman over there wants to say hi.'

Paul and I turned to see a young, pretty girl waving madly.

'Who's that?' I asked.

'Don't f—ing start.'

'Well, she obviously knows you.'

'I don't f—ing know her.'

Paul was adamant: she was just a 'pissed-up crazy slag' and he had no idea who she was, but the girl continued to wave frantically at him. Paul was embarrassed, the American couple were staring, Jay and Ami were asking questions, but all he said was that he'd never met her and told me to shut up. He was getting even more agitated and I knew, or thought I knew, that she was another girl he'd been shacked up with behind my back. Sure enough, the waiter came back and said, 'I'm sorry, Mr Gascoigne, but she says she does know you. She met you at the flat of one of the chairmen.'

We looked round again and now, I kid you not, she was standing on the chair, waving at us. Paul said she was the girlfriend of one of the chairmen of the football industry. But I'd met that man's girlfriend and this woman wasn't her. Emboldened by having Ami and Jay there, I pointed out this glaring inconsistency.

'Don't f—ing start, you fat slag!' He started pinching and

twisting the skin on my thigh, jabbing me with his knuckle. 'Don't f—ing embarrass me!'

But it was too good an opportunity to miss. I wasn't allowed to speak or look at anyone – I was accused of sleeping with every Tom, Dick and Harry, every friend's husband, and now a woman was standing on a chair, waving at him, and he was claiming he didn't know her. Finally, because she wasn't backing down, he said, 'Well, maybe I might've passed her on the stairs to his flat.'

'First you didn't know her and now you met her on the stairs.' There it was. The cardboard box all over again – the little boys my mum used to look after who had turned out to be her sons, my brothers, whom she had given up. It was Ray, and all the half-truths about the older woman he had been seeing behind my back. It was Paul, over and over and over again. I was pissed off – pregnant pissed off, and not to be messed with. Eventually she came to the table, said, 'Hi,' and kissed his cheek.

I just looked at her and said, 'Sorry, he doesn't know who you are.' I wasn't going to be made a fool of by her. I didn't want to be all smiles only to read in some tabloid the sordid details of what had gone on between them during a time when he was telling me that all he wanted was me and that he'd do anything to keep our family together. I knew he wouldn't do anything obvious in front of her or my friends but he carried on twisting the skin on my leg under the table. I wanted to know if he'd recently had or was still having an affair with her.

'You remember,' she said, and then turned to me. 'We met at the chairman's flat last week.' And then back to Paul, 'You were a bit pissed . . .'

I kept quiet as they chatted. I knew Paul was uncomfortable. When she walked away, my leg was sore and Paul was irate. I was embarrassed and angry. Paul said, 'she's just one of his girls' and nothing to do with himself. He was furious that I'd challenged him and might have got him into trouble with a powerful man in football. I had been given many a going-over for far less. I waited a few minutes, said I was going to the toilet, went upstairs, rang Les, the limo driver, to come and pick me up, got into the car and cried. I rang my mum, and asked her to fetch the kids and take them to her house. Then I called the babysitter, Zoe, and told her my mum was coming to get them. I didn't give a reason.

I went straight to my mum's home. I was hurt and livid. Why would a woman who didn't know Paul very well stand on a chair in a big, popular restaurant and make such a spectacle of herself? Something didn't fit.

The next day I got home and the door was hanging off its hinges. Paul had come back to Rush Close, kicked the front door in, picked up his stuff and left. He never had much with him, but he wouldn't go anywhere without his brown leather medicine bag – he's still photographed with it: it contains all his notes, his will and photos from fans. It was all over the papers that I'd stormed out of Quaglino's in a jealous rage because some girl had asked for Paul's autograph. They said she was a model. Had I made a fool of myself, or was I right? I really wanted to find out. I didn't believe anything Paul was saying about her so I called her agent and asked whether I could speak to her, not to berate her but to find out what was going on. She said she'd pass my number to her.

An hour later, the girl called me from a payphone. She said she didn't want the papers digging any deeper; that all that happened was that she had gone to see the chairman, and Paul happened to be there, paralytic. In fact, she made it sound as if Paul had been getting in the way. My question was whether she had been there with Paul, the chairman or both. She said she'd been with neither – but why was she so keen to keep the newspapers away?

Next the chairman rang me. I told him I was being lambasted for overreacting about an autograph when in fact he didn't want anyone to know he'd been up to no good. 'And if you keep your mouth shut, no one will know,' he said.

I was fuming: I had to take the rap to keep them all in the clear. I told Paul I didn't want to see him.

Yet again Paul started calling repeatedly, begging my forgiveness and saying it was all a misunderstanding: he hadn't been messing around with this girl, he only had eyes for me, I was the only one and would I please, please, come to Scotland? I had abusive messages from his mother, telling me I was ruining his career because he couldn't concentrate. Even though they didn't want me with him, they'd try to persuade me to take him back if he told them to. We all did exactly what he wanted. By now he was telling me he wanted us to be together permanently, to look for a home together, to enrol the children in a school in Scotland. I just couldn't be sure he really meant it. But he was, as ever, insistent, convincing, he was sorry, he'd learnt his lesson, he loved me more than anything else in the world, it would never happen again.

It lasted until I was eight months pregnant, tired and willing to be overruled. He told me to take the kids out of school and come up straight away, with as much stuff as possible, and spend Christmas with him. They were excited, no school, off to see their dad, a road trip – brilliant. I put everything that would fit into the car, packed it up to the ceiling and drove up to Glasgow with Bianca and Mason. We were back on track, and I was excited and relieved.

Along the way Paul called me to say he had to go to the Rangers Christmas do – he didn't want to, but he had to. It was a lads' lunch, but he'd be back by the time we arrived. Of course he wasn't. He came home late, pissed but in a good mood, telling me funny stories about the guys and then about some girls who'd turned up, at which point he'd apparently said, 'Right, I'm off out of here ... I don't want anything to do with that nonsense.' He tried to turn the conversation into an argument, saying I didn't believe him about the girls and working himself up into a frenzy. He was turning into Mr Workyticket. He threw in that it was his dad's birthday the next day. I thought that now we were a family we could all join in whatever had been organized. 'How would you know what my dad likes?' It was getting nasty, but luckily it was late and, after a long day on the lash, he fell asleep; unfortunately he did not stay asleep.

The next morning he started on about his dad again. Like a fool, I said, 'Let's all go,' thinking that was the way to please him but he didn't want me to go. Then he spelt it out: 'How the f— can I enjoy myself when you're there?'

As soon as he left to go training, I packed up my bags again, put them and the kids back into the car and drove the eight hours home. I did not leave because Paul didn't want me at his dad's birthday. I knew by then he kept us all separate. I left because of what took place during the night. I would prefer not to describe what happened. Suffice to say what occurred is sadly all too common in domestic violence and I could only live with it by pretending it had happened to someone else.

I spent the last month of my pregnancy looking after myself. I saw my doctor, not the private doctor Paul had promised when we were 'together'. A month later, I called Paul to tell him I'd had a 'show'. Naturally he didn't know what a show was, so I told him that the birth was imminent. If he wanted to be with me when the baby was born, as he'd said he did, he should come to London. He waited until he knew I was on the school run to call and leave me a short message, telling me he was going out. Then he rang Ami and told her he was going out on the lash with the boys, staying at some hotel, and that, although he was in London, he wouldn't be contactable. Ami told him to take his phone because I'd been having twinges. He turned it off.

Paul has often accused me of bringing on my labour to ruin his night out. I was 'seen' jumping up and down to start it. That evening the doctor came. The twinges weren't regular so I went to bed and timed them through the night. At some point the press turned up and rang my doorbell. I knew then that Paul was up to no good, because all the way through my pregnancy whenever he was out on the lash photographers had come to the house to take pictures of me, pregnant and with the kids. They would usually run them with some of Paul partying, drunk and probably with a couple of girls hanging off his arm. The blimp and the bad boy – it dovetailed nicely and, of course, made a monkey of me. It was like an early-warning system: the press turn up – Paul's done something.

Then the phone started ringing. Rebekah kept a running commentary of Paul's antics as they unfolded. The girls he was 'chatting up' were female journalists undercover who were calling in the story as it happened.

In the morning it was all over the papers. There were pictures of him with 'Shezza look-alikes', and quotes of him urging his mates to carry on partying – if he was up for it despite the fact his 'missus was about to drop one', why weren't they? A whole army of press were now camped outside the house.

Mum arrived. The twinges had stopped, which worried the doctor. He thought it was stress and told me to go to the hospital. I didn't want to do that so he let me give it a couple of hours to see if they started again.

Suddenly Paul appeared. I was beyond livid so before he could say a word I told him to f— off and leave me alone.

That suited him perfectly. He had permission to leave, safe in the knowledge that he'd made the effort and I'd told him to go. 'That's it. I tried, but I'm not wanted here. I don't need to stay where I'm not wanted.' He turned on his heel and started back down the stairs.

Mason, happy as ever to see him, was distraught. 'Dad, where are you going?'

'Your mum doesn't want me here so I have to go.'

Mason started crying, telling me he hated me for making his dad go. My mother kept telling me not to give in to the pressure, but I was all over the place. Now I desperately wanted him to stay, but he just picked up the keys of the Range Rover and drove off. I remember my mum saying, 'That's right, run home to Mummy!' and he did. He fled to Dunston. I called Mel, then Rebekah, and told them what I'd said to him and that I wanted him back. I didn't want him to miss the birth. I rang him: 'Please come back!'

'No, I'm not having you telling me to f— off. Who do you think you are?' And then the record started playing. Big-headed blonde bitch, who do you think you are, you've forgotten where you came from, you were pushing a pram ... I tried to ignore it, appease him, I told him the doctor was worried. He just said it was my own fault, I'd brought it on. Mel, Len and Rebekah called him too, but he wouldn't come back. He switched off his phone.

When the contractions became regular, my doctor took me to the hospital in Welwyn Garden City, pursued by the press. We went in through a private entrance, and when I'd been installed in the labour ward, Rebekah arrived, with Ami and my mum. I just wanted them to find Paul. Rebekah told me a deal had been set up through Mel and Len for the first pictures of the baby worth £35,000. People would be clamouring for them, she said, and assured me she could keep everyone off my back. She was happy to do the deal with me, rather than through Mel and Len, and since I was the one having the pain, I didn't think that was such a bad idea. When she left, I believed wholeheartedly that she was looking out for me, and I still do.

Finally they hooked me up to an epidural and everything seemed better.

When I was ready to push, they still hadn't found Paul. As I lay on that bed I stared at the door, willing it to open, thinking please, please, please come back. We'll never be able to get this back, we'll never be able to change this. This was not something I could fix, not something I could forgive and forget – this moment will be lost for ever. If you don't come, it will be gone, and we'll never get it back. Right to the last second I thought he'd come to his senses and walk into the room, but he didn't, so he missed the birth of his baby. Regan was delivered in the early hours of 18 February. Who did I call? Rebekah, a newspaper editor. She'd become a dear friend but, all the same, she was a newspaper editor. Shows how very warped my life had become. I told her the name I wanted: Regan, which means 'Little King'. I'd put my faith in a big one, and he'd let me down. But I had a little one, and he was mine. I would love him, and protect him, and make sure no harm came to him.

Rebekah tracked Paul down at his sister's house. 'You've got a boy.'

'I don't want to hear it. I don't care.'

Oh, yes, I was certainly on my own again.

Rebekah came to pick me up in a blacked-out van, and when we arrived home she had tall men holding up big sheets so I couldn't be seen and the baby couldn't be photographed. I never felt as though she was taking over: I felt protected, that someone was looking after me. I got the money for the exclusive. I put £17,500 into a bank account for Regan, used some of the rest to do up the nursery and lived off the remainder. The baby was registered as Regan Failes, so we all had the same name. The kids called him Chuckie, after the one in *Rugrats*. It was a bit chaotic those first few days because we couldn't go out until the story broke on the Sunday, but going out wasn't at the forefront of my mind.

On 22 February Paul showed up. He arrived with a huge teddy bear and some 'It's A Boy' balloons. I was pretty reserved, not unfriendly, but I kept my distance. He didn't seem concerned – he was actually quite excited, and wanted a kiss and cuddle. I thought he might like to see his son first. Paul bent over the cot and cried. He said all the right things, but it didn't feel real to me. He then came out of the room and tried again for a kiss. I was like, no way. So he said, 'Well, there's no reason to be here, then.' And once again he was off. He didn't want to go out the front because the press would know he'd only been there for five minutes, so he called a taxi to meet him at the back, jumped into the neighbours' garden, then out over their back fence. It was reported that Paul had come to visit, bringing gifts, and stayed all day.

For three days Regan screamed continuously and wouldn't sleep so I had something to take my mind off Paul. He seemed ill. In the middle of the third night, I sat on my bed rocking back and forth with him in my arms. I thought it was God punishing me. Mum tried to give me a break, but I wouldn't let her. 'No, I got myself into this; I'll get myself out of it.' The next day I called my doctor, who helped me take him into hospital, where they found out that something was wrong with his white blood cells and put him on a drip. My family and a couple of friends tried to get hold of Paul but no one seemed to know where he was or who he was with. But someone must have known because he turned up at the hospital – paralytic, loud and demanding. I'd been given a put-U-up next to the baby's cot, and though he stayed with me, all he wanted was a drink and to have his wicked way. When neither was forthcoming he went stamping around the ward, trying to work out how to get a drink. It was then that I began to think the booze was getting the better of him, that his drinking was more than boys on the lash and that he'd taken it to another level.

The next day Regan was better and was allowed home. There were pictures of us coming out of the back door of the hospital. God knows how they knew, but at least Regan was better. I was actually called up by an acquaintance who told me that the person tipping off the press was a woman, and an old family friend at that, and to be on my guard. Well, I had no idea who that could be.

Paul's partying and drinking didn't stop. He, Danny Baker

and Chris Evans made newsworthy drinking buddies. Even with Euro '96 looming and his football career seemingly safe at Rangers, Paul was playing with fire. The England team were berated in the press for the now infamous 'dentist chair' drinking game in Hong Kong. The boys took turns to lie back in a reclining chair while alcohol was poured from some height straight down their throats. It didn't stop Paul scoring a mind-blowing goal against Scotland. He lay down and the boys squirted water into his mouth. It was a f— you gesture that said, 'I can drink and still perform the Gascoigne Magic.' But he couldn't.

Paul was on a high. Loved again by the English, worshipped by the Scots, forgiven many times by the Italians, and me, he proposed for a third time. He came alone to see me from the training camp and asked if we could have a quiet lunch together at Briggins House Hotel. It wasn't planned, there was no razzmatazz, no cake, just him and me. He produced a ring, a Cartier solitaire diamond, and said this time it was for real, no more messing around. He wanted to get married and he wanted to do it now. I told him I didn't want a ring. It meant nothing. Getting married would mean something. So he took it back and told me he'd learnt his lesson: this time he was sure. Above everything, he owed it to the children, to Regan.

For the first time we set a date: 1 July 1996. I had two weeks to plan it. I thought it was a little close because of Euro '96, but he said, 'We're not going to beat Germany. It'll be fine.'

So off I went to Hanbury Manor, the beautiful country-house hotel where we'd dined many times, to make the arrangements. They were not very keen on the idea of a footballer's wedding, and less keen, I felt, on me. I got the impression they were expecting me to be the hysterical, calculating person they'd seen in the papers. They must have gradually warmed to me, because they changed their minds and said yes. Then again it might have been because it would be a no expenses spared event?

I knew the dress I wanted. I'd seen it months ago in the

window of Harvey Nichols – it was so huge it took up the entire space. Ami said, 'Isabell Kristensen does dresses like that,' and pointed me in the direction of her shop in London. Off I went to Beauchamp Place in Knightsbridge, armed with the video of *Coming to America* in which, at the end of the film, Eddie Murphy marries his girl and she wears a really OTT dress like the one I'd seen.

As soon as I met Isabell I liked her. She was tall and beautiful, and we got on well. She told me that the Harvey Nichols dress had been hers. A good omen, I thought. We planned a huge dress with beading, and she said she'd get her friend Jimmy Choo to make matching shoes. She introduced me to a florist and the musicians. It was a great two weeks. I was excited, positive, more in love than I'd been in a long time. Why? I honestly thought it was the end of the violence. However much Paul professed to love me, I knew he loved his money more. He didn't want a pre-nuptial agreement and he said that if he ever hurt me again I could take half of everything he had. That was a promise I thought I could believe.

Our big day arrived. As Paul had predicted, England had lost to Germany and the footballers had come home. Paul's family arrived from Newcastle and were picked up by limos from the station and taken to the Swallow International at Waltham Abbey. Later I found out that they'd been taking bets on how long the marriage would last. One month, two? Would we make it through the honeymoon? I don't know who collected the pot, but someone was more clued up than I was. But I can't pretend I wasn't worried that Paul wouldn't turn up at all, and refused to leave Rush Close until I knew he'd left the Swallow, where he was staying, and was on his way. I kept checking with the security guard, Weir, that he was still there. He thought I was mad, but I really thought there was a chance he'd jilt me.

When I knew he was en route I left home in everyday clothes and got ready at Hanbury Manor. Mel and Len had negotiated a deal with *Hello!* and the magazine's photographers were taking pictures of me. Isabell was still sewing sequins on to the bodice of the dress in the back of the car as she was driven to the hotel.

I checked the flowers, and everything looked lovely. I couldn't have been more happy, more excited. My new hairdressers, Harry and Zekki, were invited to the wedding so they sent someone else to put my hair up.

Then Isabell squeezed me into my dress – she said I could faint and still stand up, and I reckon she was right. The strapless bodice was tight and bosomy but it was a wonderful, wonderful dress. Cinched in at the waist, it burst into a vast skirt of layer upon layer of peach tulle. I was the Good Witch of the East. A princess. A fairy queen. The veil fell to the floor creating a twenty-foot train. I was a little nervous but generally calm. I knew it was the right thing to do. It was the only thing I hadn't tried with Paul. Did anyone say I was mad? No. Would I have listened if they had? Of course not. I'd waited a long time for this.

We took photos beforehand, of me and the kids, me with Dad, the usual stuff. The man who ran the security company Paul used was checking everything – his wife kept my lip gloss with her for touch-ups. Bianca and Mason were my bridesmaid and page-boy. Zoe was looking after Regan. Everything was going well. I felt in charge of the day. This was the absolute new beginning.

I went downstairs. The doors to the Zodiac Room were closed but I could hear the harpist and flautist playing our song, 'Unchained Melody'. The doors opened, I took Dad's arm and Paul turned round. I had barely stepped through the door when the first flag went up: Paul gave me a onceover. At that moment I was so nervous. The dress was low-cut and I never wore anything like that usually. But he smiled so I decided it was OK. I don't know what he was thinking. He was jittery and twitching.

The lady registrar started speaking about lawful impediments and solemn vows. Each word about honour and faithfulness seemed to fall from her mouth with particular gravitas. Paul's father sat behind us picking at his eyebrow and there weren't many smiles from his sisters or mother. When we promised to be faithful to each other, Paul cried.

Ami got up and read two poems, of which the first went:

> *Love is patient and kind.*
> *It is not jealous or conceited or proud.*
> *Love is not ill-mannered, selfish or irritable.*
> *Love does not keep a record of wrongs.*
> *Love is not happy with evil but is happy with the truth.*
> *Love never gives up and its faith, hope and patience never fails.*

She had chosen it, I believe, as a message to Paul and perhaps also to me. Love should not be jealous, conceited, proud, ill-mannered or selfish – but the love Paul and I had included almost all of those failings.

Finally after six years, countless false starts, a thousand bruises and a thousand kisses to make up, the registrar pronounced us husband and wife. Paul smiled at the word. I was his wife now. He lifted my veil and kissed me. Then he brought it down again. I signed my name, Sheryl Failes, in the register while the musicians played 'Have I Told You Lately' by Van Morrison. Everyone stood and we walked out to 'Can't Help Loving That Man'. Which was true. Except I didn't know what real love was.

Outside, we were given large flutes of champagne and I heard Paul say, 'Never again.' He never wanted to go through another marriage service. 'If she thinks she's going to divorce us, she's got another thing coming.' He was polite, chatty, but his humour was edged with a hard and uncomfortable truth. He'd often follow a tease with the reassurance that he was 'only joking', and he'd get the laugh, but not necessarily because what he'd said was funny.

There were endless photographs for *Hello!*, with Chris Waddle, Steve McManaman, Bryan Robson and David Seaman. Paul had invited the footballers he believed had stuck with him through thick and thin. A couple of guys managed to get into that photo even though they weren't footballers, which was quite funny, except it turned out one of them was selling stories.

There was a long receiving line, Paul played with his false tooth and gave his nephews champagne. He dipped Regan's dummy into a glassful and gave it back to him when Zoe brought him out. Regan looked beautiful, in his cream outfit – I was exceptionally proud of all the children. Mason hardly left Paul's side, constantly giving him hugs and smiling. I didn't really drink, just trying to keep my wits about me, as usual. Paul boasted about having a wife and three kids – which was lovely to hear.

Rebekah came up to me to tell me that one of my friends was trying to get a car so that she could leave. Bearing in mind that we'd already had the tip-off that someone close to me was selling stories about Paul and me, we thought this was suspicious. I went to ask this friend if she was all right. She told me her son wasn't feeling well and she was going home to check on him. Seeing her later with a camera set alarm bells ringing because cameras were not allowed at the wedding, and everyone knew this. She was asked to leave. We'd been right. When I got back from honeymoon, I found out that it had indeed been her selling stories about me for the previous three years and that she had built a nice extension on the money she'd made. We never spoke again.

Eventually we moved into the dining room and sat down. I looked at the place card and saw, for the first time, my new name: Mr and Mrs Paul Gascoigne. The rest was smoke and mirrors. The top table overlooked the panelled dining room. Dad was on my left, Paul on my right. Carol was next to Dad and then the children. My mother sat on Paul's right, then John and Carl. It was the standard seating arrangement, but you couldn't imagine a less united family. A microphone was sticking out of the flowers in front of us to pick up the speeches, but it also picked up everything else we said so it was quite difficult to chat. There was a moment of tension: Paul told Mason to quit playing with the mic before he smacked him.

After dinner my dad stood up to give a speech. Like all dads, he thought I looked beautiful and told everyone so. 'The boy doesn't look bad either . . .' he added. He didn't want to talk for long but there was something he wanted to say. 'A lot of people are knocking them, saying this marriage will never last, but I've got every confidence in them. I'm sure it will last. They've been through so much to be here tonight, and proved that they love each other.'

Finally it was time for the groom's speech. Paul stood up. He was still twitching. He kept pulling at his false tooth and rubbing his peroxide-blond hair. He was sweating in his gold Favourbrook Nehru jacket, but he looked great and, though he was clearly nervous, he seemed happy. 'I ain't going to be nervous, cos I've been shitting myself all day. The rooms are on me, you don't have to pay for your room. If you have cameras please develop them in three to four weeks . . . We've got this exclusive.' He thanked Carl for being his best man and everyone else for coming. He acknowledged the players who had stuck by him through thick and thin, and thanked Terry Venables, who was the England manager, for 'giving me time out to go and buy the rings'. He thanked the limo company, the security guys and the hotel for putting on an amazing wedding at only two weeks' notice. 'What they've put on is fantastic. I hope you've appreciated that the food, the staff have been outstanding. Chris Evans and Danny Baker are going to be the DJs. They were going to charge twenty grand but said they'd do it for free, so I spent it all on the wedding.' And finally me. 'Sheryl, how beautiful she really looked today. I'm very proud of her for having the guts to marry me in the first place – she must be mad. I'm really looking forward to the life ahead with our three kids. I'm the most happiest man in the world. I love you all but not as much as I love Sheryl. I love you, Sheryl.' We kissed.

I had heard the speech a thousand times before, but this was different. We were man and wife and everything was going to be as it should be. I was moved by his words, but it was Bianca who sent me over the edge. My ten-year-old daughter stood up in her beautiful dress in front of a room full of people and spoke: 'Me and Mason and Regan think our mum and dad make a wonderful couple and we just want to say congratulations to the both of you.' She sat down. She hadn't really wanted to speak but she wanted to make me happy. I started crying. From happiness? I'd like to think so. But the thing was, I couldn't stop. So, deep in my heart of hearts, I knew that I was crying because we weren't a wonderful couple and her congratulations were forced. If it all turned out okay, my faith would be vindicated, but if not . . .

Carl said a few words, and when he mentioned Paul's great friend Cyril, who was in prison, Paul began to bawl his eyes out.

Then the party started. We danced our first dance to 'She Loves You' by the Beatles. It was the first time we'd ever danced together and I was just desperate for others to come and join us on the floor. Thankfully, Rebekah and her boyfriend, Ross Kemp, took pity on us. Later, when Paul was much more tanked up, pipers came into the room. They started quite traditionally at first, then went bonkers and played Guns N' Roses and other rock music on the bagpipes, accompanied by drums. It was an incredible sound. Paul loved it, was going mad for it. Mason just stared wide-eyed until he was given drumsticks to bang in time to the music.

When the party ended, I was Mrs Paul Gascoigne. Paul was insisting all the children become Gascoigne too. The passports were changed, Regan's birth certificate was changed and, at last, the five of us were a proper family. Paul and I got into the limo, which was full of food and more champagne, and drove away.

We were staying at Cliveden and flying out for our honeymoon early the next morning. How did my wedding day end? With laddered stockings and sore feet. Pretty typical of most brides. By the time I'd taken off my makeup and climbed out of my dress, Paul was asleep. So, for me it had been a perfect day.

9. A Pair of Lincolnshire Sausages

The honeymoon was in Maui, one of the Hawaiian islands, on the other side of the world. I don't think Paul had any idea how far away it was because he hated flying. But it was worth the long journey because it was breathtakingly beautiful, utterly immaculate and laid-back.

Did I finally relax? Start to enjoy myself? Maybe a little. There hadn't been any incidents on the plane – he'd drunk a great deal, and taken tablets to calm his fear. Because it was just the two of us, Paul didn't have to share me with the children, and I decided to stay glued to his side. I allowed myself to believe that the magic of marriage had worked. However, on the second night when we were sitting in an open-air lounge at the hotel, having a drink, things took a turn. Those places can be a little intimidating, and there were honeymooning couples wherever I looked, whispering sweet nothings. I didn't want us to be the only newlyweds sitting in silence or, worse, bickering. I was try-ing to chat, trying to keep him sweet, but it wasn't working. Then the subject of his family came up. Suddenly Paul was being very rude. We'd lasted just two days. I told him I was going upstairs – there was no point sitting downstairs if we were going to row. He didn't want to be embarrassed by me leaving him in the bar, and I didn't want to be embarrassed by staying because I knew he was about to blow. So we went back to our room. All I could imagine was that everyone in that bar was thinking, See? It's crap, he doesn't love her, never did – the whole thing's a sham, a money-grabbing sham. In fact, they were probably too busy looking into each other's eyes to notice.

When we got back to our room he didn't hit me but found a way to hurt me all the same. We had sex, rough and nasty. I was bruised, but it wasn't a beating. So far he'd kept his word, but I felt pretty shattered, and too afraid to admit to myself what had just happened. In the morning I lay in bed, waiting to see what mood he was in, whether it would be more of the same or we could get on with our honeymoon.

Generally all Paul wanted to do on our honeymoon was drink, fish and have sex, probably in that order. Perhaps it hadn't been just me who had expected the wedding to cure all evils. But, as we both discovered, no ceremony can do that. He was probably as freaked out as I was, but neither of us said anything. We didn't have conversations like that – we didn't have conversations. The two subjects we discussed were sex and him.

As soon as we got to the beach, he wanted to be doing something. We'd lie down, and within minutes he'd want to book a boat, a jet-ski, a banana ride . . . We never just lay in the sun side by side, reading. I never picked up a book because he'd just tell me how 'f—ing rude' I was. Then he'd make some false accusation and we'd have a bit of a set-to, which gave Paul the excuse he needed to stomp off in search of a bar. I know now that each 'argument' was manufactured, but back then I tied myself in knots trying to make something logical out of the illogical. I didn't realize that he didn't want a rational answer, that he wanted a fight. Alcoholics go looking for reasons and excuses and they always find them.

At the bar Paul switched into man-of-the-people mode: Gazza in a Hawaiian shirt shelling out for cocktails at the beach bar. He went looking to make friends, find buddies behind whom he could hide his need to drink. On one occasion he had been gone for ages when a bloke came over to me, knelt down and said hi. Immediately I panicked. I wasn't allowed to look at another man and this one was kneeling beside my sun-lounger just millimetres from my barely covered breasts. My response to his friendly overture was rapid: 'My husband's just gone to the bar.'

'I know,' he said. 'I've been watching you. Why do you put up with it? A man shouldn't speak to a woman in that way.'

I wasn't really listening. In my head I was begging him to go away. I told him I was fine and I asked him to leave, which he did but not quite soon enough. Paul saw him walking away and my blood ran cold. As usual, he went mad at me – the second his back was turned I'd been throwing myself at men, he accused me. I told him the guy had just come up to my sun-lounger. Not for the first time he told me that was highly unlikely. Why would anyone come and talk to me? What did I have to offer that was so f—ing special? 'You must have been giving him the eye.'

Again I said he'd just walked over, and pointed vaguely in the direction he'd come from.

'How do you know he came from over there unless you were looking at him? You must have been looking or you wouldn't know where he'd been! You were giving him the come-on ...' He went on and on and on. Normally I would have removed myself, which would give him carte blanche to do whatever he liked, but that day I decided that, no matter what, I wasn't going to leave the beach. He was still swearing and going on about what a slag I was, throwing myself at any bloke around, but I stayed. I didn't look over to where the man was, but I like to think that if Paul had got physical, he'd have intervened. I felt braver, a bit protected. And maybe, just maybe, I didn't want Paul to do anything he couldn't undo. In the same way that he'd missed Regan's birth, where else was there for us to go if he hit me on honeymoon?

Finally he left, his feet slapping on the pathway, enraged. It was a relief that he'd gone, but then I started thinking, Now what? I got up and went to look for him in the hotel grounds. Or to *look* as if I was looking for him, because if I lay on the beach, I was asking for the other guy to come back and that would have meant more trouble.

Finally I found Paul. I told him I'd been looking for him, and he was apologetic. It was his rage, his jealousy. Didn't mean he didn't ever bring it up again. And then he started again. Big-headed blonde bitch, busy bitch, not the best-looking fanny in the world, slag, 'Staring at blokes on the beach the moment my back's turned.' Then the usual, 'You don't love me, you never want to make love, you never hug me, can't wait to get away ...' It was exhausting.

Paul loves deep-sea fishing so he chartered a boat for a day. He caught a mahi mahi – which he had stuffed and flown home – so he was over the moon and arranged a celebratory dinner with the boat's captain, a lovely man with whom Paul got on well, and his wife. That evening the captain asked me if I was inundated with compliments on the beach while Paul was away. It was a passing remark, but to me it was a red flag and I knew I could only talk to his wife after that or Paul would decide I was encouraging him. Everything I said became measured, so it was little surprise that I sort of stopped talking in the end.

We both got on very well with the hotel manageress and, typical Paul, he bought a time share in the hotel though, to my knowledge, he never used it. I tried to dissuade him but he was always telling me he could do what he wanted. Like throwing rocks at the photographer we caught hiding in the bushes. What Paul wanted, Paul got. Few people ever said no to him. And if they did, he didn't listen. When he wanted us to take out a catamaran on our own the guy in charge told him the wind was picking up so only experienced sailors should go out. Paul told him he'd done it loads of times and hired one regardless of the warning. As soon as we got on to it he was struggling.

'I thought you said –'

'Shut up, woman, I can do this!'

We went out a little way and caught the breeze. Suddenly we took off and we were flying. Paul was swearing madly as he tried to slow the boat down, but he couldn't and the wind took us miles out. Eventually he managed to turn the catamaran, but it flipped over. Paul climbed on to the upturned hull but I couldn't pull myself up. All I could see was the sail disappearing into the cobalt sea beneath me. *Der dum, der dum, der dum* ... The first two notes of the terrifying theme tune to *Jaws* were playing in my mind.

We were rescued by a couple of lifeguards on jet-skis. One was demonstrably better-looking than the other, and he came for me. Paul watched me like a hawk as I got on to his jet-ski, and all the way back to the beach, but there was nothing he could do. As soon as we were on the sand he mumbled into my ear, 'I bet you loved that.'

Back in England the press had printed our wedding certificate, which featured our home address. This was unbelievably stupid, not to say irresponsible and dangerous, and the paper had to pay for round-the-clock security for the kids while we were away. That meant a lot of phone calls to Mel and Len, and I was furious, but the kids enjoyed having some burly guys around to keep them company.

When the honeymoon ended I was looking forward to getting home and seeing them. Paul went back to Rangers for pre-season training and we spent the rest of the summer planning our move to Scotland, but this time, although our two weeks in Maui had passed without a proper beating, I didn't pack up the house. I packed a suitcase.

Paul was based at Loch Lomond, moving around the lodges at Cameron House Hotel, but with the help of the Rangers' secretary, we started looking for a house to buy. One caught my eye. The White House in Kilbarchan was set back off the road and up a steep incline, with electric gates to guarantee privacy. All good features for the new Gascoigne family. Paul bought it, with quite a bit of the previous owner's furniture. For the rest we went to Harrods. I still have the towels Paul chose: white, with 'Harrods' embroidered on them in gold.

There was a lovely school in the village, and as it was the

holidays, the caretakers, Tommy and Margaret, showed us round. They are still my friends today, and were then like a second set of parents to me. They're a wonderful couple. Before the term started, we bought the children sturdy shoes for outside and plimsolls for the classroom – it was always wet and windy, which I never got used to.

Bianca was ten and she was moving school for the fourth time. I know she missed her friend Lindsay, but she had a nice bedroom with a four-poster bed, her own phone and en-suite bathroom and seemed all right about the move. But Paul was on edge: he ran the house like a military operation and didn't like mess. If Bianca left something out of place, he had his own way of making sure she didn't do it again. Once he emptied her drawers and cupboards into a heap on the carpet because he felt they were too untidy. I told him he couldn't do that but he was determined to teach her a lesson she wouldn't forget. I can tell you now, it had the opposite effect. Mason wasn't exempt. One day he forgot to flush his toilet. Paul made him go around the house flushing every toilet a hundred times. True to male form, that didn't work either.

In Scotland I made another great friend. Jan became a life-saver. I'd got to know her from previous visits to Glasgow – she was married to the footballer Alan McLaren and I'd liked her from the first moment I'd laid eyes on her. We had been pregnant at the same time and our babies were born close together. Paul had bumped into her and Alan at Cameron House and shouted to Jan, 'My lass likes you,' so she made an effort to get to know me. She would let me know, inadvertently, that Paul wasn't telling me everything that was going on: she'd say something like 'See you next weekend at the Rangers do,' so I'd know when I wasn't being invited. Paul once tried to have a go at her about it, but she wouldn't take it from him, and her husband never, ever condoned his bad behaviour.

It was Jan, beautiful, petite, kind Jan, who told me later that when I wasn't at Rangers Paul was the life and soul of the party, but when I was there he was a miserable lump, never leaving my side. Others interpreted it to mean that I was an insecure, needy wife, who put a stop to his fun. In a way they were right: I did stop his fun. When I was there, how could he dance on tables, flirt with girls and keep up the story that he was lonely and miserable without me? For that he needed me to be out of the way, and over the previous six years he had mastered the art of keeping me where he wanted me.

For my birthday, on 24 September, Paul bought me a Mercedes SL to match the large Mercedes saloon that he'd bought for himself. I didn't want it: I knew why he'd given me such a 'generous' present. He'd been foul to me recently and wanted to buy me off again. To add insult to injury, when Jan and I met halfway between Edinburgh and Glasgow for a birthday lunch, I couldn't get Regan's seat in it – the seatbelt wouldn't go round it. All I succeeded in doing was getting myself drenched in the attempt. 'When exactly do you get used to the weather in Scotland?' I asked Jan. She told me you never did.

In the end I didn't have to: we weren't there long enough.

Looking back, I don't think Bianca and Mason settled in very well to their new surroundings and school. They didn't make friends, so at break-time they popped round to see Margaret and Tommy. Mason liked the Salt'n'Shake crisps they gave him – he'd never had them before – and their dog, Benny, a yellow Labrador. Perhaps they were biding their time for the event that would mean we all left again. Sometimes Margaret and Tommy's grandchildren came to visit and we'd make a camp in the garden, then eat sandwiches and read stories in it. Paul must have been away at the time, or I wouldn't have let them do it because of the mess. He'd got so exasperated by family life that we'd hired a nanny – I didn't need one since I was with the kids all the time, but Paul wanted me at his beck and call.

That autumn he was jumpy – the pressure of football, the drink, or perhaps he regretted having me and kids with him again. His family was certainly getting to him. If the phone rang after nine o'clock he wouldn't pick it up – he said it would be his mother and she'd be pissed. I tried to keep out of Paul's way so as not to make things worse. I took care of Regan, taught myself to play the piano a bit, saw Jan, and looked after the kids when they got back from school.

Around that time, Rebekah and Ross came to stay, and Rebekah told me about Gleneagles, the luxury hotel in Perthshire, which they'd been to. They'd had a fabulous time, and suggested we go. I booked us in for the October half-term break. The kids could have golf and riding lessons, and there was a wonderful spa. We'd leave on the Sunday and the plan was that Paul would commute during the week to Rangers since it wasn't much further than the journey he was doing already.

On the Saturday before we left Paul's dad came up to Scotland to watch the match with a mate from Dunston. John was a bit more talkative than usual, and when we went for a Chinese meal after the game, he kept mentioning his 'partner'. I was amazed to discover that he had split with Carol. I'd had no idea that they'd separated or why – Paul always jumped down my throat if I asked about his family. I suggested that next time he came up he brought his girlfriend to stay with us.

The next morning Paul was in such a bad mood he barely spoke to me. It was about eleven thirty: John was getting ready to go to the pub and Paul wanted to go too rather than do the family bit with us. I wondered if John would like to come with us to Gleneagles. It was absolutely the wrong thing to say.

'Why the f— would he want to do that?'

I went on getting ready for our trip and said no more. You could have cut the atmosphere with a knife.

It was early afternoon on the Sunday when we got to the hotel. Paul stripped off his clothes, opened a bottle of red wine, lay on the bed and switched on the TV. I wanted to change his mood somehow – I'd thought we could go and look round, take the kids swimming, or the nanny could take them swimming while we had a coffee – but whatever I suggested he received with a grunt. He said he was tired and wanted to watch the football. When I asked what was wrong, he said, 'Nothing.' But something was going on, because he was cutting me out even more than usual. I didn't know how to handle the silent treatment.

In the end I took the kids down for a swim, they had tea and then we went back to our two-bedroom suite. Bianca and Mason were sharing their bedroom with the nanny, while Regan was in a travel-cot in ours. I started getting ready for the evening – we normally booked a table quite early because Paul was always keen to get to the bar, but that night it took him ages to get off the bed. I asked him what dress he wanted me to wear for our evening together, and told him how much I was looking forward to the restaurant. But he still wouldn't speak.

Downstairs we stopped at the whisky bar and Paul chatted to the guy behind it and tried a couple of whiskies while we chose what we were going to eat. His dark mood had cleared a little and I thought we were out of the woods.

When we were seated in the dining room, I took in the surroundings: the hushed almost reverential atmosphere, the discreet clink of glasses and the polished silverware. I started to relax and said how nice it had been to have a chat with his dad. Paul emitted another monosyllabic grunt, but I wasn't going to let him ruin our dinner. Gleneagles was a treat and I wanted it to be perfect. I told him that John and his girlfriend were welcome to come together next time – we could all go out somewhere. That was the worst thing I could have possibly said.

'What the f— are you talking about?'

'I'm just saying –'

'Your f—ing family, they don't give a shit about you!'

'Why are you picking on my family?'

'Do you think my mum couldn't get a bloke? Do you?'

'I wasn't saying that –'

'You want to remember where you come from.'

'All I'm saying is how nice it was and we could all go out together.'

'You saying my mum can't get a bloke? My mum could get loads of blokes if she wanted.'

He was getting louder and louder, ranting about uncles and being given sweets and pop, people were staring. It was hard not to notice and even harder to pretend not to notice. I was thinking, Get me out of here – this is so humiliating. He went on and on. I was the gold-digger, I was spoiling his fun, I was causing a problem, I was neurotic, I was making him angry – his family hated me.

I told him I was going to the toilet. He snarled at me, 'You better come back, I'm telling you now!'

I walked out of the restaurant, and as soon as I was out of view, I sprinted to the room. It was a pattern that was pretty well established and Paul never waited for long.

I ran as fast as I could in my heels. I could hear him pounding down the corridor behind me. I started running even faster, but just as I got to the door of our room, he whacked me round the head. The door opened and we both fell in. Then he broke a thousand promises and one stupid dream.

It was a beautiful room, a suite, crammed with paintings and heavy dark Scottish antiques. Three huge windows over-looked the gardens, and there was an imposing fireplace, a glass cabinet, sumptuous armchairs and carved tables. The first thing I went into was the cabinet – I thought the glass would shatter in my face. I bounced into a corner, sent a standard lamp flying, then was thrown against the wall between the windows. It's a wonder I didn't go through one. All the time I was taking severe blows to the side of the head. He would head-butt me, pick me up, throw me against something, pick me up, slap me, pick me up, hurl me into a corner, pick me up ... Then he grabbed me round the neck and squeezed, shouting, shouting, shouting in my face.

I was aware of banging on the door and prayed it wasn't Bianca. I can't remember screaming for Paul to stop, but Bianca told me later that she could hear me, so I must have been. I had no chance to get away from him, even when he threw me against furniture or on the floor – he'd throw himself against me before I could get to my feet. At one point he pushed me on the floor with renewed vigour and when I landed I felt an excruciating pain in my hand. I looked down: the two middle fingers were lying on the back of my hand. 'My hand!' I yelled, more in panic than in pain because it looked so hideous.

That stopped him. Or perhaps it was the hammering on the door. It was indeed Bianca and he had to go back to putting on a show. He looked at my hand, said, 'There's nothing wrong with them!', took my fingers and snapped them back into place. Everything went deadly quiet.

Bianca: *'This is still by far my worst nightmare and the one I beat myself up about most. Even though I'd been aware of the physical abuse before, this time was different. I was woken by crashing and banging and the worst sound anyone could hear, their mum crying helplessly, hysterically, for their dad to stop hurting her. I was panicking, shaking and scared, and I went to see if the connecting door was open. I wanted to save her or at least try. As I got closer to the door, the noises got louder and louder. It was locked so I just tried to make Paul aware that I was awake. I bashed and kicked it, begging him to stop hurting my mummy and pleading with him to stop making her cry. I rushed to the nanny and tried to pull her out of bed so she could help me help Mum, but she pretended it wasn't happening. I hated her in that moment – although she was probably only young herself and just as terrified as I was ... I looked for a weapon. The only thing I came across was the kettle, so I boiled it to chuck over him but it never came to that. Eventually it all went quiet.*

'I tried to stop loving Dad after that. Instead I just stopped liking myself. What sort of daughter was I if I couldn't help my mum? A useless one.'

I hate to think what might have happened if the nanny had let Bianca in, and I'm grateful that she didn't. I shudder to think of a ten-year-old running about with a kettle full of boiling water. I don't need Bianca to forgive the nanny, but I do need her to forgive herself. There was nothing she could have done – it wasn't her fight to stop.

I went into the bathroom, turned on the tap, and while the cold water ran over my fingers I slipped off my wedding ring. I don't know why, maybe to tell myself it was over, that we'd tried and failed. Or maybe it was just my survival instinct kicking in – my fingers were changing colour. My face was a mess of blood, tears and ruined makeup. I'd applied it less than two hours before with such high hopes of a perfect evening. It was almost impossible to meet my own eyes in the mirror. They couldn't hide the truth. I'd been right all along: I was better off alone. Love couldn't be trusted. I lowered my gaze.

Whatever made me take off that ring, it saved my fingers. Shortly afterwards they had both swelled to the size of Lincolnshire sausages. As the hospital told me later, the ring would have cut off the blood circulation and my wedding finger would have had to be amputated.

I went into the bedroom, where Regan had been put to sleep in a travel cot next to our bed, and sat down. The pain was seeping into my system. Paul had sworn that once we were married he'd never hit me again.

Regan was crying so I picked him up to comfort him – but I think he was comforting me. All the while I had one eye on the door to the sitting room. Paul had got straight on the phone and rung his boss Walter Smith. I could hear him saying: 'I'm quitting football. I've had a row with Sheryl and I'm quitting football. I can't take the pressure. No, I don't want you to come and get me. OK, OK, yeah, all right, I'll come.' I heard him put the phone down.

Then he came back into the bedroom. He stood in front of me, then fell to his knees and lowered his head. 'I know it's over, I know it's finished, I know we'll never see each other again – but, Shez, I beg you, promise me, promise me, don't ever tell anyone what I said about my mum.' And then he got up and left.

That was the final twist of the knife. He didn't give a shit about me, or what he'd done. He only cared about his mother. That hurt me more than anything – more than the fingers, the head-butting, the cuts and bruises, more than all of it put together. Paul has been reported to have said in the press and on TV that I called his mother a whore, which is why he attacked me at Gleneagles – and this was perhaps what he told his mother to excuse his behaviour. Who knows why he attacked me, but I swear that my account of what happened at Gleneagles is the truth.

When Monday morning came I asked the nanny to take the kids to their activities, gave her Regan and kept out of everyone's way. I cancelled my treatment in the spa. When the receptionist offered to reschedule it, I told her I wasn't feeling too well, which was true. That afternoon there was a knock at the door and the Rangers' physiotherapist, a man called Grant, asked if he could come in. He took one look at me and sighed. Then he said words I'd thought I'd never hear. 'Paul Gascoigne or no Paul Gascoigne, we're going to hospital.'

Grant drove me there, and I registered under my maiden name. I was mortified because I looked so terrible and I was with a Rangers' physio. It seemed to me that nobody wanted to know: few people spoke to me, and if they did, they offered little sympathy. If they blamed me for taking the sheen off their idol, they didn't need to: I was quite capable of doing that myself. I believed somehow that it was all my fault – I even felt a fraud for bothering the nurses with it. My fingers were fine – well, they'd be OK, once the swelling had gone down and they'd stopped throbbing. Grant and I waited for what felt like ages. Then a woman and a man came in and examined my injuries.

'What happened to you?' they asked.

What did I say?

'I fell down the stairs.'

Some stairs! If an eyebrow was raised, I chose not to notice.

They took me for an X-ray and discovered that the fingers weren't broken. When I came out Grant had gone, and the Rangers' doctor was there with Davy Dodds, one of the coaches, in his place. They had turned up and asked for Sheryl Gascoigne, which blew away my thin veil of anonymity. The hospital bound my enormous fingers together and put my arm in a sling. Once the doctor had discovered they weren't broken he left, telling me that Davy Dodds would drive me back to Gleneagles.

In the car Davy Dodds wanted to know what I planned to say. I told him I'd said I'd fallen down the stairs and that I'd stick with that. Satisfied, he told me to stay in my room because I couldn't walk around the hotel without bringing attention to myself. We drew up outside. He took off his coat and made me wear it to cover the sling. He told me to go straight to my room and made it clear that I was to stay there. 'Keep a low profile and out of the way.'

So I did. But I couldn't hide from Bianca. She came into the lounge and started shouting: 'He said he'd never do it again, and look at you – look at you! He said he'd never hurt you again ...' She was so upset and there was nothing I could say to make her feel better.

Jan had arranged to come over with her baby, Ellie, while I was there to hang out with us for the day, but Alan had phoned her to give her a heads-up. Paul had told him and Walter that we'd had a fight and he had pushed me. Now Jan rang, wanting to know what was going on, and I told her I was fine. She didn't buy it and said she was coming over. I asked her not to – I was better off on my own – but she turned up anyway.

She looked at me and said, 'Pushed you?' Immediately she called Alan, told him about the state I was in and that it had been a tad more than a push. Alan took it up with Paul, but I don't know what was said, and soon everyone at the club knew what had happened. No one ever said anything to me – I certainly didn't get any calls asking if I was all right.

I told Jan what had happened. She was furious, of course, but more furious that I was locked into that hotel room, like a prisoner, while Paul, by now in the bosom of Rangers, was playing against Ajax in Amsterdam. He was acting the merry fool and having a laugh – I know this because it was televised, and I watched, searching for a sign of remorse. It looked to me as if he didn't have a care in the world. I wanted to think he was putting on a brave face, but that was just wishful thinking. Despite his telephone rant to Walter, Paul didn't hang up his boots for long – or his gloves, come to think of it.

Jan came back the next day and persuaded me to go and watch the kids riding. The nanny had told me how good Mason was on a horse, and I really wanted to see him in action. We went to the coffee bar and then to the equestrian centre where Mason's happy little face when he was on that pony made me forget everything else that was going on – until we got back to the hotel and a photographer jumped out from behind a wall by the entrance. I ran inside, but too late.

From then everything moved quickly. Rebekah called me to say that the *Mirror* were running an exclusive but that the story was everywhere. She told me to ring my mum and dad and warn them that I'd be on the front pages. I felt an element of relief. It wasn't my dirty secret any more. I said to Rebekah, 'Do you think it might make him stop?' He'd been caught. It was out. Would it really stop now? And in that one question I gave myself what I wanted: another excuse.

I rang my dad and told him about the papers. I said it looked worse than it was. And, to be fair to Paul, it *wasn't* as bad as it looked: I'd had far worse. My fingers were painful, but I still had ear-lobes and my hair hadn't been ripped out in clumps. Yes, he'd bitten me and pushed me, but he hadn't held me over a balcony this time or flushed my head down the loo.

The following morning, Thursday, 17 October 1996, the

story made the front pages of the *Daily Mirror*: 'Gazza Beats Sheryl Black and Blue'. The hotel was mobbed by the press. I'd thought I was safe inside with the staff, but I was wrong. A member of the senior hotel staff came up to my room and said that it would be best if I left. I said I couldn't simply leave – I hadn't packed. She informed me the valets would do it for me and send the suitcases on. They just wanted me gone. It didn't matter that the kids were somewhere else, I had to go. I was appalled that they could do this to me and told her so. She said that, although it might not look like it, she was doing it for my own good, then arranged for me to be ushered out of the hotel undetected by the press. I was so angry. It was easier to direct my anger at Gleneagles than Paul, and far easier than being furious with myself.

Ian Muir, Paul's security man, came to the hotel to make sure I left as quickly as possible. He and the hotel staff stood over me as I tried to get some essentials together. As soon as the children got back, we were taken down in the service lift, through the kitchens and out to a waiting car. I sent the nanny home – I just wanted to be on my own with the children, shut out the world and hide.

A car chase followed and we drove wildly through the countryside at breakneck speed in an attempt to lose the press. Only when we were no longer being pursued did Ian turn the car towards Loch Lomond. Paul had flown in from Amsterdam early that morning and was hiding from the journalists. Ian said Paul wanted to talk to me, that he needed to see me, and I couldn't leave without talking to him.

At Cameron House, we went in through the back entrance. Paul was in his room, sitting on one of the two double beds. He didn't look at me and barely said a word.

'Haven't you got anything to say to me?' I asked.

I thought he'd beg for my forgiveness, promise he'd never do it again. Above all, I was hoping he'd give me the excuse I needed to stay. I'd realized in the car that, despite what had happened, I didn't want our marriage to end. Now that everyone knew about the violence he would stop, I was sure. He just had to apologize and I was his again.

But he didn't. A girl came in with some food, and Paul started to chat with her, over-familiar, purposefully humiliating and cruel. How much lower was I prepared to go?

'What do you expect me to do? You said you'd never do it again. You haven't even said sorry.'

'What do you think I'm going to do? Say, "Yes, sir, no, sir, three bags full, sir," to you for the rest of my life?'

It was like swallowing a cup of cold sick. I'd come to Cameron House prepared to give him an out and he'd thrown it back in my face. I could go no lower, so I left.

10. A Moment of Clarity

Someone had brought my car to Loch Lomond. Ian offered me a driver, but I was determined to drive myself to Rush Close, even with one arm. I'd got myself into this mess so I'd get myself out. I didn't need anybody's help. They insisted the driver came in the car with us. I wonder now whether they were more concerned about who I spoke to than whether we got back safely.

The drive down is a bit of a blur now. All I remember is having to stop occasionally to feed Regan and change his nappy. When we arrived home, the driver slept on the couch.

The next morning, the driver returned to Scotland. We were hemmed in by the press. My lovely view of open ground and the canal was now covered with men pointing long-lens cameras towards the house. The curtains in the old show home still didn't close properly so I spent a couple of days crawling around on all fours. It was a circus, but not a fun one. I called the police, who told me there was nothing they could do because the photographers were on public land. I think the kids were pleased to be home, though – and certainly Bianca: Rush Close was safe.

Meanwhile Paul was tucked away in Scotland, protected by Rangers' press and security teams. He released a statement on 19 October, saying he was a 'disgrace' – but it wasn't about the events at Gleneagles: he had been sent off after ten minutes in the Ajax match. He feared losing his £2 million sponsorship boot deal and, more importantly, his place on the England team: on the back page *Mirror* readers had voted 3,675 to 687 that he should be turfed out of the England squad. On 23 October he upped the ante and tried to reverse his waning public support, pleading, again on the back page of the *Mirror*, 'Don't Destroy Me Glenn'.

I didn't give any interviews to the press. I did my best to avoid them. But I had to go to the hospital for a check-up, which made the news. My dad drove me. Only three months earlier he'd put his faith in Paul and me, and we'd let him down.

It was half-term in England, so we didn't have to leave the house. But what made it more hellish than anything was that I heard nothing from Paul. So I registered the children back at their old school. The first school run was a nightmare, with flash bulbs exploding all over the place at eight o'clock in the morning. Eventually we worked out a system: I'd get Regan into his car seat in the house, get the book bags ready, then crawl to the front door, because it had a glass window. On the count of three, we'd make a dash for it. While my backside was sticking out of the car as I fixed the baby seat, the click-click-click would be going off behind me. I drove through the school gates, pulled up by the door, the kids got out and I left. I didn't have to face anyone, or talk to anyone, just went home with Regan and waited until it was time to pick up the older two.

There was a lot of press speculation about who Glenn Hoddle was going to select for the World Cup qualifying squad. Paul had been pictured out with kebab sauce dripping down his shirt when he was out on the lash. Many people were saying he was too risky to pick and not match fit. Sir Bert Millichip called for England to axe Paul from the game against Georgia in Tbilisi and for him to face disciplinary action for his violent behaviour on and off the pitch. Clearly Glenn Hoddle wasn't listening: on 6 November he named the 1996 England World Cup qualifying team. He was going to 'stand by Gazza', and when he was asked about the speculation regarding Paul's behaviour, he said he'd spoken to me and – being the kindly born-again Christian he was – had offered any help he could give.

At the end of the press conference, Rebekah Wade went up

to him. 'You haven't spoken to Sheryl. How do you think that makes her feel, you saying that on telly?' He mumbled something about how he'd *meant* to call me . . . He had my number but hadn't got round to it. Perhaps he should brush up on his ten commandments.

Paul was now being guarded by the England team, and Glenn Hoddle had said he should be forgiven. Every hotel had security, so he was totally protected. When he finally went back to our marital home, the White House, he moved his mates and family straight in. He also bought a horse and a parrot to keep him company. The horse was left in the garden and overfed until its stomach swelled and he gave it away.

The stories about us continued to appear in the press, with comments in all the columns – 'She knew what was coming'; 'She was trying to change him'; 'She didn't know what was coming'; 'She knew she couldn't change him'. All the while, Paul was cosseted. Many people thought it was my fault, not his. That's not uncommon in crimes committed against women. Rape, domestic violence: we all had it coming. I felt eyes on me everywhere I went.

When Paul and I finally spoke, he turned the whole thing round on me again. He was furious that I'd started the children back at school. 'One thing happens and you run off and put the kids in their old school. You never had any f—ing intention of making this marriage work. You say you love me, but you f—ed off as soon as you could.'

'But, Paul, you didn't call me – you didn't tell me you wanted me back.'

None of that mattered. I had left so it was my fault the marriage was over. Poor him. Evil me. It was that pattern again. He'd orchestrated something to happen, I would play ball and leave, then he'd ring me and blame me for leaving, saying it was because I didn't love him enough. But I had to get the children into school. We couldn't all be in limbo. Or should I say, we couldn't go on being in limbo.

A while later I bumped into Paul and Lorraine Merson at Brent Cross Shopping Centre in North London. Paul said, 'Everyone knows that, without you, his life is f—ed up. You're the only stable and secure thing in his life, the only thing that keeps him grounded.' I so wanted to believe that was true.

Lorraine suggested I go to see therapist Beechy Colclough, and offered to come with me. I didn't think *I* needed to go – surely it was Paul they should be convincing – but Lorraine strongly recommended that I went. So I did.

'I don't think Paul would have meant to . . .'

'Paul only does it when . . .'

'Paul wouldn't have intended to . . .'

Beechy wouldn't have it. He said I was only talking about Paul while Beechy was talking to me: he wanted to know what *I* thought. When he said that talking to me was like talking to a person who didn't exist, he got pretty close to the bare bones of it. There was no 'I'. There was only Paul. He had consumed my every waking hour for six years and in that time I had disappeared.

But Beechy wasn't going to let me off the hook. That's when he asked me that question: 'Could Paul have killed you?' I couldn't say no, because I'd come close a couple of times. Saying yes was a big moment.

At the end of the session, I said, 'It's not me that needs the help, it's him.' But that was rubbish. I needed the help to break away. I needed the help to understand that I was worth more than continuous abuse. I needed the help to understand that I was endangering my children as well as myself.

The second time I saw Beechy I told him about Gleneagles.

'It wasn't you Paul was attacking,' Beechy said.

But if I had two arthritic fingers to prove it was me, then who was he hitting?

*

As we approached the end of the year Paul's fury with me started to abate. He loved me; he didn't want it to be over; he wanted to see me and the kids again. He took us to the première of *101 Dalmatians* for a family outing. I realize now that he had me where he wanted me again: there, but not there. I started to feel guilty that he would be alone for Christmas. Poor Paul, he needed me, I was the only one who really made him happy. I was the only one who kept him safe. Paul Merson and Beechy Colclough agreed: it was pitiful and it was a lie. He started sending cards again, told me how much the other players were messing around, how they'd open the club at night to put the sauna on and get girls down there, but not him, never him: he missed me, I was the only one for him and he was never going to love anyone as much as he loved me. It was then that I suggested we go to Beechy together.

Paul put on a brilliant façade for Beechy: he said a few little things, and Beechy said that Paul was sorry, had learnt his lesson. He also said that there were many Christmases ahead of me, that it was important we were together for this first one and I should work on the marriage.

I wanted to work on the marriage, that was why I was there, but I was torn too. I didn't want to go to Scotland for Christmas. I knew that my dad wouldn't sanction it, and that therefore my beloved nan and granddad wouldn't come either. Edna May was seventy-nine now and she was getting frail. I worried it might be her last Christmas. My nan was the one good constant in my life, the only person who loved me for myself, unconditionally, as family should. It was unbearable to think I might not be with her on her last Christmas. But Paul said that if I didn't come it was proof I didn't love him, that I didn't want to make it work. He'd made a huge sacrifice by coming to Beechy and I wasn't prepared to meet him halfway. As far as Paul was concerned, if I didn't come our marriage was over for ever. Why was I always living in the past? We had to move forward now: why didn't I want to? There was no chance of him coming to England because of his Boxing Day match. Eventually, with a heavy heart, I gave in to the pressure and agreed we would go up to Scotland to join him for Christmas.

My mum came, but as I'd predicted my dad wouldn't come. Neither did Nan and Granddad. It was a big thing for me to miss what might be her last Christmas for the man who'd repeatedly attacked me. And sure enough when we arrived at the White House with loads of food, determined to make it worth it, Paul behaved as if he didn't want us there. He was off with me and bad-tempered with the kids. Christmas Day was awful: he disappeared, and when he came back, he said he just wanted to be with his family. His family always meant his Newcastle family, never us. I suggested they join us, but he told me they wouldn't leave Dunston for Christmas. I would have been happy to have them there, anything other than this hell. I felt stupid, and so utterly robbed. I'd deserted my grandmother, for nothing.

Thankfully I got to see her on Boxing Day. My nan and granddad had their sixtieth wedding anniversary and we all flew down to join the happy celebrations. Even Paul made it, flying in still dressed in his Rangers kit. I returned to Scotland for New Year's Eve. To be honest I was happy to see the back of 1996 – it had been an exhausting, painful year, even though our son had been born and we'd got married. That evening, lots of people – mostly footballers and their wives or girlfriends – came over. There were a few familiar faces – Jan and Alan, Ally McCoist and his wife Alison, Ian and Tracy Muir – she'd carried my lip gloss on my wedding day – but I didn't know most of the others. There was one man I was surprised to see, a local guy who'd helped us with the building work when Paul had made a wine cellar – Paul was always telling me he'd ripped us off, which he hadn't. Paul said that sort of thing about everyone.

No one mentioned anything to me about my return. Paul got pissed, of course, and at midnight when the bells were chiming he was on the phone to his family. I was getting worried. I couldn't celebrate or kiss anyone without kissing him first, but as he was on the phone I wasn't allowed anywhere near him. I had to let him know I'd at least tried to see him or I knew I'd pay for it later. Abruptly he ushered me away. He took the phone upstairs and I heard him saying we weren't having a party, just a few people over.

I left him alone for a while, then went back, assuming he'd finished his conversation. On the way I walked past Mason and some friends of his playing a game he'd been given for Christmas. When I went into the bedroom Paul was completely naked. I told him he ought to get dressed if he was going downstairs. He was irate.

'F— off! What do you f—ing know? I should be with my family!'

'But, Paul, you could have invited them.'

'Why the f— would they want to come here? Why should they? I can't f—ing enjoy myself when you're around . . .'

I asked him to get dressed and come down. He threw on a red and blue dressing gown and, without doing it up, strode down the main stairs.

I was going down the back stairs to the kitchen, where most people were, when I heard a terrible yelp. I ran back upstairs. By the time I got there, Mason was climbing the front stairs towards me. Halfway up he was sick. 'Dad's kicked me.'

Bianca was running up the stairs to us now, as was Jan. She was furious – she wanted Alan to sort Paul out, but I just wanted them all to stay with me. We hid in Bianca's bedroom. We could hear Paul storming around the house, his feet slapping on the stone slabs, shouting and swearing. 'Look what she's made me do now!' Everyone was trying to calm him down, make sure he was all right. But he didn't want to calm down and he didn't want to be made to feel all right. He stormed off down the drive, his dressing gown flapping. 'I can't take this any more! I'm f—ing out of here.'

People ran down the road after him. I didn't care – while Mason was still trying to get his breath, I had my first moment of clarity. I had put Mason in harm's way. Paul had always been a bit rough with him – an extra dunk under the water, a clip round the ear – but they had all been 'little' things and I had turned a blind eye. But that changed on the first day of 1997.

Paul had come down the stairs and told Mason to get to bed. He replied that he would in a minute.

'No! Now!' shouted Paul.

'I'll just finish this game, Dad.'

Bang! Mason still doesn't know whether he was kicked or punched. But he had a large red circular welt on his back. For ever after Paul denied hitting him and accused me of lying about it.

Eventually Jan managed to calm the children and put them to bed, then went down to the kitchen. The phone rang and it was Tracy Muir, Ian's wife. She told us Paul was in a B-and-B in a terrible state. How did she know where Paul was? He'd called her. Well, how did he have her number? I was immediately suspicious but I really didn't care. I was leaving and that was that.

The following morning I went to the doctor. The incident was recorded in Mason's file, but nothing was said, reported or followed up. I didn't think we could fly because Bianca had an ear infection, but we dosed her with antibiotics and went home. I was cold with fury. Do what you want to me, Paul, but don't hurt my son. It had been a pivotal moment. I knew that in going to Scotland I had let my beautiful nan down and had endangered Mason. It was too much to bear.

Nan died in January. I was having dinner with friends at an Italian restaurant in Stanstead Abbotts when Bianca rang. When I answered my phone I noticed a missed call from my granddad. Bianca said, 'Granddad's rung. He sounded upset.'

When I got hold of him, all he said was 'Nan's gone.'

'I'm coming.'

'No, don't.'

'I'm coming.'

I'd driven to the restaurant so luckily hadn't had anything to drink. I got into the car, my friend came to support me, and we drove straight to Norfolk. I couldn't believe it. It broke my heart to think I had missed her last Christmas. It always will. My dad arrived the next day and we made the funeral arrangements. So many elderly people had died recently that there was some delay: as my nan had died at home, in the bathroom, there had to be a post-mortem. She had asked to be cremated, wearing her wedding ring and the outfit I had bought her that Christmas. It was a suit and blouse with matching necklace. I arranged for a professional makeup artist to do her face. At the crematorium, the coffin was open. I found it so hard to walk into the room, and as soon as I saw her I froze, but as she had made me promise that she would have her wedding ring on I had to check. I picked up her hand, which was as cold and hard as marble – her wedding ring was in its usual place. With her hand in mine, I couldn't leave. I sat with her for ages, talking to her, telling her I'd look after Granddad, and that I was so sorry I'd missed Christmas.

One of her wishes was that people wore hats at her funeral. I went all out for her, the suit, hat, gloves and bag. I also wore her engagement ring that she'd given me a few months before.

The children joined us at the wake, but Paul didn't come. You'd think it would have been a relief for me not to have to face him, but I felt the lack of his support keenly. Nan's ashes were buried in the grounds of Swaffham Church. Granddad ordered a plaque and planted a bush. The stonemason had suggested putting her name on one side of the plaque, and when Granddad died they would turn it over and inscribe both their names on the other side. That way he wouldn't have to see the empty space waiting for his name to be added. But he wanted to see that space: he wanted to know that he would join her. (He did, but not for another eight years.) He kept the garden looking lovely, sure that she was watching. I miss them both so much, I think about my nan every day, and often talk to her. In everything I do I ask myself, 'What would Nan think? Would she be proud? Would she approve?'

I had never sold Rush Close – I wouldn't have been that rash. No promise that the violence wouldn't happen again could have convinced me to sell my house. Deep down I knew I'd be back. There was something calming about being home – the three kids and I were on our own again, and something had shifted. Paul was in our lives – I didn't want him never to see the kids – but he never touched me again after that New Year's Eve party. It's a bit like children: they'll push and push until they find your limit, and that's how they know when they've gone too far. I think Paul realized he had when he hurt Mason. This time I didn't want to go back to him. I found a steeliness in me that has only strengthened as time has gone on.

More than anything I wanted to make the children happy. Now that I had Regan there were many things I could no longer do with Mason and Bianca, simple things like going to the cinema and skating. I didn't think it was fair that they had to stop doing the activities they enjoyed, so I hired a nanny called Julie. She turned out to be a godsend, a great nanny to Regan, Bianca and Mason, and a good friend to me. All four of us needed someone stable after the roller-coaster we'd been on. Bianca often said to Julie that she wished Julie had been her nanny in Scotland – perhaps Julie could have done what none of us had achieved and stopped Paul. Thinking about it now, I don't think God sent her, but I know who did. The best grandmother in the world.

On 18 February, Paul made an appearance for Regan's birthday. And things had changed: on the home video he made, you can hear him say snidely, as I come out of the front door with the three kids, 'Take as long as you like ...' Then me saying, 'Oh, great! Thanks! Paul says we can take as long as we like!' It must have been one of the first times I began to answer back. That year he had another round of injuries so he was with us a bit more than usual. He called often to make a date with Mason, or to see the others, then usually let them down by not showing.

The drinking was getting worse and his behaviour became increasingly erratic. He started coming back from the ground with tobacco pouches stuck under his lip. You were only supposed to have one, but being Paul he'd put four up there and was barely able to talk. He told me they were harmless: they just helped him relax.

After Gleneagles he went to see a shrink who told him he was on the border between madness and genius: he should take Librium, one tablet each night, to level out the chemicals in his brain. Walter Smith told him not to take it because it affected his play – at least, that was what Paul told me. Apparently it took away his aggression on the field and stopped him doing what he was famous for. Then he'd panic and pop a few, but not when he was supposed to or at the correct dosage. He was drinking too, and it was at Rangers that he discovered Zimovane, sleeping tablets. He had to take more and more of them before they worked.

Paul wooed me back. He took me out for meals, and treated me like a princess. We'd have a lovely time and I'd let myself be talked round. It was always the same – the abuse and the pleas for forgiveness. It went from 'big-headed blonde bitch pushing a pram' to 'I love you so much, you're so special, a great mother to my kids, I'm so proud of you, you deserve so much.' I would say, 'But you don't do those things if you love a person,' and he would argue, as ever, that it was *because* he loved me so much that he got out of control. 'I know you're not going to forgive me and I can't bear it. I love you – I can't live without you.' He wanted to take us all to Disney, no doubt trying to make it up to

Mason, though he didn't have to try very hard with that: Mason would have forgiven him anything.

On one occasion Paul sent me a card. The word 'Sorry' appeared on the front with a rabbit holding an 'Apology List'. It said, 'Sorry for being prickly, selfish, impatient, hard to live with, foolish, thoughtless, but my heart is full of love for you.' Paul apologized for what had happened and said that he had picked that card because it 'said everything'. He begged me not to take Mason away from him and pleaded that he didn't want to lose me.

I let Paul take Mason swimming or to the sports ground, and sometimes I left Julie with Mason and Bianca so that Regan and I could fly up to Scotland to see him. He used to say no one else would understand the love we had. He was always off with other girls, but he assured me that what we had was unbreakable, precious. It was his jealousy that got in the way, he said. It was because he loved me so, so, so much. By then he was mostly living at Cameron House, but once I went to the White House and while I was there a fan letter arrived – normally they went to the Rangers ground. The writer talked about how distant Paul had been 'the other night' when she'd seen him, yet they'd had 'such a great time at Christmas together'. So much for not being able to live without me.

I agreed to go to Disney with him. We spent two weeks there, and he took us, with Julie, on to Barbados to stay at Sandy Lane. It coincided with the break in the football season, and Paul doesn't like to be on his own. Perhaps he'd decided to try to win me back when he'd have time on his hands. On the flight, Regan was in his car seat next to Julie, the two older kids sat together, then Paul and me. We went first class, of course, but I couldn't sit back and enjoy it because Paul hated flying. It was the usual thing. He'd drink B52s, huge ones, and gulp down painkillers. I had to stay on top of my game and keep my wits about me. He would go into generous-dad mode: the kids would point out things they liked in the airline's duty-free magazine and he would buy them everything. I would tell him, 'Not another watch/ Walkman/ whatever.'

'Don't f—ing tell me what I can and can't do. If I want to buy my f—ing kids a present, I'll buy them a f—ing present.'

Then he'd pass out, usually with a drink in his hand, which he'd spill all over himself, then wake up, get angry and buzz for the stewardess: 'Where's my drink?' He'd question the kids: 'Where did you get those watches from?' It was the same every time.

We had a lovely time in Barbados. There were no violent incidents. Paul was still controlling and there were verbal attacks, but despite walking on eggshells we managed to have fun too. He treated the kids to endless jet-ski rides, gifts, ice-creams, pizzas. We made friends with a lovely lady called Marnie, and she helped Mason to water-ski. We were even witnesses at someone's wedding. As ever when other people were around, Paul was the life and soul of the party: 'Gazza' was on show – a real good bloke. As soon as they left, he'd pull faces and slag them off, and we'd be back with Paul again.

I remember a meal with Julie, Paul and the children. Mason was messing around, and we were trying to get him to stop before Paul blew up at him. Julie kept squeezing Mason's thigh gently under the table to make him stop but it wasn't working. He wasn't being naughty, just a typical little boy. She made sure Paul didn't see her trying to keep Mason in order, because if he did, he would have an excuse to lay into Mason. It was always uncomfortable with Paul: we were all waiting for him to blow. We had to make sure he was the centre of attention. The kids and I spent a lot of time trying to please him, but Mason couldn't do anything right, however hard he tried. Bianca didn't try so hard – the scales had fallen from her eyes – so, perversely, Paul left her alone.

But it was one of our nicer holidays – no security guards were called, which is a pretty low benchmark. Why were there no incidents? Because I had reached a point at which I simply would not allow it. If he created a row, I no longer ran off to a private place in my mind, leaving him to do as he liked. People knew, which gave me a backbone. And I had Julie with me, which helped more than she could ever know. Julie was never scared of him, and couldn't be bought. Paul bought people all the time – it was how he functioned – so he didn't know how to approach Julie. Once he tried to set her up, telling me she'd stolen some cigarettes, but he had given them to her. It was a weak stunt, which backfired.

Poor Julie hurt her back in an accident on a doughnut inflatable, which eventually stopped her being our nanny. She was in her room, immobile, in a neck-brace and Paul wouldn't let me go to her. Eventually I managed to convince him that she needed help to wash. Then she and I shared a few stolen moments when we could laugh ourselves ragged, breathe easily, and I could be myself. Paul told me he had paid for her to fly home first class and had ordered a wheelchair for her. It turned out not to be true. He lied about things he didn't have to lie about. She'd flown home premium economy, which was generous enough. Honestly, if he told me it was raining outside, I had to check. His lying was compulsive.

But the kids were happy. They loved those pockets of time on holiday, when they were given the world. Those were the good times that I was hanging everything on and which I couldn't give them on my own. But it was a smokescreen because, as Julie said, when Paul wasn't around family life was very different. It *was* relaxed. It *was* happy and easy. So I *could* give them what they needed but I didn't know it at the time.

And what about what I wanted? Sexual chemistry is often high in abusive relationships. Passion requires uncertainty. Well, uncertainty ruled our relationship and it was passionate to the end.

11. Dolls Against Addiction

During the summer of 1997 Isabell Kristensen, who had designed my wedding dress, asked me whether I would consider doing a fashion shoot, in her dresses, for *Hello!* When I told Paul, he said, 'If you do that, I swear on your life I will divorce you.' (It was always my life, never his). 'I'm not having my wife parading around, showing her bits off.'

I thought about it. He'd kicked Mason, scared Bianca, let us all down; I decided to go ahead and do the shoot. He stuck to his word and filed for divorce, citing my unreasonable behaviour. But I wasn't going to take that lying down and engaged a lawyer of my own. The result of the shoot was published on 23 August and I shared the magazine's cover with Princess Diana – I was bowled over by that.

The divorce proceedings had begun but that didn't mean our roller-coaster was at a standstill. We carried on as we always had. It may sound weird but it underlines what our relationship had always been like. To stop the divorce would have required Paul and me to sit down and talk about us, but that conversation never took place. As always, we talked about him or sex. Occasionally Paul might mention something his lawyer had said, and I would explain that it had come out of something Mel or Len had said or done. Then Paul would resolve the issue.

One time we were staying at Hanbury Manor with Alan and Jan and went out for dinner. When we got back we went for a drink at the cocktail bar – Alan had to borrow a tie so that we could go in. Paul was on form. He was drinking sambuccas, setting light to them and generally messing around – until his top lip and eyebrow caught fire. It was funny, we were all having a laugh. As we were leaving, someone had a dig about Paul and his entourage. Alan didn't like this and responded. Paul and I left Alan to it, but then Paul began picking on me. Little things, all verbal – did I know the bloke? He was shouting and swearing, so Jan told him to calm down. He ignored her, and when we got back to our room he started punching the wardrobe, then man-handling but not actually hitting me.

Suddenly Alan was at the door, shouting at Paul to open it. Paul didn't want to, but Alan insisted. He told me to leave and said he would stay with Paul. I didn't need to be asked twice. I ran out of the room and went to join Jan. That wasn't the only time it happened. When the four of us stayed anywhere, Alan would suggest we should check in like that because that was how it would end. Paul would kick off, but he never lost control. I wonder, could he have controlled his temper and stopped attacking me years before?

The next morning was Princess Diana's funeral. Jan and I ordered some tea and toast, and were sitting up in bed watching the television when Paul and Alan knocked on the door. Alan sat in the chair next to the bed and Paul got into bed with us, pushing us along so he could be right next to me. 'Didn't order me any tea then – you only think of yourself.'

'And you're so special?' said Jan – she was forever trying to make things more bearable for me. We watched the funeral, that terrible, poignant moment as Princes William and Harry stood behind their mother's coffin and Earl Spencer touched Harry's shoulder. I kept thinking about my children and what would become of them if anything happened to me. Bianca was thinking exactly the same because later, when I got home, she wanted to know what *would* happen. 'Who would look after us? Where would we go?' It didn't bear thinking about. But as Beechy had pointed out, it was a possibility and my daughter knew it. Sitting in that bed I knew it too. It was another moment of clarity.

I was lost in my thoughts, staring at the screen, when

suddenly we heard banging from the other side of the wall. 'What's that?'

It soon dawned on us that they were putting the wardrobe back together. If it hadn't been such a dreadful day, it might have been funny. But it wasn't. Last night it had been the wardrobe, but I wouldn't always have Alan around to protect me. I could never let myself be in that position again. Final. And so, thanks to the women around me, to those young princes and their dreadful loss, I found myself getting stronger. I found my voice. Paul wasn't going to hurt me or the children again, and they didn't have to be scared any more.

After seven years, I had learnt the power of owning the problem. It was no longer 'How can I get Paul to stop?' I couldn't. I never had been able to, and I never would. The question was, what did I have to do to make sure it never happened again? It took me a while to find the answer. I knew I didn't want to be that wardrobe door any more. The trouble was that I didn't have a watertight exit strategy.

Isabell Kristensen and I became good mates. After the photo shoot she was asked to donate dresses to a charity fashion show, called Dolls Against Addiction, and asked me to model them. So in October 1997, Mum, Jan, Maggie – my ex-boyfriend David's mum – and friend Dianne came to watch me. I wore, among others, a lime-green off-the-shoulder dress I had modelled in the *Hello!* shoot. No doubt the split was high, and I was conscious of the photographers below me, but it looked fabulous and so did the photograph. This big event marked another big change of course in my life. The positive press I got was a nice confidence booster.

Paul tried his best to wring out any pleasure I felt. On the morning the pictures were published he called me at the hotel and yelled, 'How dare you embarrass me by showing off your fanny? Who do you think you are? I'm going to get so much rap from the lads – "Your wife showing off her fanny!" You never think about me!' Jan grabbed the phone and yelled right back at him. She gave me the courage to ignore him. Isabell, Jan, Julie and Ami were my personal Dolls Against Addiction, my addiction to Paul. I started to see it for what it was – a terrible need to be needed, wanted, adored, coupled with the fear of repeating the life of loneliness and boredom I had had as a child. They reminded me of the promise I had made to myself years before to be a better mother than my own. They taught me to value myself – if women like them thought I was worth something, then maybe I was. I am for ever indebted to them: they gave me enough strength to stop myself doing anything stupid, like going back to Scotland, despite the continual promises of a better life.

Paul was having a much better time without me anyway, constantly on the lash with his drinking buddies Danny Baker and Chris Evans. They 'borrowed' cars and once drove one of them into a loch. They commandeered a London bus and a London cab. Paul appeared on Chris's show and generally pissed about – he was trying everyone's patience, particularly Walter Smith's, and sailing, as ever, far too close to the wind. I tried to pretend that it wasn't my problem, but it was. Paul's self-destructive behaviour affected the children just as much as his errant parenting. But at the time I didn't know that. I thought we were safely out of harm's way because we were out of arm's reach.

And when Paul and I were together I wouldn't put up with that sort of behaviour. We had Christmas all together at Loch Lomond: Cameron House gave us a room for the day and served us a proper lunch with all the trimmings. Afterwards, Paul was pretty drunk. He'd spent a fortune on a bottle of wine and he was swigging from it as we walked back through the hotel. There was a blazing fire in a hearth in the reception area. As Paul took a swig, he lost his balance and fell backwards over the fender. As he fell he grabbed Mason. The glass smashed, he cut himself and was moaning about the blood, but

I went ballistic. Mason could have been badly burnt. How many warnings did I need?

I wasn't the only one who'd had enough. The press seemed to be turning against him. After another stupid mime with imaginary Celtic pipes, Paul was receiving death threats. He only did it because they were chanting, 'Wife-beater,' at him, so he managed to pin that one on me too. Then one day I woke up to a story about a fifty-two-year-old woman called Irene: she'd sent a photo of herself to Paul and they'd met up and started an affair. Paul denied it, of course. 'I don't so much as look at another woman when you're away. I haven't had any sex for ages – they're all doing it but I only have eyes for you ...' She called Paul to say she would never have leaked the story, her husband was furious and she didn't know how they'd found out. Paul told her to deny everything, just as he was. Unfortunately she was taping the conversation and it was printed verbatim the following day, with the swearing blacked out. He told her he was angry because the story was stopping him attending his son Regan's second birthday party. Not because I had told him he couldn't come. I still wanted him there, for Regan's sake. I never stopped him seeing the children.

All the dalliances that came up prior to Irene happened at times when we weren't officially 'together'. Paul may have engineered that so he could have a fling and, if he was caught, give a plausible excuse. At least I could say to myself, 'He hasn't cheated on me.' Again, the benchmark was low. But, according to Irene, the affair had been going on for ten months, during which Paul and I had been on holiday together, he had begged me to take him back, told me I was the only one, and made me go to Scotland for Christmas. I was angry. Apparently he met up with her at Chris Evans's house whenever he was in London. The detail in the paper spoke for itself.

On Regan's birthday, the press rang the doorbell and presented us with a cake and balloons. I'd given Regan a tricycle, and after a lot of pestering I let him go outside to ride it. Why shouldn't he go outside on his birthday, even if his dad had been caught with his pants down? They got their photo. Why? Because I was hurt. The revelation of this affair hurt me more than the others, which was perhaps why I was less bothered about the photographers and feeling more vindictive than usual. It was portrayed as Gascoigne versus Gascoigne, which it was.

We split up again. Paul partied hard, left Rangers and, in March 1998, signed with Middlesbrough. He lived in a hotel for a few weeks, then rented a property in Seaham, a pretty rough area by the sea. By now he had bought houses for his mum and dad, his two sisters and brother, but not for himself. His mate Jimmy was with him more often than not, and his team mate Andy Townsend moved in too. It was a big house and the kids went to stay with him there, but they didn't like it because it overlooked a graveyard.

I was getting better at protecting myself. I was trying to keep my distance, look after the kids and, for once, create some sort of normality for us. I put things in the diary so that I had something to look forward to and that when Paul rang, promising love and excitement, I wouldn't go rushing back. We did go on holiday together in May, but the divorce proceedings that Paul had started were still going ahead.

I carried on building a life of my own. I agreed to do another fashion show, this time for a cancer charity in Coventry with Matt Dawson compèring. There, I met a guy called Gavin, who was tall, handsome and gentlemanly, and when he asked for my number, I gave it to him. We chatted for a while on the phone. I was planning to take the kids to Alton Towers at half-term and he suggested I come to see him on the way. Julie and I went up first and the new nanny followed with the children the next day. Gavin invited us out to dinner with him and his friend, which was fun, and the following evening he arranged to pick me up and take me to a country pub.

That evening, as I stepped out of the hotel, twenty photographers emerged seemingly from nowhere, clicking away.

I jumped into the car and told Gavin to drive. I warned him to tell his parents, but he thought I was being ridiculous. I told him that someone was talking to the press – 'They knew you were coming to pick me up and they'll know who you are and everything about you in seconds.' He wouldn't listen. He was at the very end of a relationship and I thought he should warn his ex-girlfriend but he didn't think for a minute she would talk.

Two days later news of my hot date was out. Gavin had fallen for Gazza's woman, filled her room with flowers (which he had and there were photos to prove it) and was head over heels. Of course it was exaggerated, but the information had come from his side, and when we talked, he suspected he knew which 'mate' had passed it on.

Paul called and left long messages on the answerphone. He was so upset. His reaction was totally different from what I'd expected. I'd been accused of sleeping with any man who came within fifty yards of me and I'd been on a real date, but Paul was not calling me every name under the sun. He was so sad that he was losing me and that I'd met someone else, but he wasn't angry. It was weird to hear his voice on the phone, gentle, sorrowful and quiet. He was reacting like a normal person, almost genuinely. But I didn't crumble straight away. I liked Gavin, I was getting stronger away from Paul. I had heard it all before and gone back too many times.

Paul had called from La Manga in Spain where he was training with twenty-seven other players to finalize the 1998 World Cup squad. No one thought for a second Paul wouldn't be in it: despite his regular appearances in the press with Chris Evans, he'd been playing well for the new England manager, Glenn Hoddle. But then he was caught drinking on the golf course, which was banned by the England coaches. When Hoddle called each player into his room, one by one, to tell them whether they were in or out, Paul lost his temper. He did not like to wait and barged in while Hoddle was talking to Phil

171

Neville, and knew immediately he was out. He went ballistic because it was unfair. Lots of them had been drinking, but Glen Hoddle, whom Walter Smith had warned was 'trying to make a name for himself', had singled out Paul. Enraged, Paul hurled furniture but never hit Glenn. One more piece of evidence that even when he was in a ferocious rage, he could control whom and where he punched.

It was then that I had a phone call from Paul Merson. 'You have to help Paul. He's been kicked out, and no one knows what to do with him.'

As usual, Paul had found an emissary, one I liked and trusted. Paul Merson asked if Paul could come home to me – it was the only place he wanted to go: 'You're the safest place for him.'

Paul was devastated and he needed me. The two things I found hardest to refuse. My exit strategy wasn't working.

I called Rebekah for advice. She told me Paul was Regan's father and that I should have him back: 'He's beside himself – what if he does something stupid? You'll never forgive yourself.'

It was the permission I needed to take him back. He'd said he loved me – maybe it was worth one last try. He came straight home to us and I was happy to have him back. Rebekah got the scoop. She and I had a good friendship but we played right into each other's hands: I needed her permission to take him back, she wanted the story.

Paul wanted us to get away, out of the country, as far from the World Cup as possible. But I didn't want to go anywhere with him on my own, so we planned to go to Miami. I begged Jan, now pregnant for the second time, and Alan to come with us, so they did.

This time, because he'd been kicked out, he was, for once, grateful to me for being there. We sat by the pool, ordered wine, watched the kids till the sun went down, and didn't rush around at Paul's demand. On the beach he said, 'Let's go to

Disney – we're so close.' We took two limos and had a lovely time. He was on his best behaviour: he wanted us to get back together, although the divorce was still going ahead. I wasn't sure about that.

Poor Gavin, his ex did talk. A lot, and not particularly kindly. And he had to deal with it on his own when it hit the newsstands, as I was in Miami. However, Rebekah passed me messages from him, that he was 'looking at the moon' and thinking of me. I was touched, but I was back in Paul's arms and thoughts of Gavin soon evaporated. It was a shame because after that Paul's behaviour deteriorated.

As far as I was concerned, the evidence showed that Paul was now a problem drinker. On a couple of occasions that autumn he turned up at Rush Close and was unable to stand or get up the stairs. He'd sleep it off, then I'd take him to the station and send him back to Middlesbrough. For days afterwards I'd get lots of abuse on the phone, I was a bitch, he hated me, until it changed to, 'I love you, I can't live without you.' He'd drink on the train on the way down, carrying a bottle in his bag – he usually came with one of his friends, Jimmy, Cyril or Hazy. Hazy's ten-year-old daughter was regularly brought in to play with Regan on the few occasions Paul had him to stay. When he had any of the children with him, he would call me up to twenty times a day, knowing I would pick up the phone – which I might not if he was on his own. He even called in the middle of the night, crying and begging for help. He rarely remembered those calls when we next spoke. Alan told me he'd seen lines of cocaine on the coffee-table in the Seaham house. Although Paul denied it, I suspected things were getting out of control.

One week he came to stay at Hanbury Manor to see the kids, but the doorman called to warn me not to bring them. Paul had been in the bar until five that morning, then back there at seven. Now I was convinced he needed professional help and asked Rebekah how I could get it for him. She put me in touch with the Priory but they told me I could do nothing without a doctor's letter. I had no idea how to get one, and it was impossible to make Paul do anything he didn't want to do.

A few days later Paul called in a terrible state: a friend had died in his hotel room after he and Paul had been out on a bender. A week later he got on a train, apparently intending to come and see Regan – I think he went AWOL from the club because no one knew where he was. He called me from Stevenage station, pissed and ranting, out of control. He hated everyone, Jimmy, Chris Evans, his family, everyone except me, of course – but it was all nonsense: he was pissed, dangerously so. He wanted me to come and get him but I had the kids and there was no way I'd put them through that. I told him he had to sober up first.

The manager of Middlesbrough, Bryan Robson, rang: Paul had given him my number because I wouldn't go and collect him. The pressure on me to help him started up again.

'Please go and get him. He won't go to anyone but you. You have to.'

'Okay, but you have to do something for me. Get him a doctor's letter. I think he's an alcoholic.'

'What do you mean? He told me he'd spent a weekend with you and the kids and wasn't drinking.'

'Bryan, we've hardly seen him, and when he did come he couldn't get up the stairs.'

I found out later that Paul had gone on a four-day drinking marathon in Dublin.

'Right. I'll bring a doctor down, but you will go and get him? I can call him and tell him you're coming?'

They were understandably worried about their investment, but I wasn't going anywhere until I knew he'd made the appointment with the doctor and alerted the Priory. I told Bryan I wasn't taking him home. I would take him to Hanbury Manor and Bryan had to pick him up from there and get him to the Priory.

'How?'

'He'll pass out eventually. You can get him then.' I got Mum to leave work early and come to watch the kids, and after the Priory had confirmed Bryan's call, I went to the station to get Paul. I was waiting at the bottom of the steps when this unrecognizable creature appeared at the top and staggered towards me. He was trying to talk to people – trying, because his mouth was stuffed with toffees. He used to eat sweets to take away the smell of tobacco because he knew I didn't like it. But this was excessive.

'You won't kiss me cos I've been smoking.'

His chin was covered with sticky brown dribble, his clothes with spilt food and drink, and he was clutching his leather medicine bag, dragging himself along the wall for support.

'I wanna go to yours.'

'No, Paul, we're going to Hanbury Manor.'

I drove him there and dropped him off.

His head kept falling forward and his words were so slurred. 'Come in for a drink, just one drink.'

I lied through my teeth: 'I've got to go home, I'll come back later.' I was thinking, Please, God, just get the doctor there.

'Just one drink, please, one drink.'

The doorman who'd warned me that Paul wasn't capable of looking after the kids was on duty. He helped me to get him in and took him to his room. I went home, terrified about what would happen when Paul found out what I'd planned. I spoke to Bryan again and discovered how far away they were. I gave Bryan the room number, then all I could do was wait.

Finally Bryan called. Paul was in the clinic. I put down the phone and cried. What a terrible thing I had done. I'd had him locked up, incarcerated, and I felt as if I'd betrayed him. I thought he might never forgive me.

He woke up in the Priory and was soon asking for me. He was furious, as I'd suspected he would be, and disputed that he needed to be there. His notes record that he was in total denial and did not accept he had an alcohol problem. Eric Clapton went in to talk to him, but whatever he said fell on deaf ears. I went every day, from Stanstead Abbotts to Roehampton, but I was scared to be alone with him.

After five days I'd had enough of the abuse. A counsellor said, 'You don't have to stay here.' But I was worried Paul would walk out if I didn't come. The counsellor said it wasn't my responsibility, it was Paul's, so the next time Paul had a go at me I told him I could leave any time I wanted to. He didn't believe I would, but I did. He smashed up the room.

They gave him pills to stop his body going into toxic shock and sedatives. Apparently if you take heroin, you can stop it straight away, but it's not the same with alcohol: if you stop drinking suddenly you can die. He started stashing them, so that he could take seven or eight at a time.

The moment the news broke that Paul was in the Priory, lots of stories were published about his drunken antics and the women he'd groped. As usual, he denied everything. A famous British model was also in the clinic and he told me he'd taken cocaine with her. Allegedly she'd had it all over her body and let men and women inhale it off her. I wasn't impressed. I just thought it was painfully sad that Paul was wasting all his talent and opportunity on drink and drugs. Unsurprisingly he didn't stay the full twenty-eight days and left on 25 October. I had done what I could.

On 5 November I received a letter that told me Paul was now using against me the very place I had wanted him to go for help. Our decree nisi had come through on 26 August. Six weeks later it should have become absolute, by which time all financial arrangements had to have been settled, including, most importantly, maintenance funds for the children. I was very sad when the divorce came through. Our marriage was over, and the financial wrangling was only just beginning. We would meet in court. But Paul used a report from the Priory, which said he was in no state to deal with such matters, to stop that happening. With this report Paul had his get-out-of-jail-free card. The court case was postponed. He went back to Middlesbrough, and started playing well again. He seemed willing to do something about his addictions and was trying hard. As he had stayed sober, we headed up to Scotland for Christmas – another chance, another disappointment.

12. The Charm Syndrome

It was a strange Christmas. There were the usual excessive gifts, but an unusually sober Paul. It was a miserable time because he was on edge, presumably because he was struggling to stay sober, so everyone else was on edge too and the kids were unhappy. We didn't celebrate New Year's Eve because Paul wasn't drinking and instead of joining the Hogmanay celebrations with Alan and Jan, we stayed in at Cameron House to support him, watching the telly. On New Year's Day, with no warning, he left us and went home to Dunston. When he called me I could hear there was a party going on in the background and it was obvious that he'd had a drink. I'd ruined the children's Christmas again, this time bending over backwards to accommodate Paul's recovery, and as ever doing exactly what he wanted me to do, only for him to leave us behind. No one in Dunston was going to stop him drinking. I went home to Rush Close.

Paul had been so generous when we'd been together, and I eked out the money he'd given me so that I had enough to live on while the courts were waiting for him to 'get better'. In the end it took a year. I had more friends than I'd ever had, supporting and helping me, and I think that where they were concerned the Gazza Glow had finally started to dim. He had fewer emissaries to send to me and I had stronger defences, but it was a difficult year. I tried to make sure the children saw their dad but it got harder and harder. He would say he was coming, tell them he was taking them out, then, more often than not, let them down. His excuse for not seeing them was always the same: he couldn't handle it because of me. It was like Colin all over again – a man was putting aside his child because he was so angry with the child's mother. When Mason and Bianca saw Paul, they weren't allowed to mention me. By now they were thirteen and ten. They'd been through so much, but it wasn't over: 1999 was the year of the legal pad, when everything was listed, all our expenses and Paul's visits, and the details sent to the lawyer. Behind every sporadic and infrequent entry is a messy story of cancelled plans and haphazard visits, but you probably have the gist of it by now.

We saw him in March, but by accident. Alan and Jan asked me to be their new son's godmother, but Alan said they couldn't ask me without asking Paul to be godfather. Jan was apologetic about that but neither of us thought he'd come. He was supposed to be sober now, but I knew he was drinking again because I had had so many drunken phone calls.

The children and I went to Scotland. Halfway through the ceremony Paul arrived and after it ended he asked me to get into the car and drive with him to the party – it was only round the corner. I didn't want to make a fuss, or a scene – it wasn't our day and the kids were there – so I did as he asked. At the party I could tell he wanted to talk to me, but he was keeping his distance. There was a bouncy castle, a wonderful tea, but I could tell Paul was drinking. I was talking to Jan's cousin when he came over. 'Who the f—'s that? They've asked me here and you're f—ing shagging that bloke.'

Like a fool I tried to explain: 'He's Jan's cousin.'

He jammed me between a door and a wall and started to have a go. 'You're a f—ing big-headed blonde bitch! Who do you f—ing think you are, you stupid f—ing slag?'

I was still trying to appease him. 'Paul, you're drinking.'

'No, I'm f—ing not, you stupid big-headed . . .'

Luckily for me two guests were behind the door and they fetched Alan. He listened for a little while, then decided he'd heard enough. He appeared, grabbed Paul, and said, 'That's enough of speaking to her like that. Get out.'

Once he'd gone I felt an incredible sense of relief – it was as if a world of possibilities had opened up to me. The bouncy castle, my kids, we could have fun together without worrying that later I'd be dragged over hot coals for 'showing off and making everyone look at you'. My children deserved a mother who didn't cower, cover up, look at the floor and put them in the way of danger.

I would always ask the children if they'd had a good time when they were at Paul's. They almost always said they did. But between scant visits to Middlesborough, we would rarely hear from Paul, unless it was to speak to me, shout abuse or ask for help.

There was light at the end of the tunnel. By the end of 1999 our finances had been settled. For the record, once and for all, my divorce settlement was £660,000 cash. (All the newspapers reported £700,000 or a million – one even said £8 million.) Along with that I was allowed to keep the cars he'd bought me for my birthday, a Jaguar and a Range Rover, Rush Close (my own house, which I had bought with the *News of the World* money after I'd signed the gagging order), and two chairs from the White House, my grand piano, which Paul had given me one Christmas, and Bianca's bed. We both kept the jewellery we'd bought each other; the total value of mine was £23,000.

Throughout the negotiations Paul wanted to make sure that I couldn't touch his Guernsey money. He wanted to implement a list of restrictions as long as his arm, the most ridiculous one being that if I went out with someone for a number of weeks, he would stop maintenance. I didn't have to fight that one as everyone agreed no judge would accept it. There was a chandelier from the house in Scotland that I wanted, but he said if I gave it up, he would lift those restrictions. In the end I gave in, and he kept the chandelier. I had visions of him hurling it off the cliffs in Seaham. We settled out of court because the maintenance arrangement he offered was generous. At this point Paul's monthly basic salary was in excess of £60,000, which meant that out of his annual basic salary of £720,000, which excluded all his sponsorships deals and bonuses, the children and I got £120,000 a year. It remained at that generous level for almost two years.

My plan was to move somewhere secluded, away from prying lenses. I found a house in Much Hadham, which everyone loved – it had a walled garden and an indoor swimming-pool – but it was quite far out and I would have spent even more time than I already was as a taxi service. Two days before we were due to exchange contracts, the vendor asked for another £50,000 on top of the £820,000 we'd agreed. On principle, I pulled out of the deal. I wasn't going to have my back over a barrel, balcony, or anything else for that matter, any more.

I went back to the agent, who said he had a house he thought was perfect for us. Bianca and I fell in love with it immediately. We ended up with a better house, in a better location for £775,000, and I sold Rush Close to my friend Ami. On 27 October we moved into our new home: Pepper Hill House, Pepper Hill, Great Amwell, Hertfordshire. It was only five minutes from Stanstead Abbotts so Bianca could stay at her school, Presdales. Mason was still struggling at his state school. One day he told me, 'They think I can spell "the", and I can't.' That was it. I decided to send him to Duncombe, where Bianca had been several years ago. I applied for places for both Mason and Regan. First I had to pay the outstanding £3,000 from when Bianca was taken out of school. Luckily the headmaster waived it. Within six weeks Mason had been diagnosed with dyslexia and I was told he was three years behind. He made up two in one and was soon winning cups for almost every sport. It was the beginning of a more settled, happy time for them all. At last, I felt ready to take control.

One day shortly after we'd moved into Pepper Hill, I found Bianca lying on her bed and sobbing her eyes out. I sat down next to her and asked her what was wrong. 'This really is a new start,' she said. 'No Dad, no memories. I can't believe it, Mum, you finally did it. Thank you.' She was crying because she was safe, and she believed Paul had gone. They were tears of pure relief. 'It's our house and he can't come here.'

I promised her I wouldn't let him back. I hadn't realized until then how much I had put my daughter through over the previous ten years, and how much it had affected her. But someone knew: Sandra Horley, chief executive officer of Refuge, the charity that helps women who are victims of domestic violence.

Back in 1997, about a year after the Gleneagles incident, I was sent a copy of *The Charm Syndrome* by Sandra Horley. It was about domestic violence. I didn't know why anyone would send it to me – honestly, it baffled me. I wasn't a victim of domestic violence. I was just . . . Well, I didn't know what I was. I hadn't stopped to think about it. I started to read it, and after a page or two, I stopped to pick up a pen. A line had jumped right out of the page: 'I was accused of looking at someone in the restaurant.' I underlined it twice. How many times had I been accused of that? Restaurant, street, car, house, hotel – anywhere and everywhere. After a short while with Paul, I only ever looked in one direction. Down. I have a great friend now who met me once years ago when he and I were just back from Italy. She'd thought I was standoffish because I wouldn't look up when I talked. I didn't dare look at anyone. Even a woman. Because I would be accused of talking to them to get to their husband or boyfriend. Ordering in a restaurant was traumatic. Try giving a waiter an order without catching his eye. It's impossible.

I carried on reading. Another line jumped off the page, then another, and eventually I put the pen down: I'd realized that before long I would have underlined the whole book. I felt as if someone had put a camera in my house, filmed me secretly, then written a description of the action and sent it to me. I also realized that what had happened to me was happening to hundreds of thousands of women every day. There was domestic violence in every street, in every town, all over the country, all over the world. It was a pattern and I'd been stuck in it, just like every other woman in that book.

The book explained that, to everyone else, the perpetrator is the life and soul, deeply charming, a people person, usually much admired, dashing, the sort of man others seek out at a party, but behind closed doors he's completely different. In my case, the world got Gazza the charmer while I got Paul the abuser. I don't know if it was always the case, but by the end Paul's violence was attached to alcohol. He always tried to get people drunk and he could never leave half a glass of wine. He was always topping people up – no one could ever drink fast enough for Paul. Then he'd have one too many and turn violent or abusive.

When I finished the book, I understood that class, creed, colour and age didn't matter: it was all the same. Like death, domestic violence is a great leveller. I felt distressed and elated at the same time. I didn't have to be a victim any more – and Paul and I weren't so very special, after all. He was just a violent man who controlled me to make up for his own psychological deficiencies. I was no more the cause of his rages and jealousy than I was the cure.

I should have been bounding about with joy at the fact that I was free, but instead I was sad. How had I thought that what Paul and I had was love? Instead of answering that vital question, I made Paul the focus of blame, my anger and disappointment. I had a great deal to make up for with my children, and now that we were happily settled at Pepper Hill House I would ensure that their every need was met.

I was lucky enough to meet Sandra Horley. When I did, I said to her, 'That book is my life.' She said it was every abused woman's life. I went to her house often and, over a year, we built up a friendship. She took me round the Refuge offices and told me she thought I would be a great spokesperson for the cause. I couldn't imagine talking about it – how could I? Paul would kill me. By the end of 1999, though, I was considerably stronger and probably considerably angrier and she convinced me I could do it. There was no denying it was a good cause. So, in November I launched Domestic Violence Awareness Week. Bianca was ecstatic. Now everyone was going to find out what the real Gazza was like.

Just before the story came out, Paul called me in tears. He just wanted us to be friends, he said, able to get on. I was all in favour – I didn't want to waste the children's money on lawyers. He told me he would not fight back: we could go ahead with the campaign and speak freely. But later that day I was served with an injunction, with a penal notice attached to it saying if I did not comply I could face a jail sentence. Undeterred, Rebekah went ahead with the story, publishing the article with the restricted sections blacked out.

My diary of that week was published in the *Independent*.

Monday

I appear in the *Sun*, launching the Refuge awareness-raising campaign against domestic violence. The campaign is designed to bring domestic violence out into the open and dispel the myths surrounding the issue. I then go to film the Martin Bashir interview for the *Tonight with Trevor McDonald* programme, to be screened on Wednesday. This takes up most of the day.

It's very difficult talking about my own personal experience of domestic violence. I have to stop the filming four or five times because I become too emotional. Some of Martin's questions are tough, but I'm more than happy to answer them because I want the people at home to understand. It's exhausting.

I then go to my home in Hertfordshire to see my children, aged 13, 10 and three. I find out that Paul has served me, the *Tonight with Trevor McDonald* programme and the *Sun* with an injunction forbidding me from talking about any allegations of domestic violence that are not already in the public domain. I don't sleep very well.

Tuesday

The *Sun* prints the story about the injunction. [Rebekah was now the editor and decided to print the whole article with the bits that Paul wouldn't allow blocked out. It was a brilliant editorial decision.] The whole of today is taken up with lots of faxes and telephone calls between the *Sun*, the lawyers and Martin Bashir – the injunction will affect the programme. My youngest, Regan, is recovering from a gastric flu bug, which he contracted on Saturday, and wants to be cuddled, so it's good that I'm home all day. I eventually collapse into bed and don't sleep too well again.

Wednesday

I take Mason, my 10-year-old son, to the dentist. There are calls all day about the injunction and how it will affect the *Tonight* programme. I'm scared about what will happen with the legal stuff. In the evening I take the children for a Chinese meal with my parents. We come home, I put Regan to bed, and we watch the programme. I've been worried about people's reaction, but I get calls straight afterwards saying it was fantastic and moving, and that I managed to get my point across even though the questions were quite difficult.

Thursday

I wake up at 4.10 a.m. and can't get back to sleep. I leave the house at about 6.45 to go to London to be interviewed on the *This Morning* show by Richard and Judy. We discuss the reason women stay when they're being abused: because their confidence has been knocked out of them.

I come straight home and have lots of calls saying how well it went last night and this morning, which is fantastic. I'm told that the crisis line at Refuge was flooded with calls after the programme last night, and that the first time the lines became free was at 4.30 in the morning.

They even had men ringing saying how they had been affected

as children by domestic violence. There were women crying, saying: 'Can you believe she's done this to help people like me?' It makes me feel so humble, and makes all the soul-searching for the last few months over whether to do the programme worthwhile.

I take Regan to McDonald's. I walk in and four women immediately approach me and say: 'My God, what a brilliant programme last night.' One woman says she went through it five years ago and really relates to what I said. It's great to get that response. Then the manager comes out and says, 'Fantastic.' I'm told that the donations to Refuge are flooding in. I'm over the moon. The icing on the cake is the news that the National Lottery has awarded £250,000 to the charity. It's superb.

There's a flood in the kitchen – the third in three weeks. I don't mind too much. Today has been a particularly special day for me.

Friday
In the morning, I'm interviewed and photographed at home by the *Observer* for an article about Refuge. I then spend some time with the children because, although I've been around during the week, my mind's been on the campaign. It's been an amazing week, one that I will never forget. It started with a lot of trepidation over whether I was doing the right thing. From then on it has been amazing to know that women out there are listening, and I know they are responding.

Not everyone was as pleased. Because of the injunction, the programme makers had got scared and much of it was toned down. Bianca was beside herself. She cried inconsolably, cross with me because I hadn't told Martin Bashir what it had been like for her and her brothers. They had spent their life being told how great it must be to have Gazza for a dad and every press report stated he 'doted' on them. But the kids didn't have Gazza as a dad: they had Paul, and Paul was not a doting father. The rest of the world got Gazza. They wanted the other kids at school to know that having a famous father was not the fun they imagined it was. Mason was always told he was only good at football because Paul had shown him all the tricks, but in ten years Paul had probably kicked a football with him on five occasions. Bianca told everyone at school to watch the programme. Finally they would understand what it had been like for her.

Paul rang us on Christmas Day 1999, the first we'd spent without him since 1990. I was in Loch Lomond with the children, my mother, my father and his new flame, Jan and Alan and their parents. He asked to speak to Mason and Regan, but they were opening presents and it was utterly hectic so I couldn't get them to the phone but I told him they would ring him back. Paul called me an 'ignorant c—'. I didn't let it affect me.

Dad had been single now for nearly ten years, so I was happy that he had finally met someone and brought her with him. He wanted to take her out on the lake, the full works, champagne. I'd never seen him be affectionate, but he held her hand when we went out for a walk. It was a fun, frivolous Christmas – well, it would have been: Paul wasn't there.

We didn't hear from him again until 7 January at three a.m. He was drunk. Which was now typical. Then he rang us on the eleventh, said he'd speak to us again the following day, but didn't. The children asked to see him but Paul kept making excuses and didn't ring. We only had one mobile number for him, which he never answered. It was destructive, and hard for them to be picked up and dropped time and time again. In total he only saw Mason seven times and Bianca four times.

As Bianca saw Paul so little, it wasn't surprising that she looked for another, more reliable father figure. She found one in Ian Hart, who taught her and Mason football. As 1999 went on, he became part of the family and both children adored him. However, he went to the papers: he said he and I had a relationship and that we were so close he had a key to our house. There was a photo of him leaving Rush Close in the interview. I went to court because it was nonsense and was offered an apology. It wasn't so much because of the damage to my already pretty damaged reputation, but I was aware that now I was on my own, I had to let the papers know they couldn't go on printing whatever they liked about me. The worm had turned. But it was really distressing that we'd lost another trusted friend – he'd sold us out.

When would Bianca find an adult male she could rely on? I wondered. I'm so thankful for my dad, because, actually, she did have one – and so did the rest of us. Sometimes you can't see what's under your nose. My dad was more of a father to my children than either of theirs were. He helped me when I couldn't be in two places at once, and when Mason needed male guidance. He helped me put up shelves and paint walls. He was never very talkative but his presence was enough.

Still, Bianca wanted a dad, not a granddad. She was becoming more savvy about what life was like for other children. She had friends with divorced parents and knew how 'normal' separated parents behaved. Her friends didn't live with their dads, but their dads contributed to their upbringing, visited every other weekend and took them on holiday. So, Bianca started visiting Colin. Within months something happened that soured their relationship. I don't want to go into the details, but Bianca didn't see him for years after that. Colin blamed me, of course. But I know what happened, and he knows I know.

13. The Monster Awakes

In the early part of 2000 Paul had another career setback. He was drinking again, and broke his elbow on another man's head during a brawl. By now Kevin Keegan was managing England, and not only did the incident put Paul out of the game again, it guaranteed he could not be trusted with the England shirt. In May we went with him to Dubai for his birthday, and my protectors, Alan and Jan, came too with their kids.

Why did I go? I was still trying to fix it for everyone. But I felt safer and stronger and knew that if he erupted I wouldn't be so embarrassed that I'd run to a place where he could hit me in private. We would sit on our balcony watching Mason and Bianca running around the water park and had a great time. We slept together but I knew that if anything happened all I had to do was bang on the wall and Alan would be there.

After Paul ran into more trouble at Middlesbrough and was voted 'most disappointing player', Walter Smith took pity on him and, on 17 July, signed him to Everton, but he was out with a hernia before the season was over and continued to struggle to maintain his fitness.

I was determined to enjoy myself with or without Paul. The girls and I went to a charity 'Men For Sale' auction in London in which you bid for a male celebrity – Gordon Ramsay would come and cook, a TV gardener would do your garden, that sort of thing. I bid £10,000 to go to Rome and see Michael Bolton in concert. I didn't really want to see Michael Bolton, but I longed to go back to Rome, stay at the Hotel Hassler, and wash away all the horrible memories by taking Jan with me. I owed her a big thank-you. I was determined to win that prize, and I did.

Michael Bolton was on stage, suddenly they were putting a mic on me, and I had to join him while he sang to me. I didn't want to be serenaded. I'd bid a month's money so, clearly, we were a little tipsy at this point. It was thanks to Dutch courage that I went up there. I was so embarrassed – but I have to admit it was hilarious!

When we arrived at the hotel in Rome our suite was full of flowers and there was a card from Michael. He offered to pick us up and take us to see his live performance. I would have pre-ferred a girly evening at my old haunt, Sabatini's, but we agreed to go. He was wearing a cashmere scarf to protect his voice. We went to the studio and afterwards he asked us to dinner with his friends. So we went. The photographer/film producer Gianni Bozzacchi was there. He told me, 'Your eyes are beautiful but dead.' That line again.

After dinner Michael asked me up to his suite for coffee. He had the penthouse in the Hotel Hassler, there was a huge balcony overlooking the city of Rome. It was phenomenally beautiful and as we sat there out on the terrace, it felt like a real *Pretty Woman* moment. We talked about Nicolette Sheridan, (Michael's then ex-girlfriend), his beloved daughters and ex-wife, his charitable organization for battered women, and Paul. The next day Michael was to have lunch with the Italian prime minister at his house and asked me to go with him. I said I couldn't because I was on holiday with Jan so it seemed we wouldn't meet again. We had a kiss and a cuddle, then I went back to my room, where Jan was still awake, wanting to know all the gossip. There was none, but it had been very romantic. On the Sunday Jan and I went round the Vatican where we bumped into Michael's entourage who told me he was looking for me. When we got back to the hotel there was a message from him: he'd cancelled his lunch with the prime minister, moved his flight time to later and invited us to dinner. It was all pretty daunting, but exciting and fun. When Michael asked me if he could see me again, I said that would be lovely but never expected to hear from him. As he left, he asked Gianni to look after us and gave us his driver for the night. Gianni took us out on the terracotta tiles and we met an extraordinarily handsome actor who was rather taken with Jan. She was sorely tempted, but she was a good girl, and we went back to our hotel to dissect the night and laugh about it.

That weekend was utterly surreal and one of the highlights of my life. I'd laughed so much. The funniest thing was walking back through Heathrow with a huge bouquet of flowers that Michael had sent me before I left. And he stayed in touch. I saw him a bit after that and we had a few dinners together when he was in England.

In January 2001 I helped launch the Metropolitan Police Appeal for Domestic Violence at the Globe Theatre in London. We were campaigning to have a special court system set up in Britain so that more women could come forward safely and be heard. I was more than happy to do whatever I could. I once went to Newcastle and did a programme with BBC3. Liza Tarbuck had just won some money on *Celebrity Who Wants To Be A Millionaire?* and given it to Refuge. They needed the money: in 1990 there was only one Refuge house in the whole of the north-east.

The following month I thought Paul might like to come to a family party at Pepper Hill. I left a message but sensed when we spoke that he was irritated at having to come all the way to ours. He arrived late, and I think he'd been drinking on the way down. He walked in just as a friend of mine was leaving. He blanched when he saw her, said hello, then walked into the house. She had been one of the girls who had hung around his house years ago when he had lived in Dobbs Weir, and her younger sister had lost her virginity to Paul. We had become friends through the school, and one day she'd told me all about it. Their affair had happened when Paul and I were supposed to be passionately in love – the love that was deeper, better, truer than anyone else's. It was further confirmation that the Paul and Sheryl love story had always been a lie.

At the party Dad told me he'd seen Paul downing bottles in the utility room, and things soon got out of hand. He lost his rag with Jan and nearly punched her: she said she saw his eyes change and he didn't blink as he drew back his fist. He was literally shaking with the effort of not slamming it into her. He chased me round the house, and Bianca, who always wanted to protect me, hid with me. Sick of the constant drama and the threat of violence, we called the police. I'd been introduced to Sir John Stevens on the back of the Refuge campaign and had worked closely with the police on how they should handle domestic violence situations. Taking the abuser away, and keeping him away, was always my main point. I had faith things had improved. When they arrived, Paul went into his routine of offering them signed shirts, promising he'd calmed down. Relieved, I watched as they took him away. We all relaxed. Twenty minutes later they brought him back. Just like that. They told my dad he had calmed down and could come back safely into the house. Paul had fooled them again, and not just the police. I was in my room, when Dad came in and said, 'Sheryl, please, he's begging. He just wants to come up and say goodnight.'

'No, Dad, it won't be like that. Please don't let him.'

'He's promised he just wants to say sorry and goodnight.'

My pleas fell on deaf ears. Dad brought him up.

As soon as he sat down on the bed, the name-calling and accusations began: slag, sleeping around, who did I think I was, I'd forgotten where I'd come from ... Dad charged back in. 'You promised blind you wouldn't start, you wouldn't do anything. Now you're out!'

But Paul didn't want to go anywhere. He wasn't calm, he was drunk, angry and looking for a fight. He went on saying terrible things to me and Bianca, who had come in to find out what was going on. We all went downstairs. Bianca and I were in tears. This was Pepper Hill House, the place with no bad memories, the place with no Dad, the place where we were safe and Paul wouldn't hurt us again. No wonder Bianca was distraught and my dad was so angry. I knew the situation was out of control and that something was going to happen. My dad exploded: 'Look! You're making them cry and I'm about to lose it.'

Paul was rude one time too many: there was a crack and he staggered backwards. My father had head-butted him. Expecting the worst, I was amazed when, immediately, Paul backed down. 'Sorry, Rick, you're right. I don't want to fall out with you. I'm sorry.'

Dad looked at him. 'I should have done that ten years ago.'

By the summer of that year Walter told Paul it was either rehab or leave. He chose rehab. Having little faith in the Priory, he decided to try Cottonwood in Arizona. He rang me and asked me to go with him. I agreed to help. He came to stay at Pepper Hill and we went out to lunch at L'Auberge du Lac. He was drinking, but not excessively. On the plane, though, he drank a lot. I asked why. Because it was his last day before rehab and he was scared – scared of flying and scared of where he was going. He cried a bit and we talked, just more about poor old Paul and what they were making him do. They could have picked us up from the airport but he wanted to stay in a hotel for a night before he checked into Cottonwood. He hired a limo to take us there, a three-hour journey through ghost town after ghost town until we arrived at our motel. There was no mini-bar, just a vending machine in the corridor, and although Paul liked to think he was still a down-to-earth kinda guy, he wasn't impressed by the plastic chairs and basic décor.

His Cottonwood mentor came to the motel to introduce himself and told us he'd be back first thing in the morning. Paul wanted to know that I would be there to collect him after his treatment – then we'd all go on holiday somewhere in America.

*

They arrived in a van and told him to say goodbye to me, but Paul wasn't having it. He wanted me to come with him. They allowed me to do so. On arrival they took everything from him – his watch, his phones, everything. The Priory hadn't done that. He started crying, really crying, and didn't want me to go. When he saw his room and discovered he had to share, he hit the roof. He was getting more and more agitated, and one of the attendants was saying to me, 'Maybe it's time to go.'

I didn't know what to say to Paul. I couldn't fix it for him. I couldn't get him a single room – I couldn't do anything. For once he was going to have to accommodate someone else. The rules were strict. If you broke them there was no conversation, you were just put out with your bags. They wouldn't even call you a taxi. I left Paul there, went to buy a candy-floss machine for Regan, then flew home. I felt distraught – but I was happy too: I thought I was going to get Paul back, that he'd be better with the children, that we'd have our life back.

We faxed messages and spoke when we were allowed to. Paul would moan about the guy he was sharing with – he talked all night and kept him awake. He felt very sorry for himself and told me how hard it was and how sad all the other people were. He went through the hideous detox – they were much more severe than at the Priory: they wanted their addicts to feel it. After that he had terrible mood swings while they got his medication right. At the end there was supposed to be a family week and the lady who was supervising Paul's programme asked me if we would come. Bianca was happy to go, and I wanted all of us to be there – his family, Jimmy, everyone. But Paul wouldn't allow that.

After Paul's treatment was over, Regan, Bianca, Mason and I flew out to see him. I had high expectations, and he looked much better, much healthier. His supervisor asked me a few questions, then said to Paul, 'Have you ever tried to control Sheryl by threatening to embarrass her, shouting loudly in public?' He said he had. That was a big breakthrough for me.

Up to that point he'd always claimed he'd done nothing wrong, his rants and rages were my fault, and here he was admitting he had done it to control me.

We went to Florida again, and he wasn't drinking, which was brilliant, but he was still angry. Angry with me? About his career? The injuries? Not being able to drink? I don't know. He didn't want to talk about it. When we got home he crashed his car on the way up to Everton, where he was playing. He said it was the jet lag, that he wasn't drinking.

At Christmas I was planning to go with my friend Lorraine and her family to the Belfry, which is off the M1 on the outskirts of Birmingham. Paul asked if he could come too, so I called Lorraine, asked, and told her he wasn't drinking. I rang Mum and Dad too, and everyone agreed. But Paul didn't want to be in the dining room with everyone else because he wasn't supposed to be drinking, so he booked a private room for us all. I told him not to drink but he insisted that he was allowed one or two. He was on good form but it was clear that he was drinking more than one or two although it was hard to catch him in the act. He'd disappear or make an excuse to leave the room, then come back in and nurse his one glass of wine. Because Christmas had been planned at the last minute, and Paul wanted, as ever, to give me something memorable, he signed over to me his three-week time-share on Loch Lomond, saying that the kids and I deserved it. Lorraine had brought her karaoke machine, so we all had a good sing-song and it was a happy Christmas.

That evening he picked up Mason's phone and, scrolling through the numbers, saw Colin's. It was listed as 'Colin Dad'. Paul hit the roof. He went mad at me and mad at Mason: 'If you want him as your dad, have him. F— off, then.'

'You can't go mad, then pick and choose when you see the kids. They need a father. They're bound to be curious about Colin.'

I tried to explain to him that a few months earlier Bianca had got cross with me because I hadn't let her go out with people much older than she was. She was fifteen, she argued, why couldn't she go clubbing or to the pub? I was at loggerheads with her and eventually she'd said she'd ring Colin and go to live with him. I said, 'Fine,' and gave her all the numbers. She took Mason into her bedroom and rang Colin. They hadn't talked for years, and they arranged to meet him at his five-bedroom house.

When they came back they were raving about his home, how lovely it was, with a swimming-pool, cream carpets and lots of ornaments. I pretended I didn't mind, but inside I was dying. After another visit they told me Colin had said what a shame it was that we were going away for Easter because he wanted to take them to Naples, Florida. 'Don't worry,' I said, 'if you really want to go, you can.' Immediately they called Colin and told him they could come.

Then he called me and said, 'You've done a really fantastic job with the children.'

'They say they want to go with you, and that's fine by me.'

'I don't think I can get them on my flight.'

'But you've told them they can come, so best you tell them that.'

He booked them on to another flight, but they had a bit of a shock because they had to fly economy.

Shortly after they came home, they stopped seeing Colin again. I think the holiday had been uncomfortable, with a few too many comments about me. But Mason still had Colin's number in his phone.

On Boxing Day Paul left to go to work, but the next thing we knew, he was back. He had smelt of alcohol so they had tested him, then sent him home because he was unfit to play. When we went back to Hertfordshire, he returned to his hotel in Everton where, I now know, his drinking got progressively worse.

Nearing Valentine's Day Paul got in touch again and arranged to see me on the most romantic night of the year. He

Christmas Day, Belfry, 2001. Lorraine took the photo; Paul kept complaining I wasn't close enough.

By the third photo, I was practically on his lap!

A quick photo before dinner at Hotel Hassler on the Spanish Steps. Mason loved their bread.

Universal Studios, 1993.

Mason and I at a celebration
dinner in Norfolk, 1994.

A family holiday
snap taken in
Barbados, 1997.

Sandy Lane, Barbados.

I don't remember why this picture was taken – we're on the drive of my house in Stanstead Abbotts – but I like it.

Paul, Regan and I were stopped for a photo at Glasgow Rangers Football Club.

My amazing wedding dress.

My wonderful friend Isabell, who designed my dress.

I was very proud of my handsome family that day.

The Zodiac Room, Hanbury Manor, 1996. The setting was stunning.

Me, Paul and his father.

Me, Paul, my two fabulous children and the infamous Jimmy 'Five Bellies'.

Paul and me with my dear friend Rebekah and her partner Ross.

Mason in awe of his hero David Seaman.

The three stooges.

Tommy and Margaret McCormack, my Scottish parents, a wonderful loving couple.

Regan and his nan in Dubai, 1998.

Regan and me on the beach – the first of many holidays in Dubai. Paul used to keep this photo in his wallet, but in 2004 he sent it, along with some other photos, back to us.

June, 1997: Barbados eight months after Gleneagles, trying so hard.

Regan and his dear friend Ellie McLaren.

I took the children to California to spend time with our American family.

Paul and the children posing for a local paper in Barbados.

After Paul's first stint in Cottonwood in 2001, he asked us to meet him and holiday in Florida.

Pre-Christmas celebrations in Edinburgh with the McLarens – here we are watching the children ice-skating.

Me, Regan and B celebrating Mary Poppins's – aka JuJu's – birthday.

was asked to be the ce of a new jewellery ne called Joy.

Paul and Regan in Sandy Lane, Barbados, in the summer of 1997.

Modelling for Isabell in Copenhagen.

The day before we were to fly Paul to Cottonwood we had a family lunch at L'Auberge du Lac.

Regan and me in the lounge at Pepper Hill.

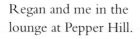

Aaahh . . . butter wouldn't melt! Mason and Regan.

Jan, Alan and Ellie McLaren.

Me and my very dear friend Jan at Cameron House.

Alan McLaren, me with my godson Sam, Jan and Paul. Shortly after this photo was taken, Alan had to ask Paul to leave.

Family pic with a sober Paul in 2003.

My strong family unit in our garden at Pepper Hill.

My stunning daughter on her way to Love Island.

Regan finally got to EuroDisney with his dad in 2004.

Paul showing Mason, Ellie and Regan his 'dance' moves, 1998.

You can see the joy in Mason's face at spending time with his dad.

Get a hat . . . get ahead! Paul is delighted with one of his Christmas presents.

Bianca decided to give her dad a new hairstyle.

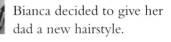

Paul's brother Carl with Jane.

Christmas, 2001, in a private
room at the Belfry – at
Paul's insistence.

Father's Day, 2003, in my garden at
Pepper Hill – a sober Paul looking
for a new addiction.

Tea at the Gascoignes'
John-Paul King, Jane,
Carl, Lindsay, Darren
and Carol.

My lovely sis Vicki during her struggle with cancer, my niece Julia, me and David.

Trying to change attitudes and reaching out to society at the fifth Annual Domestic Violence conference in London, November 2007. I was honoured to speak alongside the Rt Hon. Harriet Harman, QC MP.

Bianca and I, pictured here with Cherie Blair and Sandra Horley, OBE, were honoured to be invited to Chequers.

My gorgeous three, 2009.

My last holiday with Nanny in 1995 – for me, the most elegant lady in the world.

My incredible grandparents.

sent a car to take me to a private airfield in Stapleford Abbotts where I got into a small plane. When I arrived at Manchester airport he was waiting on the tarmac and greeted me in a black Moschino waistcoat he'd bought years ago in Italy, with a great big red heart covering the front. He took me to a huge suite in the Lowry Hotel where he gave me a diamond baguette cross and diamond Rolex watch – as ever, it was much too much. Years later he caused a big scene, demanding to know who had bought the cross and watch I was wearing. He was drinking a lot, in front of me, bottle after bottle of champagne, but we had dinner in the suite, which meant he could drink as much he liked. In the morning a car came to collect me, and as I got into it, I saw a photographer. Again, I hadn't told anyone where I was going.

Before I left, Paul had said he wanted to take me and the kids to the Burj Al Arab Hotel in Dubai. We went but Paul only stayed for a few days because he had to go home and play football. One day, Regan and I thought we could see dolphins, so I texted Paul to tell him, since he was always on the lookout for them. 'Guess what we've just seen?' He thought I was going tell him I'd spotted Neil Sedaka, an old crooner who'd just arrived in Dubai to perform. Next thing I knew, there were dozens of calls about me having sex with this man that I'd never met. It ruined the rest of the holiday, because he was ringing all hours of the day to check I wasn't shacked up with Neil Sedaka.

In March, after Everton lost to Middlesbrough, Walter washed his hands of Everton, and Everton, fed up with Paul's drinking, washed their hands of Paul. He found a place at Burnley, a second-division club, where he had to wash his own kit and take a significant drop in salary, but he boosted their gate and merchandise sales considerably.

Meanwhile, perhaps perversely, my life was still improving. I was asked to be a reporter on ITV's *That's Esther*, fronted, of course, by Esther Rantzen. I felt privileged to be invited to work alongside her. We covered things like training guide dogs, volunteering, mentoring ... I loved it. I could work round school hours and it got me out of the house. It was nice to have my own money and nice to be considered a valued member of a team. Also, I was still doing bits and pieces for Refuge, going to the houses, listening to the women there and helping to raise the charity's profile. I don't know whether I was of any help to them, but listening to those women helped me enormously. Once again, it brought home to me that I was one of many, that what had happened to me was happening to many others. I wasn't the only one who went back time and time again. I wasn't the only one who believed the promises. But I felt guilty too: I was the fortunate one among them – I hadn't ended up in a refuge because I had a house, my *own* house, and I didn't have to separate my children. I could keep them with me even though they were in their teens. If I hadn't had my house, would I have been strong enough to leave Paul? Had I really left him? Had I really moved on? It helped me to know that I hadn't been mad, that those things had happened and, more importantly, I didn't have to let them happen any more.

Isabell asked me to do a private fashion show for her at the Ritz Hotel in London's Mayfair. Bruce Forsyth was there, with his beautiful wife Wilnelia, and other celebrities. There was also an oriental gentleman called Andy Wong, a very good friend of Isabell's. When I went back into the dressing room to make a quick change, Isabell's PA, Andi, said to me, 'Did you see Andy Wong out there?'

'No, where is he?'

'At a table by the bar.' Next time I sashayed around the tables, I was to look out for him, say hi, smile and carry on. My mum and a friend were there watching, and when it was over I joined them. We were going to have afternoon tea. As I sat down, a manageress came over and said, 'Mrs Gascoigne, a gentleman here would like to say hello.'

I turned and saw two oriental men walking towards me. 'Of course.' The one I assumed was Andy came over and introduced us to his cousin. They sat down and had a cup of tea with us. Then Andy suggested I joined the Ritz Club and persuaded the manager to oblige with a free membership.

'Andy,' I said, 'I'll never get to use it.'

He stayed until my taxi arrived and we had to leave. When we got up to go he said, 'Here is my card. If you ever need anything, please ask.' He pressed his card into my hand and gave another to my mum and her friend. I went to the dressing room to pick up my bag and on the way glanced down at the card. There, in big letters, it said, 'Jimmy Choo'. I've never left anywhere so quickly – I'd been calling him Andy for a whole hour! I wailed about it to Isabell, but she assured me he would see the funny side.

I remain hideously embarrassed to this day. I couldn't even bring myself to call him and apologize. I said to Isabell he was amazingly polite not to say anything, I hope he has forgiven me. Not so Bianca. Jimmy Choo, the greatest shoemaker in the world – how could I?

By now Mason was at secondary school, St Edmund's. I'd had to fight to get him in, but succeeded with the help of his learning-support teacher. Regan was attending the primary school. I made a very good friend there, Adele, who, like Jan, remains a huge source of comfort and strength. Her daughter and Regan made friends too. Adele and I started going out to a place called Barroosh in Hertford. It was my weekly treat. One night I saw a guy across the bar and a friend gave him my number. His name was David and we met up and got on very well. I met his friends and on a couple of nights we went out as a group. I told Paul I was seeing someone, and shortly afterwards I received calls from his family about maintenance. Lindsay told me I had to leave Paul alone.

'He hasn't got any money. You want to go and get a job.'

'I don't have to discuss this with you.'

'Yeah, but you've got someone else!'

'So? It's the first time, and Paul and I are divorced now.'

David came up to Edinburgh and met Jan. Mason was a little wary, but the others liked him. We had some good times, but after a couple of months it fizzled out.

From then until 2003 we had erratic contact with Paul. Slowly and steadily he slipped further into the grip of alcoholism, but refused to admit it to himself. Soon he started taking illegal drugs as well as prescription medication, and his football career gradually fell apart. His tics, obsessions, anxieties and drinking escalated, in direct correlation to a drop in his performance on the pitch. He tested positive in the USA for a drugs test, fought with his brother putting them both in hospital, and spent most of his time in hotel rooms either with strangers or alone. He'd train manically and injure himself, then drink manically and injure himself. Nothing in his life was working. I would get calls at odd times when he thought he was having a brain haemorrhage, a stroke. It all came to a head when he moved to China to become part-player and part-coach for the club Gansu Tianma.

In March 2003 I had a call from him. Around that time he called often, talked for ages and was drinking far too much – a bottle of vodka before training. He hated China, was lonely and bored, pleading with people to play tennis with him at three in the morning. He would ask me for help but it was hard to understand what he was saying because he was so drunk.

The next thing we heard he was back at Cottonwood in Arizona. The kids wanted to send him a message, which they did. Then I had a phone call from him: he was at Heathrow airport, in tears, begging me to let him stay at my house. I was very wary. We hadn't heard from him since he'd gone into rehab a month ago and we were going to watch Mason play football at a weekend tournament. Eventually I said he could come for one night. I think he was genuinely fearful of going back up north where he would be tempted to drink again.

Bianca and I went to collect him from a garage. He'd shaved off his hair, was wearing lots of mascara, possibly foundation and diamond earrings. He looked like Right Said Fred. Bianca and I were staggered. She teased him about the mascara but all he said was that people had told him how nice his eyelashes were. He had good taste in makeup – Yves Saint Laurent, no less. For a man who'd just come out of thirty-three days in rehab, he seemed neither clean nor serene. Much later I found out that he hadn't come straight from Cottonwood: he'd been to Miami with a bloke he'd met there, gone drinking, popped pills and collected a few more tattoos. We took him home, cleaned him up, removed the makeup and put him to bed.

At the time he was making a documentary about his move to China, but in true Paul fashion, they got much more than that. The production team followed him from China to America and back to my house. In it his obsessions and tics were more pronounced than ever and were finally diagnosed as Tourette's and OCD.

When he asked why he could only stay one night I told him it was because we were going away. He wanted to know where we were going. To Devon, I told him, for one of Mason's football tournaments. Immediately he wanted to come. I knew it was a bad idea: there would be all of Mason's team, plus lots of people we didn't know, and I couldn't be sure that Paul would behave himself. When Mason came home from school he was over the moon to find his dad with us.

'Oh, son, you've got a football tournament – I'd love to be there to see you play.'

I talked to Mason: did he really want Dad standing on the sidelines when we all knew what he could be like? Mason said he'd love Paul to be there – and what son wouldn't want to give his parent a chance to redeem themselves? I had watched Mason every Sunday, come rain or shine, from those sidelines. I discussed the prospect of Paul accompanying us with my dad, who was coming anyway. I didn't think it was a good idea:

for a start we didn't have a chalet big enough for him but also I was getting angry. It had been me, on my own, doing everything for the children, and now Paul had walked in, the returning hero, and it seemed that his being there was more important than anything else. For Mason it was a dream come true: finally he would have a dad on the sidelines like the rest of his mates.

I drove Dad, Paul and the boys to Devon and we arrived at our accommodation, which was pretty basic, on a cliff over-looking the sea. For the first time in our relationship, Paul and I actually went for a walk. I thought it was ridiculous that we'd never done anything simple like that. Our conversation was still all about Paul. That evening we were supposed to be going to a talk and Paul and I discussed whether he should go. It would be full of football dads. He suggested that he stay behind to babysit. My dad reassured me that he would be fine, but I was nervous. I told Mason I was going to listen to the instructions for the weekend, but then I was coming back to the room. My weekend was spoilt: those mums and dads were friends I'd made during the season. I'd been looking forward to the camaraderie.

My dad, Mason and I went to the hall to listen to the talk, but after twenty minutes I left Mason with his granddad. He didn't seem too upset because he had his friends, but I'm sure he would have preferred me to stay.

When I got back to the room, Paul had gone. The room was empty. I went out to look for him. When I passed some kids, they said, 'Where's Gazza?'

'I don't know. Have you seen him?' I asked.

'We saw him in the sweet shop – he had loads of sweets.'

'Where did he go after that?'

'Dunno.'

I ran out to the car park but my car had gone and I started to panic. I went back to the room, back out into the grounds, round and round. I went down to the beach, checked the cliff, my heart pounding. How could I have been so idiotic as to leave him? I went back to our room to check again and he was there, smiling inanely at me. The sofa was covered with the souvenirs and sweets you find in seaside shops. Sticks of rock, lollipops, kites, buckets, spades, wind-up aeroplanes, marshmallow sticks, candy floss, bubble gum, balls. There wasn't one of anything, there were groups of them, all lined up on the sofa and the floor, as if they were on display. He'd bought them all for the boys.

Paul was still grinning at me and his speech was so slurred I couldn't understand what he was saying. Then he slid down the wall. 'What the hell have you taken?' I asked. We'd brought no alcohol, and there was no mini-bar. 'Where have you been?'

I went on and on at him. What had he taken? I was so angry with myself and livid with him. I called Johnny Mack, his therapist, and told him Paul was in a mess and that he'd taken something but wouldn't tell me what. Paul told me he'd taken one pill, but I didn't believe him. He had so many bottles in his leather bag. Johnny Mack asked me to find out what he'd taken, but I was so angry I just wanted to wash my hands of him. Paul had ruined Mason's weekend, and I had put them in that situation.

'Don't take him to hospital,' said Johnny, who was worried that someone would find out that Paul wasn't quite as clean and serene as he was supposed to be. 'Just find out what he's taken. Is it the blue one?'

'Did you take the blue one?'

'Is it the white one?'

'Did you take the white one?'

It was like trying to talk to a five-year-old. He couldn't answer. Instead he started crying.

'Sheryl, walk him up and down!'

I couldn't pick him up, let alone walk him up and down. Luckily Mason appeared at the door – checking up on us, I think. I told him to go and get Granddad and Bob, the manager of Mason's team, Broxbourne Rangers. Luckily for Paul, his wife Rai was a nurse. They came and got him up off the floor, then started walking him up and down. Rai happened to be working towards an exam and had some of her books with her. She went to get them, and we tried to work out which of his pills he would have taken, and how many. She took his pulse. 'This isn't the way, Paul. What were you doing?' she asked, in a soothing voice.

'I just want Sheryl back,' he sobbed.

'You're not going to get her back like this, are you?'

'I just love her.'

Everyone thinks they can fix him. Including me. None of us knew how bad he was, even then. We spent the night walking him up and down, spoonfeeding him water. All the time Rai was being so sweet and supportive to him, but I was still livid.

'I can't function without her – I just want her back.'

He made us all complicit in his drama. Even Rai said, 'He loves you so much,' but I'd heard it so many times, and now it just made me sad. Paul was an anchor round my neck, making it impossible for me to move on. Everyone was worried about him, cared about him, loved him because he was a national hero.

First thing the following morning, we were on the pitch. Paul came out and, of course, caused a bit of a stir. We tried to keep ourselves to ourselves but he would wander off. I told him I'd get him anything he wanted, but if he went wandering around, he'd be mobbed. But that was what he wanted. He wasn't getting the usual adoration from me, because I was so angry, so he went looking for it elsewhere. He offered to go and get everyone hot dogs. I told him not to but he insisted. It seemed to me that what he really wanted was everyone to see him being the generous dad, the down-to-earth geezer. But I wasn't taking the bait. I was beginning to find my voice – or the monster, as Paul called it.

Everyone was watching Mason because he was Gazza's kid. He was good at football but only because he'd taught himself to play. He's always had to be the best of the best. When he'd arrived at Duncombe, he was upset because he wasn't in the cricket team.

'But, Mase, you've never played cricket.'

Every night after that we had to go out into the garden so he could practise batting, with me bowling at him. Two weeks later he was in the team. That's just Mason. He has to be the best and he plays to win. On the football pitch he usually took the throw-in because he had such a long throw. During the tournament a boy stood right in front of him, blocking him. Finally Mason snapped and threw the ball into the boy's face. Everyone was talking about it, and I worried that Mason, who had a tendency to be rough on the pitch, had done it because Paul was there.

On the way home Paul asked whether we could go away with him for his birthday. But I said he had to sort out his life. He hadn't got a job lined up – China hadn't been the success he had hoped. He didn't want to talk about it: he just wanted to go to Dubai. He offered to buy me a car. I didn't want a car. 'Mason, does Mum want a new car?'

'Yeah, she likes those cars.'

'I don't need a car – I don't want a car.'

All the way home he was trying to buy us stuff. I didn't want any of it. He got on the phone to the travel agent, then spoke to Bianca. The next thing I knew I'd given in to my children and we were off to the Royal Mirage in Dubai.

When we got to Dubai I started on at him again. What was he going to do? He began to tell me about how this person and that person had stitched him up, and that, basically, he had no money. The Chinese hadn't paid him, which was why there wasn't any money when he'd expected there to be some.

'So what are we doing in Dubai?' I wasn't going to pay for it – I didn't have that sort of money. First-class flights and suites were way out of my league. Paul thought everyone was trying to pull a fast one on him and that was why he'd ended up short. He asked me whether we could do a family photograph for one of the papers to earn him some money. I refused. But they got a picture of us on the beach anyway.

At the end of the holiday I realized he really couldn't pay so I had to hand over my credit card. Thankfully, I had a Centurion American Express card with a high limit. He promised he'd pay me back when we got home – but at home he still didn't have any money. However, I knew his money in Guernsey was safe. We rang the bank. I couldn't believe what I was hearing. I looked at Paul. 'Where is the three and half million in Guernsey?'

'I don't bloody know.'

It had gone.

14. In Sickness and in Health

The SARS virus broke out in China which gave Paul the excuse not to have to go back. When we got home he stayed with us at Pepper Hill and remained sober. But it was hard for everyone to adjust. One morning he insisted that he would drive the boys to school. I called out of the bedroom window, 'Paul, I'll take them.'

'No, they're f—ing coming with me! Get in the bloody car!'

I closed the bedroom window and began to go down the stairs. When I got to the landing, I heard a scream. I ran down the rest and threw the front door open. I couldn't believe my eyes. Paul had Mason up against a tree with his hand around his neck. 'Stop it!' I yelled.

I pushed him away, and got Mason into the car. 'Get out of our house! Leave us alone!' I shouted, as I drove off.

Mason was crying: he was sorry, he hadn't meant to upset his dad, he had just wanted to stop him being violent. I told him we wouldn't go to school, we'd just wait until Paul had gone. But Mason had an athletics competition and it was a big day for him. He really wanted to be at school. I was worried because he was upset and he was worried because he didn't want me to go home on my own. I dropped the boys off and spoke to Mason's house mistress. I told her there had been 'an incident' at the house, Mason was upset and I thought he might get angry at school. She agreed to keep an eye on him.

Then I went to my dad's flat and rang Johnny Mack and left a message for him.

By the time Johnny called me back, he'd spoken to Paul. 'It's not going to be easy for anyone. The thing is, he hasn't run. It's a big improvement. If anything happened before, he'd run away, and this time he's facing up to what he's done. He knows it's wrong and he wants it to work. The Paul of old would have run. This time he's stayed because he wants to make it work.'

'No, Johnny, no more, I'm not having it.'

Johnny insisted: he's changed, it's not going to be easy, he's trying, he's had such a great time being with you, he really wants to work it out, you're so important to him, he needs you.

Once again I gave in; I wanted Paul to get better. Johnny was a professional, and I was led by him. I let Paul stay, but reluctantly. It was easier for everyone else if he was with me: he was becoming too erratic and difficult for anyone else to cope with. I was going to Mason's athletics competition and he came too. When we arrived at the stadium Mason was pleased he was there. Paul apologized to him, said he was stressed, that he wasn't well and that things would change. 'I'm going to get better for you, son.'

But Paul didn't know how to get better. And he didn't know what he wanted.

So, Paul came home and we started trying to sort out his financial situation. As he said in his book, he didn't have the energy to work out where it had all gone, so I did it for him. Over the next month I went through all of his accounts: he'd always been suspicious he was being ripped off by various associates, would fall out with them and move on. It left a chaotic trail. My dining-room table was taken over by his papers. Eventually I had to talk to Anna, who had been acting as his assistant. I thought she was the person most likely to know what Paul had done with his money. She wasn't best pleased to have to speak to me – but the money had come out of the bank and gone somewhere and I wanted to know where. I asked to see all of the bank statements and spoke to the Guernsey bank.

I discovered he had put millions into some film company. He had also put a lot into dollars when the dollar was high, but now the value had dropped. He had county-court judgments against him for failing to pay his Barclaycard bill. I set up a meeting with my bank manager and accountant and I took out a loan of £40,000 to pay off Paul's credit-card bill. I kept records of all the phone calls and all the missing money. We traced some to a Pentad fund, which basically financed arms deals! I was shocked that he didn't know where it had all gone. His sister said that if Paul rang her up and told her to move money, she did it, no questions. When I asked Paul what he'd been investing in, he simply said, 'If someone comes up to me and says, "Give me a million and I'll make it two million", I'll sign it.' He didn't understand any of it and he didn't want to have to do anything about it. 'Get my money back, Shez. Find it and get it back.'

In the end I did get most of it back. I told the people who'd taken it from him that they'd had it under false pretences and he hadn't been in a fit state of mind to make such decisions. He tried to get shirty about his sister. 'What the f— has she been doing?' But she'd only been doing what he asked her to, which was part of the problem: no one said no to him.

When we went to the film company I asked questions but didn't understand the answers, so I went on asking and asking. It appeared that they didn't want me to understand. Eventually it transpired that the money was sitting in one of their accounts. If that was the case, I said, I wanted it back.

He'd cashed in a pension every time he wanted some extra money and each time he did so his bank charged him a huge sum. We froze the standing order to me because he couldn't afford to pay it, so all maintenance ceased at that point. I told him he had to do the same for his family. All standing orders had to be stopped, because every time payment of one was refused his bank made another huge charge. He was living with us, so he didn't need money, which meant he had a chance to figure it all out.

I knew that money was due to him. He had signed a book deal with Headline; there was a Rangers' video from which he would getting 50 per cent of the Christmas sales; a McDonald's ad featuring Paul was showing; a computer soccer game and a mobile phone game were in the pipeline; and there was a competition in the *Sun*. On top of that there was always the possibility of doing interviews for money. I chased the unpaid funds, which came in, and immediately he transferred the money to his family. He couldn't say no to them, but I didn't feel I could remonstrate with him. I didn't want for anything, and it wasn't my money. He could do what he liked with it. But I thought it was sad. And so did he, I know it.

While he was at Pepper Hill he worked on his autobiography with Hunter Davies. It came out in time for Christmas 2004. They sat in the garden together, Paul regaling Hunter with stories of his pranks and jokes, the time he put poo in the mince pies, then replaced them in the fridge for Cyril and Jimmy to eat, loaded paralytic friends on to trains naked, and drove quad bikes to training. He talked about the comedy breasts, the belching, the farting, pulling down other people's trousers, pouring water over people in bed, fishing for carp in a hotel's ornamental pool, all the 'fun' stuff. He brushed over the rest. We were supposed to go to stay with Hunter in the Lake District where he lives, but after the meeting in the garden Paul ducked his calls, made me answer them and in the end we didn't go. The autobiography was intended to be a truthful account of Paul's life, but my friends often move it to the fiction section in the bookshop.

During the four months Paul stayed at Pepper Hill our sex life waned, perhaps because I'd listened to the testimonials of other abused women and knew that sex had played as important a part in the controlling as the beatings had, and I had found my voice. I told my friends I would start as I meant to go on. He wasn't going to have his wicked way with me ten times a day, and I wasn't going to be at his beck and call. In the mornings I would get up, get the kids up and carry on with my day in the usual way. If Regan came into my bed in the middle of the night I let him stay, even though Paul hated it. Before, I would have taken him back to his own bed (as I had with Mason) so Daddy didn't get annoyed. But I wasn't going to put Paul first any more, especially if it was to the detriment of my children. I still went out and met my friends for coffee. I went to the gym. My life didn't stop because he was back.

But the verbal assaults went on. I was told so many times that I thought I was something but I was nothing. Sometimes I went to sleep with my fingers in my ears while he ranted and raved. 'They all know what you're like. Terry Venables knows what you're doing to me. Jimmy knows what you're like – everyone tells me to keep away from you. Your family are shit. What's wrong with you? Why aren't you close?'

Occasionally I'd take my fingers out of my ears.

'You want to remember where you came from, you were nothing . . .'

I'd put them back in and eventually he would run out of steam or I would fall asleep. I didn't defend myself: that was what he wanted, for me to engage with it. Saying nothing was the best defence I had.

Yet he still wanted to hold my hand, keep me close. He needed physical contact all the time. I mastered the art of detaching myself. I would look at my hand and think, That hand is not my hand. The arm round his body is not my arm. If he held on to my leg, it was not my leg. I worried about showing him affection because it was one of the things that set him off, so now I would give him a quick hug, a squeeze, stroke his arm in a bid to keep him sweet, always trying to pre-empt his mood. And I could never be affectionate to the children when he was around because he hated it.

*

In August me and the kids planned our annual summer holiday to La Manga. Paul wanted to come with us. It was another disaster. Regan and Paul didn't get on very well. Regan wouldn't compete with him as Mason used to: he walked away. Paul broke the window in our room when he threw a phone at Mason. Mason, by now a tall fourteen-year-old with an understandable angry streak, had discovered he could wind up Paul. Once he pulled Paul's swimming trunks down – a prank Paul had perpetrated at least a hundred times. Paul got so cross he smashed something over Mason's head. Paul didn't like it: he couldn't mess Mason around any more, and Mason was less gullible, less grateful, and stopped seeking his approval. Paul didn't like being by the pool because people were drinking, and he decided he wanted to go home.

Paul badly needed a job – and not just for money: he had to be occupied or he would get bored and cause trouble. He was searching for one – at one point it looked like he was going to sign for Al Jazeera in Dubai. When he went out there to talk about it, Regan asked whether Dad had gone. I said he had. 'Good. Now you won't have to do all his work for him.' Unfortunately the deal fell through, and Paul came home again.

Shortly afterwards I was tidying up Mason's bedroom when Paul walked in. He grabbed me and tried to kiss me. When I turned my head away, he shouted in my face accusing me of not wanting to kiss him, or have sex with him and all the usual list of other accusations. Finally sick of it, I pushed him away and told him I didn't want to make love to him any more. While he'd been in Dubai I allowed myself to look at my family and knew for the first time in twelve years that life without Paul was happier, calmer and easier: despite his sobriety, I didn't want him back.

*

When Paul Ince suggested Paul went to Wolverhampton Wanderers to train, and sit on their reserves in the hope that they would sign him, I thought it was a great idea; this was my chance to get him to leave once and for all. I waited for the kids to be safely out of the house and when he started packing to go to Wolverhampton I told him to take his stuff, all of it. However irate he got, I stayed calm. I left the house telling him that when I got back he had to be gone. And he was. Our relationship was over, but as with Colin, I never stood in the way of the children getting in touch. That, however, became increasingly difficult.

He changed all his numbers except one, but he rarely answered it so the kids couldn't get in touch with him if they wanted to. The maintenance payments never resumed. In November 2003 Paul's doctor called to ask me why Paul had requested he send a fax to his solicitor stating he could not work. Dr Brenna hadn't seen him since September when he had seemed fit and couldn't understand why he had to do this. It was all about money. I had to go back to court.

The long-term side effects of our family life were beginning to show. Mason was getting into trouble at school: he was struggling in lessons and hid it by becoming increasingly disruptive. As he was popular, others followed his lead. The school didn't think they could help him: they were trying to become more academic and Mason couldn't cope with the changes. The headmaster suggested he needed somewhere with more pastoral care if he was going to reach his potential and not get left on the side. As my dad had always said, if you play the clown, the last laugh will be on you. While all his friends were getting on, Mason had been falling behind. He also had to be top dog, beat everyone, thought he knew it all and wanted to go out all the time. He wouldn't toe the line.

We went to visit some other schools. As soon as we walked

into Ellesmere School in Shropshire Mason loved it. Regan liked it too, so once again, we were packing our bags and moving. By now Bianca had left school and was working at Harrods, so I rented a two-bedroom house for her and her boyfriend, Dan, in Hertford so she had somewhere to live and we could stay when we visited her and my parents.

At the end of the summer of 2004 we rented and moved into a beautiful house in Shropshire called Kidnal Farm, surrounded by forestry and fields. Mason fitted into year nine at his new school, throwing himself into sport and being given extra help in his GCSE subjects. It was a good decision for him, but tough on Bianca, who had relied on the stability of Pepper Hill and wanted to put down lasting roots. It was tough on Regan too: he didn't like his new school very much, though he loved being in the countryside. An American couple moved into Pepper Hill and paid enough rent to cover the mortgage and contribute to what I was paying my landlord at Kidnal Farm.

I threw myself into the PTA and soon made friends. In Shropshire there seemed to be an open-door policy and soon people were dropping in all the time. I did flower-arranging, decorations for the school productions and music teas. I made more new friends, one the former wife of an alcoholic who said to me something I will never forget: 'I had the easy way out – he died.' Only the partner of an alcoholic could understand that sentiment. No one wishes an alcoholic dead, but the addiction is such a drain on those who have to stand by and watch. I met a couple of nice guys, single parents like me, and had the bizarre experience of being cooked for by a man. It had never happened before. He did Christmas dinner, the whole shebang! Impressive.

Nothing lasted – I wasn't looking for anything serious. And as together as I might have appeared, I wasn't capable of giving anything to anyone. There were times when everything I'd gone through came tumbling down on me, and I felt overwhelmed, then empty and exhausted. I had been on high alert for so long that I'd burnt out. Then I would close the door, stop answering the phone and wrap myself up in my children. I needed to heal my family. I still do.

There were bleak moments. Mason and Regan had a row and Regan, angry with his brother and wanting to get him back, asked me for his dad's number. I gave it to him. We hadn't heard anything from Paul for over a year.

'Is my dad there?'

'Who's that?'

'It's Regan.'

'Who?'

'It's Regan, his son, Regan.'

The phone went dead.

Paul could never cope: things would get too much for him. Once, he and I had arranged to meet on the M6 when Regan had been visiting him. But Paul turned nasty on the phone because he didn't understand where we were supposed to be meeting. The service station on exit twelve, I'd told him.

'Where's that?'

'Exit twelve.'

'Don't talk to me like I'm six! Stupid f—ing cow.'

He was working himself up into a state, and by the time he arrived at the service station, he was in one. 'Stupid big-headed blonde bitch, slag! You think you're something, but you're nothing, nothing, nothing . . .'

I wanted to drive off, but I desperately needed petrol. I waited until I'd seen Paul leave, then went back for petrol. I was on edge the whole time I was filling up the car. As I drove away I thought, Thank God I don't have to deal with that any more.

After that we didn't see Paul for a while. A year later he came down and took Regan to stay in a hotel near the school. When he picked him up, Paul insisted on getting out of the car so, of course, he was surrounded by the boys all wanting autographs and photos. Then he was offering to come in and talk to the juniors at assembly. The teachers, the boys, everyone made a big fuss of him, and Paul loved it. It wound me up: he was the hero father . . . the hero father who didn't even pay the fees. He stayed all morning and the teachers took him into the canteen for lunch.

As for Bianca and Mason, Paul made no effort to see them. The only contact they had with him was abusive texts and drunken messages.

15. Have You No Pride?

In June 2005 Paul's book came out in paperback with a few amendments and added extras. It was pretty vile about me and upset the children, especially Bianca, who still found it hard to live with the misconception that Paul was the greatest dad in the world, loved kids and would do anything for his own, and that I was a money-grabbing slag.

The gagging order that Paul had slapped on me over the interview with Martin Bashir and the *Sun* still stood, so I couldn't respond to the accusations in the new edition of Paul's book even if I wanted to. Which I didn't. But the children were beside themselves. They wanted the right to reply and asked to go to court to have the injunction against them quashed. Rightly or wrongly, I agreed that they could, and we went to court. Paul, of course, didn't show up, and neither did the Shropshire police, but the children won their right to reply. They did a big piece each in the *Sun*, which quietened a few of Bianca's demons. But the public's adoration of Gazza was bigger than all of us, and in the main the consensus remained that I was a vindictive, money-grabbing blonde vulture, and he was the daft, funny, albeit troubled national hero.

But not everyone believed him to be all that lovable.

One of the great things that came out of the *Sun* interview was that Refuge asked Bianca to speak on behalf of children brought up in abusive households. She went on *This Morning* to talk about how she had felt, not to detail what happened. She was absolutely fantastic, portraying the guilt and heavy burden of responsibility that children carry when they can't stop the violence. (On the back of that interview, she was asked to audition for the reality TV show *Love Island* and was given a part.)

In recognition of our support for Refuge, we were invited, with other supporters, actors, comedians and benefactors, to a Refuge evening hosted at Chequers by Cherie Blair. It was an absolute highlight of my life and a privilege to walk around the imposing house yet stumble across toys and family photographs. Everyone at that event was against domestic violence – I didn't have to prove myself, convince anyone or defend my actions. Everyone understood and I felt supported and honoured to be there.

The summer of 2006 was, for Bianca, the summer of love. She won ITV's dating show *Love Island*, with the beautiful Calum Best, whose background was similar to hers. Everyone knew about the trials and tribulations he'd had to go through with his father, George. We were glued to the television watching her. I thought she handled herself brilliantly and I could see she was enjoying being out there, making her own mark. Paul, however, told the press he didn't want anything more to do with her – like he'd had so much to do with her up to then. However, a few weeks after she'd won I had a phone call from him. He was in tears again.

'Tell B I'm really proud of her. She's really beautiful, tell her.'

'I'm sure she'd love to hear that from you, Paul.'

'You tell her.'

'OK.'

He eventually told her himself, pissed, of course.

Paul and I had no reason to talk but when he rang, no matter how a conversation started, it always reverted to abuse. 'You only moved up there because you're shagging some bloke. Who you shagging?' Eventually he started calling Bianca – all the time. I still feel bad about that: it was as if she took over the task of being responsible for him. When he was in a bad way, which he often was that year, he would keep her on the phone for hours. He'd say he'd kill himself unless she promised to meet him. Then he'd cancel or, worse, not answer the phone on the day they were supposed to see each other.

Mason had done really well with his GCSEs and got himself a place in the sixth form, but after a few months he decided it wasn't for him. I knew he had struggled academically so I wasn't going to push him. However, I told him he couldn't leave school unless he had a job to go to. He said it was easy for everyone else: they were going to work for their dads – which was probably what prompted him to call Colin and ask him for a job. I was stunned but also pretty impressed by his determination. Colin took him on at a basic salary to learn the ropes of the property business.

Mason quit school at the same time as my tenants left Pepper Hill. We were sitting at Kidnal Farm over Christmas with friends when I realized I had an empty house with no one paying the mortgage. I also had to find rent for the farm and the school fees. Meanwhile Bianca, Mason and my parents were all back in Hertfordshire, so Regan and I decided to leave Shropshire. We packed up the house in two days and on 2 January 2007 we moved south. Once again, I had to pay a school for removing the children without giving due warning.

Trouble was, I simply couldn't afford to pay. I was having the most serious cash-flow problem. I had put Pepper Hill on the market to release some capital but there was no imminent sign of a sale. In the end, because I was left with absolutely no option, I wrote to Colin, asking if he would help me pay Mason's final school fees. I constructed the letter carefully, enclosing a copy of the school bill. I asked him if there was any way he could help me out, he didn't have to speak to me, he could just go straight to the school and pay them direct. I wouldn't have done it if I'd thought there was no chance. It was his opportunity to be the hero. Mason had just started to work for him and perhaps Colin would take this chance to prove to him that a proper father-son relationship was in the offing. I explained to the school that they might hear from Colin and told Mason what I had done. He wasn't pleased, but I'd had no choice. A few days later a letter arrived. Inside was the school bill with 'HAVE YOU NO PRIDE?' scrawled across it in big red letters.

I was left with no option but to remortgage the house and then finally, thank God, found a buyer who paid £1,375,000 for it, which doubled my investment and gave me money to live on. The couple who bought it wanted to move in quickly, so we rented an antiquated house in the countryside. Regan and I loved it, but Mason and Bianca weren't impressed by the gas-canister-fuelled oven that had to be lit with a match. The views were breathtaking, and there was a huge pond with ducks in the garden. My cousin Debbie taught Regan how to fish with the Chinese rod Paul had used to hook a carp from a hotel's ornamental pool one day when he was bored in Beijing.

When Regan auditioned at the Arts Educational School in Tring and was offered a place, we moved again. By this time things between Mason and Colin had deteriorated. Mason threw himself into learning about the business, but Colin refused to put him on commission. After six months, he let him go and instead kept on the other junior. Mason took it hard, although he said otherwise: he believed he'd put everything into Colin's business.

It had been quite an eventful summer. Bianca was still living off her new-found celebrity and all that comes with it. She'd been busy and we hadn't seen much of her. She went on holiday to Marbella with some friends and discovered Paul was there too. He called her and told her to meet him straight away. She told him she could see him in an hour but he went mad. At the same time he wouldn't tell her exactly where he was staying, so she couldn't go and find him. She called me in tears. 'Why does he keep doing this?' I couldn't protect her from him – I never had been able to. He would always talk about sex with her: first he'd say he hadn't slept with anyone since 'your mother', and once, 'I've not slept with anyone since your mum, not even a dolphin!' These comments made her feel uncomfortable.

We bought a house near Hemel Hempstead, a ten-minute drive from Regan's new school, that needed renovation and modernization, with a view to doing it up and selling it on a year later. I started a big refurbishment job. I gutted the house so for a while I had no kitchen. Stories were being published about Paul getting on a plane drunk, not paying his bills and going into rehab, but we didn't hear from him directly.

I had other things to worry about. On my birthday, 24 September, my friend Lorraine organized a lunch for my crack-team of girlfriends and some new neighbours, Bianca surprised me with a huge bouquet of flowers and we had a great day. Then the husbands and boyfriends turned up to join the party. Bianca had drunk quite a lot and decided it was time to go home. We put her into a taxi and saw her off, then paid our bill and were about to leave when Bianca phoned, no more than twenty minutes after she'd left, crying and saying she'd crashed. I screamed at her to put the driver on the phone.

'No, Mum, *I*'ve crashed!'

She had gone home, written me a note to say she was going to see a friend, then jumped into her brand-new car and set off to see a friend in Essex. She'd crashed into another car on a steep bend and the airbags went off. The police were called. I went with her in the ambulance, and couldn't stop saying how lucky we all were that I wasn't visiting her in the morgue. Bianca was charged with drink-driving and, quite rightly, lost her licence.

Now that he was no longer working for Colin, Mason was doing odd jobs, not earning much, and kept asking my mum to lend him money. I asked her not to since it stopped him looking seriously for a job, but she gave him her cashpoint card and pin number and let him withdraw money whenever he liked. I was worried: both Bianca and Mason had started partying hard. I have always had a no-drugs house rule and had let the children know I had purchased home drug-detecting kits from America. They have never been under any illusion that if I caught them taking drugs they would be fending for themselves. In November I found myself in exactly that position and knew I couldn't renege on my threat. Mason thought I was overreacting, but I was adamant: if he wanted that sort of life, he had to leave. If he wanted to stay at home I would shadow him for a month, twenty-four hours a day, until I was sure he didn't have a problem. He left.

I cried all night and then all day. Of everything we'd been through, watching him leave was the hardest thing I'd ever had to do. I knew that drugs could destroy my children and condoning drug-taking might prove the equivalent of handing Mason a death sentence. Asking him to leave was tough, but I believed it was right.

Mason moved into my mum's flat. I told her he'd never stop if she went on aiding and abetting him – I thought, apart from being unsupportive, it made her no better than a drug-dealer and told her so. She went on giving Mason money and letting him stay. It wasn't the harsh dose of reality I'd wanted him to experience and it wasn't going to persuade him to come home either. He stayed away, except for Christmas Day. We spent it quietly at home, with no kitchen or dishwasher, and for the first time ever, my mum wasn't invited. She passed the day alone in her flat. Mason went back there afterwards, which was awful and painful and strange, and it wasn't until he had run up £3,000 worth of gambling debts on my mum's account that things changed. She rang me: 'Are you going to pay me back this money or not?' I said no. I wasn't prepared to bail my mum out again, and it came to a nasty head when she came round and I accused her of trying to make up for the loss of her sons by giving everything to my children. She screamed at me and said, 'But he doesn't do it in *my* house,' as if that was okay! I told her to leave and we did not speak for a year.

Now that the coffers were finally bare, Mason was forced to come home and prove to me that he had stopped taking drugs. He did his month, and he admits now that perhaps I wasn't such a sad, evil woman to have put him through it. Being a parent, especially a single one, is rarely about making friends with your kids.

That Christmas we didn't hear from Paul, the third in a row that we hadn't. I was disappointed for the children not to have so much as a card.

The next we heard of Paul, he had been sectioned on 21 February 2008 and sent to an NHS psychiatric unit in Darlington. We saw it on the news. Bianca wanted to send him a message so she left one saying we were thinking about him, with our house and her mobile phone numbers. He started ringing, and as soon as he was out of hospital it was clear that he'd started drinking again. He'd call at three in the morning – 'Help me, help me.' I'd tell him to go back to the hospital, but he swore blind he didn't need to. He needed my dad, then Bianca. He wanted Bianca to come and get him. But she couldn't because she'd lost her driving licence.

'She can drive. I know the Queen – you more important than the Queen, are you?'

'When it comes to my daughter, yes, I am.'

'I'll get it sorted – hang on, I'll ring you back.' Then he rang back. 'Right, she's on her horses and she's walking with the corgis and when she comes back she's going to say Bianca can drive her car. I'm in the know. I know people.'

Another night he called crying because he'd been with a prostitute and he thought she was press. 'I didn't do anything, I didn't do anything.'

He told me he had another one in Newcastle and just asked her to watch a movie with him and have a cuddle. I don't think that is an uncommon request, but then again with Paul's sex drive, it seems unlikely. But he was obviously very lonely. Sometimes when he rang it was tragic, sometimes it was funny, and sometimes it was impossible to understand what he was saying. It was clear, though, that he had serious mental-health issues that needed to be tackled.

If I had been in any doubt about my tough stand on drugs with the children, my faith that I had done the right thing was confirmed when an ex-lover of Paul's went to the papers following his sectioning in February with a sad, sordid story of how cocaine had taken hold of Paul. He was regularly going on twenty-four-hour drink and drug binges during which he'd line up the cocaine, then take only the lines that followed some strange sequence in his head. He thought aliens were coming to get him and his compulsions were out of control. His ex claimed he would become violent for no reason and was regularly reduced to tears before and after sex. She also said he sometimes tried to kick both habits, but that 'it wasn't pretty' and he soon started drinking again, beginning his day with six hot whisky toddies and following them with neat alcohol. It made depressing reading.

Once he asked to come and see the kids, and got it into his head that he needed to see my father. But the next time he called, he asked, 'What's that fat cow writing to me for?'

'Who?' I had no idea who he was talking about. He told me my father's new girlfriend was sending him cards. That made no sense – why would she? I mentioned that he'd missed all of the children's birthdays and Christmases. That set him off.

'What's happening to my cards? Who's taking my cards?' He said he'd always sent them but somehow they had never appeared.

He'd been in and out of the Priory, he said, and had stayed once for four weeks, but he wasn't taking part in any of the treatments, just living there, not making any progress. He was using it like a five-star hotel without a mini-bar. At one point he said he wanted to leave but had no money to get home, and no one was offering to get him or travel with him. In the end, worn down, I offered to pick him up and drive him to

Newcastle. I thought that was what he wanted and maybe he just didn't know how to ask.

'What? You'd do that for me?'

'Yes, Paul, if that's what you want.'

But he didn't want that. He just wanted to go to a hotel and get pissed.

Because of the refurbishment the new house was still a mess, full of builders, and our belongings were still boxed up. Paul was begging to come and stay because he thought the hotel where he was living was bugging his room. He truly believed that he was being spied on and he couldn't sleep for anxiety. Next thing I knew he was in a cab and had put me on the phone with the driver.

'Talk to my wife. She'll tell you where she lives. Talk to my wife.'

I gave the man our address.

Then he was shouting at the driver: 'Just f—ing turn round. Why are you f—ing looking at me? I'll f—ing smash your face in. Stop the car – stop the car now!' He was trying to get out on the M1. 'The press are following me – I've got to come to you. I'm getting out!'

I spoke to the driver, who didn't know what to do: he didn't want to let him out on the M1. So I drove to the nearest junction to meet him. When I saw him I was shocked. He was weak, thin and had a horrible crusty layer of gunk around his mouth. He was so irate that he'd smashed a phone in the car. The boot was full of flowers. I apologized to the driver, who then politely asked Paul for his phone back. Paul had taken it off him because he thought the driver was bugging him. The sim card and battery were on the car floor.

I got him into my car. I'd warned the builders, who were nice guys, that I was bringing Paul back to the house. One by one they said how sad it was to see him looking so frail, and what a terrible waste it was. Mason was chuffed that he was back. Paul wanted a drink – just one glass of wine. Mason told him he couldn't have one, that he wasn't with us to drink, but as ever, Paul went on, just one glass, then he'd relax, he'd be okay.

'One glass, then, but you've got to sip it.'

Mason gave it to him. He walloped it back in one, then started trying to neck the bottle. But Mason took it from him. Paul started going on about the Newcastle Mafia, and how hard he was, which made Mason laugh – his dad was this shrivelled little man trying to act big. Paul was furious and wanted to take Mason outside – I could see Mason was actually tempted to go. Teach him a lesson once and for all. But I stopped him joining Paul in the garden and after a while Paul came back in. The taunting didn't stop.

'You don't want to take me on? You just ask your mother how hard I am – she knows!'

After that there was no stopping Mason. He threw Paul on to the floor, grabbed his bags and flung them outside.

Paul reacted strangely: 'Good. I wanted you to know how I feel. Good, good, that's what I wanted to see. They make you bring the anger out. That's what I wanted to do. That's good, good.'

He was almost pathetic, so we went upstairs and left him to sleep it off downstairs. That night he rummaged through all our labelled boxes, and eventually found the booze. He drank everything he could find, pushing the corks back into the bottles with his thumb and emptying the contents down his throat. Oblivion, always in search of oblivion.

We would frequently find him on the phone. 'It's Gazza. It's me – Gazza.' Pause. 'Paul Gascoigne. I'm with my family in Hemel Hempstead – I'm with my son! In Hemel. Regan in Hemel Hempstead. Right!' In his mind he was checking in with the FBI, one of his regular delusions. When we checked the phone we discovered he was making 999 calls and talking to a confused operator.

When he was in a taxi he'd frequently call Mason, who would

have to listen to some song on the driver's CD. 'Just put this on. Go on, put it on! Tell my son how much I love him.' Five minutes later he'd do it again, but this time with me. He asked the builders to play music, which made them feel uncomfortable. He'd sing his head off in the garden, wearing just a pair of boxers. 'I love you! You're my only one! Marry me! She's my life.'

One of the builders took the piss. 'He's really quite romantic, isn't he?' But it wasn't funny.

He was always, as ever, playing one child off against another. He'd sit in Bianca's room and slag off Mason. He'd slag me off to Mason, and Bianca off to me. A wedge would be driven between me and the children while we all tried to protect Paul. Mason offered many times to take him out of the house for a change of scene, for a drive, or to the golf driving range, not to talk, just to get him doing something. But when he came back, he'd start where he'd left off, going on and on at me about some comment I'd made, something I had or hadn't done, and another row would erupt.

Mason dealt with a lot during those frenetic, chaotic, worrying months. I know he tried to take control, thinking that he might be the one who could make him better. When he found that his patience had a limit he'd tell Paul to behave himself or get out. Then I'd receive a text: 'Mason's had a go at me, one down, two to go.' He would often accuse the children of taking my side. But they did try not to, they were simply reacting to what he was doing to all of us.

He'd go around the house doing odd sums. The letters in people's names, the numbers on the digital clock, he'd be adding up constantly, making everything come to the same total. Thirteen. We thought it was nonsense – his arithmetic was so fast and furious, it couldn't be accurate. Yet when my friend Adele's bright little girl checked the numbers, it turned out Paul was right every time. It was oddly brilliant – and utterly incomprehensible.

As quickly as he'd arrive, he'd want to leave again, usually to go to the pub. We wouldn't drive him so he had to order cabs. He'd call seven, then cancel them, or take one and refuse to pay, so after a couple of weeks they stopped accepting his bookings unless he paid upfront.

One day when he rang to tell us he was on his way back, Mason ran all the alcohol we had in the house over the road and left it on our neighbour's porch. We had wised up: we never drank when Paul was with us. It didn't help – he simply brought his own. That day, he downed a bottle and a half of gin, plus a bottle of wine in the taxi from London. When he arrived, he'd passed out and was lying on all the flowers he'd bought. Mason had to carry this dead weight into the house. He was foaming at the mouth, this terrible froth leaking from his lips. Every cab journey took hours because he'd get abusive and either jump or be thrown out. When the cabs refused to take him he found another form of transport.

Once, Paul called and asked me, as usual, to give the driver directions.

When the man came on the phone, he said apologetically, 'I'm not a cab driver.'

'You're joking.'

'No, he just jumped into my car. I love him, but I'm working – I can't drive him to Hertfordshire.'

'I'm so sorry. Please just take him to a taxi rank.' I was forever apologizing for him.

He'd come to my home, pass out, and when he came round he'd leave again in search of booze. Another time, when he turned up I was heading off to Dubai for half-term, so I left him with Mason. When he woke up and found out I was at the airport, he left. He rang all the time, and once when he'd been arrested. He said he'd got mugged and banged into a lamp-post chasing the thief. The police had scraped him up off the pavement and, for once, not taken kindly to his bad language and threats.

Often it was impossible to understand a word he said. His clothes were covered with food and vomit. We'd clean them. Sometimes he couldn't stand. Once he fell backwards, missing the corner of the stone island unit in the kitchen by millimetres. We'd try to feed him, give him coffee, but all he wanted was to drink. And when we wouldn't relent, he'd leave again. Once he jumped into our neighbour's car. Mason tried to get him out, but he just sat there hugging his medicine bag. Another time he tried to jump out of my car when I was driving along a dual-carriageway at 50 m.p.h.: I had refused to drive him to some horse field because I'd promised Regan we'd go for coffee. Mason grabbed him and pulled him back in. Paul was convinced he could train horses: 'You go up to a horse and say, "F— off," and you turn your back on it. Then you've got it eating out of your hand.' He was furious that I'd chosen Regan over him.

He often disappeared for hours and Mason would go from pub to pub looking for him. One day he and a friend finally tracked him down in a pub garden with a bottle of cider, a bottle of wine and three treble whiskies. Mason's friend worked in a pub. He knew they shouldn't serve someone who was so completely inebriated and went up to the barman to tell him so. The staff claimed he hadn't been drunk when he'd arrived, but the truth was that Paul was never sober. Mason collected him, but before Paul had got into the car he caught a woman looking at him and launched into a verbal assault. 'What the f— are you looking at? I'll f—ing kill you.'

Mason apologized to her, grabbed him and threw him into his friend's car.

Seven young lads in the corner piped up, 'Leave him alone! Stop them! They're kidnapping him!'

Mason went mad, and his friend had to hold him back, but there was a lot of bad language.

Paul's deranged, confusing behaviour went on for four months and took over our lives. Especially Mason's.

Paul often had thousands of pounds in his pockets, all in fifties, and just handed it out to people. It's impossible to know how much he lost, was taken off him or he gambled away. He was mugged about six times – well, that was what he said. On one occasion when he turned up, passed out as usual in the back of a cab, he woke up to find that £5,000 was missing. He was furious. He had no idea how much he'd paid the driver, although the driver had told me he *had* been paid, and insisted he hadn't paid him anything and the money had been stolen.

Mason begged and pleaded with him not to drink, but he always got hold of more money and he always got served. Then on 27 May Paul walked into Barclays Bank on Kensington High Street and withdrew £13,000 in cash from the account I had set up for Regan after the *News of the World* photos were taken at his birth. It was a joint signature account, but I imagine that because he was Paul Gascoigne they let him have it. Not only was it not his money, he was not sober enough to be given such a large amount. In the end the bank paid it back to Regan. Not Paul.

Paul went up to Newcastle for his birthday, and when Mason called to speak to him Paul's sister Anna's boyfriend wouldn't let him talk to Paul. For three months Mason had been trying to keep him alive, clean, fed, and now he wasn't talking to him. But by the end of the week he wanted to come back to Hertfordshire. Mason told him he couldn't until the next day because he himself wasn't going to be there and he didn't want me to have to deal with Paul without him. Mason recommended a local hotel and at six the following morning the phone rang: 'Tell the driver where you are – they're listening and I've got to get out of here.'

I gave the driver my postcode.

When Paul arrived he could stand, but he was rat-arsed and stank. I told him to go upstairs to bed. Then I heard a bang, a crash and a scream. I found him on the floor – he'd lost his balance and fallen backwards into a five-foot mirror that had been propped against the wall. The mirror was now in two halves, and he had large, bloody gash on his back. He asked me to give him a plaster because he didn't want to go to hospital. So, I ended up trying to pull the skin back over the gash with Sterostrips.

Regan stood by helplessly. 'Dad, you've got to go to hospital.'

'No, son, no.'

But the skin wouldn't meet over the cut. It was a mess – *he* was a mess, and there was nothing we could do to help him. The abuse that came out of his mouth was irrelevant now – it was pitiful. I thought he would soon die or kill someone, if he didn't sort himself out.

'Take me back to the hotel.'

'What hotel?'

'The hotel! The f—ing one I came from. The one with the f—ing lake!'

I had no idea which one he meant and neither did he. But he knew he had a bottle of wine there. 'I've left my jacket!' It was nothing to do with his jacket.

When anyone phoned me, he'd shout and scream at me. Normally I would have put the phone down, but not now. That morning he found another way. He just walked out of the house. He had no shirt on and was carrying his medicine bag. We had no idea where he'd gone. All I knew was that the hotel had a lake. We tried every one we could think of, until an older woman turned up at the door, shaking: Paul had got into her car and now her husband was driving him around, trying to find his hotel. He took him to one, and Paul went in, necked a bottle of wine, then came out and said it was wrong. The poor man was terrified.

Luckily Paul had left his phone charging at the house. I looked up his sister Anna's number and called her. She admitted he'd been a nightmare in Newcastle. 'We don't know what to do with him, he should never have been allowed off the section. We pretend we're out when he comes round – the kids are terrified of him.'

'Well, someone needs to get him help or he'll kill himself. He's got some old guy driving him around, he's gashed his back open and he's after a drink. Have I got the family's support if I try to get him sectioned again?'

'Yes! Yes, absolutely.'

She told me there was a crisis team looking after him, and gave me their number.

I called Paul's therapist, who agreed, and then I called the police.

The woman, who was still with me, spoke to her husband again. Now Paul was begging him to go to Sainsbury's to buy a bottle of gin. The man did as he was asked but said he was going to put it in the boot. I remained on the phone to the police. They told me that when Paul got back I couldn't let him in and I couldn't let him see me.

Paul and his 'driver' arrived before the police. He was slurring his words, and couldn't get out of the car. 'Where's Sheryl? Where's Sheryl?' Then he passed out. He'd drunk half the bottle of gin.

The police arrived. There were a lot of questions, most of which I didn't know the answer to – what had he drunk, what had he taken, when had he last eaten? They put a mask on him in the back of the car, and after about forty-five minutes he was moved into a waiting ambulance. I didn't go with him, but apparently when he came round he was shouting my name. I thought he was going to die so I went straight to the hospital.

I could hear him shouting before I got down the corridor. He was in and out of consciousness. 'Sheryl! Sheryl! Sheryl! Sheryl!' Then he'd fall asleep. He'd had twelve stitches in his back. Then he'd come round. 'You've got to get me out of here!' He was so rude to the staff, making horrible personal comments. I told him I'd leave if he went on being rude. Then he'd drift off again.

When he opened his eyes he demanded to see Mason: he must come to the hospital and bring him some fags.

Mason didn't need asking twice. As ever, he was prepared to drop everything and come to his dad's side. Paul was playing the fool, joking now with the nurse and putting on a pretty good show. Even when she was trying to get a drip into his arm, he summoned up a gag from his booze-addled mind.

All the time I was trying to get through to the crisis team to have him sectioned. A policeman said there was little they could do, unless Paul ran, and then they'd try to bring him back. The hospital let me use an office so I spoke again to Johnny Mack and left messages for Dr Collins. We were all in agreement: Paul needed to be sectioned under the Mental Health Act. The doctor needed a fax, so that was done, but it wasn't enough.

They moved Paul on to a ward. 'Why are the police here, Sheryl? I'm not stupid – they're going to section me.'

'No, no, you're fine.'

He told me he was going to jump out of the window. I tried to go to the loo. 'Don't tell them, Sheryl! Don't tell them what I've been doing – they'll section me! Don't let them section me.'

I told the police he was planning to jump out of the window. That was all they needed. They walked into the room and told him they were sectioning him because he was threatening to harm himself. At first he went mad. Then, when he realized he was stuck, he went into get-out-of-here mode. He wanted food, he wanted water – he was stuffing food down his throat just to soak up the booze. Occasionally he'd try to make the police laugh, but then he'd cry. 'Hold me – I'm scared. I'm scared, hold me.'

All I would say was that I was just trying to help him. I lay on the bed with him until about two in the morning, when the alcohol in his blood had dropped to a level at which he could be moved. Coming out of the toilet I heard the policeman on the phone at the nurses' station, talking to someone I presumed to be in the psychiatric unit. I hovered a while to try to over-hear.

'An hour ago you told me you had a bed. Now the level's down and you're telling me there are no beds?'

I was worried, but when he came back into Paul's room he told me Paul was finally being moved. What about the bed situation? I assumed they'd found one because it was Paul Gascoigne. Finally we could move him. Every doctor and nurse I'd spoken to had the names of his doctors, all of whom agreed that he had to be sectioned because he was a danger to himself and others.

We arrived at the psychiatric unit in another hospital at about five in the morning. I hadn't slept and the staff there told us we had to wait a bit longer for the doctor and social worker who were going to assess him.

Paul was staring at me with wild, frightened eyes. 'Don't tell, don't tell, don't tell them, Sheryl. Don't tell them – promise me.' It was pleading, desperate, but there was a snarl in his voice that made me check the door.

'I just want you to get well, Paul.'

'I will, I will, I promise.'

Finally they arrived. The woman sat down opposite us. 'Well, Paul, where have you been living?'

'I've been at Sheryl's.'

I stayed quiet.

'How long?'

'Well, I've been staying at hotels sometimes. I'm fine – absolutely fine.'

I still stayed quiet.

'And what is the difference this time?'

'Sheryl's been helping me, and the kids have been helping me. I want to do it for the kids.'

'Has there been any psychotic behaviour?'

'No.'

I couldn't stay quiet any longer. 'Yes, Doctor, there has been.'

I listed everything that had been happening: the Queen, the delusions, the horses, the Mafia, jumping in people's cars, jumping out of other people's cars, the paranoia, downing bottles, threatening people, thinking he was being followed, everything I could think of. I was determined I was going to get him that help. I was determined I wasn't going to let him down. The doctor and social worker listened to it all, then left the room.

Paul turned on me. 'You promised me you wouldn't tell them.'

'No, I didn't. I promised I'd help you and this is what you need. You need this help.'

'I'm not staying here. I'm not f—ing staying here.'

Five minutes later, the woman came back in. She sat right up close to him and placed her hands on his lap. I breathed a sigh of relief. It was over.

'Well, Paul, we've assessed the situation and we don't think you need to be sectioned. You're free to go.'

The air in my body rapidly left me and the blood ran to my feet. The smugness in her voice made me want to retch. 'What?'

'Well, it's obviously an alcohol problem, not a mental one.'

'But one is linked with the other. Surely you can see that!'

'No, it's an alcohol issue.'

'But everyone's said he should be sectioned!'

It was the final straw. I just broke at that moment. Exhausted and emotionally spent. I cried and cried and cried. It didn't faze them, but it shocked Paul. I had rarely cried in front of him. I was prepared to beg – Colin had been right: I had no pride. I would do anything to get him help. I begged them to change their minds. 'Please, please, just wait until eight o'clock. Paul's psychiatrist will be on duty and you can talk to him – the psychiatrist will be on duty here! He needs proper assessment, please. It's just another hour – I'm begging you. Please wait. Talk to his doctors – they're all saying he has to be sectioned! Please listen to me.'

'No, Mrs Gascoigne. It's an alcohol problem.'

'What if he drinks to cover the mental problems?'

Paul was over the moon. 'I can go, Sheryl! I'm going! I'm going! Get me a cab!'

Now I was just angry – angry to my core. I stood up. 'When he's dead, you come to my house and explain to my children the decision you've just made. You all make me sick!'

'Can you get me a taxi?'

'Where are you going, Paul?'

'To Sheryl's.'

'No way. I can't do this any more.'

She looked at Paul again, with those sympathetic, kindly eyes. 'Can you get the train back to Newcastle?'

At that point I walked out.

I was waiting for a taxi, still bawling my eyes out, when they came and stood next to me.

'Sheryl, you've got to understand.'

'Understand? As long as I live, I'll never understand the decision you've just made. Never. I don't have to listen to what you say.' I couldn't stop crying.

They asked the policeman to take me home. I cried all the way and he never said a word.

That phone call I overheard about the beds has always haunted me. There had been a bed, then there wasn't. Was it simply a matter of housekeeping?

When I got home I couldn't speak. I felt as if I'd let them all down. Mason, Bianca and Regan had pinned their hopes on me, and I'd failed them. Mason knocked on the door. 'Mum, what happened?'

'Just give me five minutes.'

Between the sobs I stared at the wall. I almost couldn't believe what had just happened. Of all the nightmares I'd been through with Paul that had been the worst. All that hard work, that interminable night, the hundreds of phone calls had been for nothing.

Mason came back. 'Please, Mum, I can't stand it.'

I went downstairs.

Mason stared at me. 'He's dead.'

'No, darling, he's not dead. I'm so, so sorry – I tried everything but they've let him go.'

Mason's head lowered. 'He may as well be dead, then.'

16. Blue in the Face

I was exhausted. I took Regan to school, then came home. Bianca, Mason and the neighbours were as shocked as I was when I told them what had happened during the night and early morning. All I could do was sit on the sofa and cry. Finally I got the strength up to text Anna.

> 2 jun 07.52 I tried my absolute best Anna he was sectioned then taken to psych hospital then they let him go after 10 mins!! I got home 06.20 I walked out in disgrace they wouldnt even try and speak to Johnny or Dr Collins, he is obviously elated. They have left him to get a train back to Newcastle.

Anna replied.:

> Ah god its unreal. Thanks 4 trying. I will let his crisis team know. Take care x

At about three that afternoon my friend Carol pulled up outside and I was talking to her when Mason called, 'Mum, phone!'

'I'm talking to Carol.'

'It's the police. They've got Dad.'

Reluctantly I took the receiver. The policewoman told me Paul had gone to the barber's on Kensington High Street and passed out in the chair so they had called an ambulance. 'Now he's asking for you.'

'I can't do this any more,' I said. 'I'm not getting any help from anywhere. I don't know what to do – just take him to hospital. I don't know what to say to you.'

'He says he wants to go to the Priory.'

'That place is a complete and utter waste of time but, fine, whatever.' I'd fought for him all night and had nothing left to give.

When I spoke to Johnny Mack he assured me that this time they would get him sectioned. I rang Anna again, told her what had happened, then got into the car and drove to London.

It had only been a few hours, but Paul looked even worse than he had when I'd last seen him. He started crying as soon as he saw me, then asked if he could talk to me alone. The staff agreed, as he appeared so upset and scared. The cocky smirk had left his face, and the swagger with which he'd left the previous hospital had gone: Paul was a wreck. He said he didn't want to stay at the Priory – it was too easy, too soft for him. He knew all the tricks and how to get away with anything. But we both knew he'd never been sectioned at the Priory before, never really participated in the programmes. He would say anything to get out of there but it had become obvious to anyone that Paul was suffering from a major mental breakdown that went far deeper than problems with drink.

The following day the Priory brought in an independent psychiatrist and social worker and Paul underwent the same questioning as he had had before, but now they had the record of his previous stays there as back-up. Of course, he tried to make out he was all right, but the psychiatrist mentioned a few of the things he had been doing. I'd known he had been in and out of the Priory over the last few months, and that it was rarely more than a couple of nights at a time, although apparently one stay had lasted nearly five weeks. Each time they'd got a little more information out of him. They were aware of his delusions, of how he believed his watches and lighters were bugged and that his phones contained listening devices. I told them that Paul would make Mason go into Tesco and buy ten lighters, all different colours, then keep one and throw the rest out of the window.

The psychiatrist and social worker left the room. When they returned they announced that Paul was to be detained under Section 3 of the Mental Health Act, which meant he could be held for up to six months and had to stay wherever they put him. I heaved a sigh of relief.

I got home at about ten o'clock that night, absolutely spent. Johnny Mack rang me to tell me to switch on the television. Anna was on *News at Ten*. I collapsed on the sofa and listened to her talking about Paul's section. I had kept her informed of what was going on over the previous forty-eight hours and had the family's full support, but she said nothing about who had been with him throughout the whole heart-breaking, hideous ordeal.

When I'd left Paul at the Priory he was begging to be placed somewhere else. Up to that point when he'd been at the Priory he had never been subjected to intensive treatment. Now, confronted with the accumulated evidence of his increasingly erratic behaviour, he realized he wasn't going to be able to get away with it there any more. I believe he thought that at another clinic he would have more chance of spinning his yarns and worming his way out of taking responsibility for his actions. He had no qualms about telling me who else was in there, who was drinking, who was taking drugs, who was having sex and who was going out at weekends, so when I visited I kept close to Paul and away from almost everyone else. I'm sure now that when I was out of the way Paul was their best bud, and probably doing everything he was accusing them of doing.

Johnny knew I had reservations concerning the Priory and he promised he'd try to find somewhere else for Paul. He had in mind a clinic in Kent. He suggested I try to make a case to Paul for Tony Adams's place, Sporting Chance. Johnny knew Paul was anti-Tony – I think this went back to their playing days: once Tony had found God and was sober he became an uncomfortable mirror that Paul did not want to look into.

Apparently Tony was no longer involved with the clinic. My main concern was that Paul went somewhere with a stricter regime than the Priory's, somewhere more like Cottonwood, where his superstar status wouldn't get in the way of his treatment. He needed people who could see beyond the Gazza glare to a man in critical need of serious help.

Johnny told me that the Professional Footballers' Association, who had set up a fund to assist with Paul's rehabilitation, were refusing to pay out any more. It wasn't a bottomless pit of resources and the money spent wasn't getting results. I was pleased: I thought it would be much better if he were sectioned under the NHS, which would undoubtedly be stricter. Johnny told him that if he was willing to contribute to his treatment then the PFA would perhaps release additional funds. I said to Johnny that if Paul wouldn't, I would – I had to get him the help I believed he'd been denied so far, even though I hadn't received any maintenance payments for the previous six months. The last lot I'd received, I'd had to threaten Paul's lawyer with court action as I hadn't had it for several months previous to that.

When Paul heard that he would have to stay at the Priory for a couple of days, while a place was found for him somewhere else, he went ballistic. He screamed that he'd go mad if he was left where he was and begged to be moved straight away. He was so distraught that he was put on suicide watch and he wanted me with him all the time. I would rush back from London to collect Regan from school, drop him back the next morning, drive to Roehampton and spend as much of the day as I could with Paul. It was tough going – and other patients weren't allowed visitors with them all the time. As ever, Paul was being given special treatment.

After he had been there for two or three days, he asked me to bring him some razors when I next came. I laughed and said, 'Nice try.' I knew he shaved himself compulsively, but there was no way I was going to give a man on suicide watch a razor.

When I arrived the next morning at about ten, I was told he had gone to have a bath and that he'd been in there a while. Because of the razor conversation, I got worried. I raced to the bathroom and made him open the door. Somehow he'd persuaded someone else to bring him a razor and he had shaved every inch of his body. It's not easy to kill yourself with a disposable razor, but it's not impossible.

Johnny rang to say that he hadn't been able to get Paul moved. The place he had been considering wasn't a psychiatric hospital and didn't even have a psychiatric unit. Paul was furious, and felt utterly betrayed, but how he expected Johnny to wave a magic wand and get a treatment centre to take a man sectioned under the Mental Heath Act, I don't know. Clearly, he was still in catastrophic denial.

We started making plans for his in-patient treatment at the Priory. Some sessions he refused to do, but I told him that this was his last chance to sort himself out and he had to take it seriously. The children and I would be there for him if he was sober and drug-free. At first he wanted me there all the time but I felt embarrassed eating lunch with him every day and sorry for the other patients. After ten days of this, I said to Johnny, 'Do you really think it's a good idea me being there all the time? When will he do his classes, his group sessions?' Johnny agreed, so after that I went at weekends.

Paul threw himself into the new regime. He went over the top on sessions, ramming in as many as possible, convinced that the more he went to the sooner he would be let out. He asked the doctors constantly how long 'exactly' he would be there. Eventually he wore them down and was told that he might be free to leave after six weeks. He kept on at them to drop it to five, then four and so on. It worked.

I was adamant about one thing: if the treatment was going to work, the whole family had to come together, forget their differences and work to get Paul well. In all of Paul's clinic stays he'd never attended the pivotal, essential and potentially life-changing meetings when an addict's family comes to the rehab centre and talks through their feelings, so that when the addict leaves he or she is in no doubt of the consequence of their actions on those who love them. The only time we'd come close to doing this was after Paul's first stay at Cottonwood, but then it had been just him and me, had lasted about half an hour and taken place on the day he was leaving. It is meant to happen about a week before the patient leaves so that they are supported as they face up to what they've put their family through. It's a very tough thing for an addict to do, and up to this point I had never insisted on it because Paul was always so agitated. But this time I was determined.

I wanted it to be everyone: the children, myself, Jimmy and all of the Gascoigne family. Johnny agreed – but he knew the idea would enrage Paul. Indeed, when he suggested it to him, Paul was very angry. Johnny didn't push it. He asked me later if I really thought it would make any difference. I believed that until we'd stripped bare the years of yarns and lies, we would never be at peace among ourselves. Paul had told each of us so many lies about the others, convincing ones, that it was impossible for any of us to have honest relationships with each other. This meant he could maintain control. We needed a fresh start based on a good foundation. It was the only way we could let Paul know that there was nowhere to hide. Paul felt ill at the thought of us all in one room and him having to confront his lies. Few of us knew, even at that point, how compulsive his lying had actually become.

Meanwhile, Paul had refused to put any of his own money into paying for his treatment and told me not to either. I contacted Gary Mabbutt of Soccer Services, who managed the Tottenham Fund. I had agreed to pay £4,000 towards it. Gary informed me that Paul's treatment so far had been paid for with £40,000 from Tottenham Hotspur, £15,000 from the PFA, £10,000 from the Football Association and £12,000 from anonymous donors. He was also trying to get contributions from Everton and Rangers. So far the treatment had come to £50,000 in total and they were now looking at bills of about £1,000 a day. He provided me with bank account details of the Fund, but with everything I had been through, I wanted to make sure of where my money was going. I told Gary I would be happier to pay £4,000 directly to the Priory.

Eventually the family meeting was set up, but only with me and our children: no one from Newcastle was asked to come, though I felt the Priory should have forced the issue. The meeting only took place because I had stated that Paul could not come home without it. He had no alternative but to agree.

Johnny contacted us the night before and talked us through what would happen. He told us all to write down one bad experience and three good things about Paul, which we could read out to him. Bianca was furious: once again we were running about after Paul, putting ourselves through turmoil and heartbreak. When would we be able to move on? I think her anger hid nerves: she was frightened of what we were going to do. I didn't force them to come, but I thought they would regret it if they didn't take the chance.

Mason wasn't keen to write anything down. He wanted to speak off the cuff, which was fine. Later, though, I found a piece of paper on which he'd written his thoughts, so I knew that although he said quite a lot in the meeting he didn't get to say it all. How could you? There was so much.

On 23 June at 2.30 p.m. we arrived at the Priory. As soon as we were outside the meeting room Bianca started to cry. Part of me wanted to protect her and cancel the whole thing, but I knew if the children were ever to have any relationship with Paul, which was what they continued to say they wanted, this meeting and, hopefully, subsequent ones were vital. She managed to compose herself.

When we walked into the room, the chairs had been arranged

in an oval. We sat on one side opposite Paul, who was dressed in shorts, a T-shirt and flip-flops and was flanked by the doctors with their backs to the window. Johnny and Dr Collins gave us an update on how Paul was doing, then encouraged us to speak. Mason began. He asked the questions that had burnt inside him for so long. Why didn't Paul ever just call and suggest a game of golf? Or to say hi. 'I love you,' Mason said, 'and it's fun sometimes when you're around, but why does it always have to be about Mum?'

Paul started to get narky, and Johnny stepped in to say that Paul's childhood had been very rough.

I said, 'But he's never really explained that to us.'

Johnny told us more about Paul's childhood, which helped both the children and me to understand his rejection of love and why he tested us all the time. Paul admitted that he found it easier to have us all hate him and the reason for that lay deep in his childhood, which had been tough. Mason said that what had taken place in his own childhood had made him realize how *not* to behave with his own future family.

Paul sat with his head bowed, occasionally blurting out that he wanted to leave the meeting, and Johnny would praise him for staying.

Mason had a final plea: 'I hope and pray that you keep my dad in for the full section time. Otherwise he'll just relapse and this meeting will mean nothing.' Then Bianca, who'd been hiding beneath a peaked cap, started to cry again. She told Paul how all his rejection of her had made her feel and how horrible it had been for her that he had had no room in his heart for anyone except me.

At one point Paul shouted, 'Well, I am a love addict, as well you know!'

Dr Collins cut him off: 'Paul, let's not hide behind titles.'

I nearly jumped up and yelled, 'Hallelujah!'

Regan spoke clearly and made some valid points that belied

his age, and we all agreed that we were happy to continue to help and support Paul so that he could hopefully be a happier and more fulfilled father.

After the meeting, Dr Collins said it was obvious how much love there was for Paul and that he was a very lucky guy.

One of the best things to come out of Paul's stay at the Priory was a therapist called Colin Blowers, who helped Paul tremendously with his obsessive-compulsive disorder. Colin would put his shoes out of order, leave appliances on, nudge picture frames out of line and hang towels hang messily, then make Paul leave them. No longer could he have his toothbrush, paste and comb in the preferred order. It was very difficult for Paul. But he did it. Colin said that Paul's OCD explained his liking for hotels rather than homes. Hotels were minimal, there was no clutter; everything in a bedroom had its place.

Colin never pussy-footed around Paul. When he made Paul do exercises and Paul complained, Colin would say, 'Tough.' He made the most sense of anyone. Paul would cry for ages on the phone to me after a session with him, but he knew Colin was helping him to understand his behaviour. It was Colin who told me that when Paul started with his accusations and quick-fire questions, I had to reply, 'Paul, I am not allowed to discuss that,' and repeat it a million times if I had to. At first I was nervous. Paul would go mad and get nasty. Colin said Paul had to learn that it didn't matter if I'd slept with two thousand other men: nothing justified his behaviour. I was most indignant at that – it was like admitting I had! And it was so far from the reality. But Colin insisted it would work and that if Paul did go mad I was to follow up with 'What would Colin say?' That sentence was like a barrier: I could finally deflect his incessant badgering. For the first time since we'd met, I didn't have to listen to Paul's rubbish and I didn't have to keep reassuring him till I was blue in the face that I hadn't slept with this person or that. All I had to say was, 'Paul, I'm not allowed to discuss that.' Fabulous. As predicted, Paul hated it, but for me the sense of support and relief was immeasurable.

Colin also helped Paul hugely with his fear of dying by making him say the words 'death' and 'dying' over and over again. 'It happens to us all in the end.' Paul would freak out but Colin was unapologetic. We would all die in the end. Him, me, Paul, everyone. Paul had often said to me, 'When I die, I'm not going alone! You're coming too.' It had begun to scare me, but I tried not to let myself think about it.

Generally Paul seemed able to do as he pleased. Although caffeine was not allowed, he knew exactly where the coffee was kept and frequently made himself a cup. In the shop they sold every kind of sweet. His favourite were the charity bags, sold for a pound each and kept in a box on the reception desk – I once heard another client saying, 'We'd better get there before Gazza clears it out.' I only understood what that meant when I found his drawers stuffed with bags of sweets. He wasn't only hoarding them, he was eating them too.

Our weekend visits continued and sometimes he was allowed out for a few hours with me or the kids. Our first trip as a family was to the cinema. We went to Yo! Sushi first – it was Paul's first time and he made up a saucer of wasabi and soy sauce, then drank it.

'Dad, are you getting a buzz from that?' asked Bianca.

'Yeah! It's great!'

Oh, my God, I thought, is nothing safe? An addict looks for anything. We came out of the cinema and got on the escalator to leave the complex. Paul asked me for a kiss, and as I didn't want to cause a scene, I obliged, then pulled away almost immediately. We never saw the camera, but the picture was in the press the next day. I hadn't told anyone where we were going, but Paul blamed the security men at the Priory's gates. I've no idea whether he had any basis for doing so or whether it was another of Paul's tall stories. A couple of days later a *Sun* reporter knocked on our door and asked if I would allow them to print a picture of me giving Paul a goodbye hug that they had taken in the grounds of the Priory. 'Why are you bothering to ask me now? You didn't ask me about the one on the escalator.' She said they hadn't taken that one, and that it looked as if it had been taken on a phone camera. The one they wanted to print was of Paul resting his head on my shoulder, but I refused. When I told Paul he was angry with me and accused me of knocking his confidence – why wouldn't I want a picture of us hugging unless it was because I was shagging a dozen other men? He brought this up again and again – I have many abusive texts referring to it.

I continued to make it clear to Paul that, while I was happy to be his friend and confidante, I was not going to have a sexual relationship with him. I'd had too many phone calls from him in tears, after yet another prostitute, to consider it.

Paul was supposed to be coming home for a trial weekend, but I felt unsure about it. A few days earlier Paul had launched into a verbal attack, accusing me of all the things he'd always accused me of; he worked himself into such a state that he stormed off, leaving me feeling like I'd been catapulted back ten years. A place I did not want to return to.

The weekend had been controversial from the beginning. It was the same weekend that Bianca's win on *Gladiators* was to be televised, 4–6 July. We had invited Julie, our old nanny and good family friend, my dad, Adele, Florence and Nick, Bianca's boyfriend, to watch it at our house that Sunday on Sky One. Paul had told me to cancel our plans or he wouldn't come home. Apart from Nick, Paul had known all these people for years, and no one was staying over. One of the children's main stipulations in regard to Paul coming back was that they were still allowed to have their friends over and that we were allowed to go on enjoying family life. I was not going to cancel Bianca's friends so he sent a series of abusive texts. All in all he sent 122, starting on the afternoon of 4 July, before he apologized on the ninth, and sent another thirty-one, attempting to undo the damage. Paul was always sending me angry and demanding messages, then asking me to top up his phone because he was constantly running out of credit.

Finally, I sent a text telling him I would not be coming to pick him up because I hadn't had confirmation from the Priory that he was allowed out. He got it into his head that I was relieved not to have him, and I can't say I wasn't.

We planned another trial weekend, to coincide with Regan's school Founder's Day, the end-of-term prize-giving. I'd told Paul about it weeks previously, but when I reminded him, he claimed not to know, and flew into accusations about how I was inviting friends (which I hadn't) when he didn't want me to, and how he wasn't happy about having to sleep on the sofa and, anyway, he'd booked in to have a facial treatment on that day. I wasn't prepared to go through the nonsense again.

> 09.01 Me: Just seen yr first text ... what can i say to that its far too childish to comment. Why dont you just admit you are not interested AT ALL to be a dad or to be part of this family then we can all get on with our lives. Why keep playing games

> Paul: I can be, but not this weekend

> 09.15 Me: Ok just let us know when you can fit them in! Good job julie adele and foo etc can make it this weekend, Im going to leave it now Paul, as always you have managed to hurt everyone

They came thick and fast all day long. In one text he asked me why I wanted him there on the Saturday when I had already invited everyone.

> Me: As usual you have totally missed the point ... I think the real question is why wouldnt YOU want to be there? Plus if you didnt want to cause an argument why carry on with nasty texts all weekend?

249

Finally, knowing he needed me to get himself out of the Priory, he reined in the abuse, and apologized. When he needed to stop, he could.

His main concern about coming home was where he would sleep. My main concern was his medication. He always over-prescribed for himself and never took his tablets at the right times, so I wanted to know exactly what he was supposed to take, how much and when. He was on so many pills, it was difficult to keep track. I left message after message for Dr Collins and managed to stall Paul until Saturday morning because I hadn't heard anything.

Early on Saturday morning, Regan's Founder's Day, Paul arrived in a taxi and had been there for forty-five minutes when the Priory called to tell me Paul was coming home that day for the weekend, without having double-checked with me that it was all right for him to do so, or that he had enough medication to last him until Sunday.

'Tell him yourself,' I said furiously. 'He's been here for almost an hour and says he's staying until Monday.' So he didn't have enough medication.

'Oh, OK. He'll be fine.'

It was at this point that I lost faith in the Priory.

Despite the fuss, Founder's Day went off without any prob-lems. Paul was a bit quiet and reserved, but it was nice for Regan to have his father there. We went out for an early dinner, the five of us, to a fish restaurant. Paul had a bad turn when a couple at the next table ordered a bottle of wine – he got breathless and agitated, and wanted to leave. Bianca and Mason went with him to have a cigarette outside. When they came back, Paul had calmed himself down. A lot was at stake: the following week he was hoping to leave the Priory for good.

While he had been at the Priory, Paul had received job offers, one of which was from a documentary team at Endemol, a television production company. He was considering it and had spoken to me about it.

Since it had become public knowledge that I was visiting Paul I, too, had been approached by television companies. One stood out and my agent wanted to arrange a meeting. It was called Spun Gold and seemed very trustworthy. I met the owner, who explained he wanted to cover the story of what it was like trying to help someone in Paul's situation. He told me that many female journalists supported me – I'd felt that the papers were against me, and even if some journalists were on my side, they would soon turn, as they always did. He said Paul's story has been done so many times before, and he wanted to show things from the perspective of the family. Although he seemed very nice, I turned his offer down because I didn't think it would aid Paul's recovery. He asked if I would approach Paul about doing a documentary, so I said I would discuss it since I knew Paul was interested in the Endemol offer.

Paul was elated at the thought of Spun Gold's documentary. He had plans about how they could follow him to Newcastle and, with Colin's help, face his ordered and untouched penthouse apartment with everything neatly in its place. The OCD had stopped him living in it because everything would get messed up. He'd rented it for three years, but told me he'd lived in it for just three weeks. He agreed that I should go ahead with Spun Gold and sort everything out. The maximum they offered was £50,000. Paul was happy with that and asked my agent, Jan, to act for him too.

She looked into the Endemol offer and discovered it would involve a rehab programme with hardly any pay but lots of treatments thrown in. I went to meetings with Spun Gold to Channel 4, then went back to the Priory to report to Paul what they had said. He remained very excited about it and wanted to organize a *News of the World* story to coincide with the documentary so that he could double his money and, hopefully, get a free holiday out of it as well from the newspaper or the production company.

But then one night in the Priory, a week before he was due to leave, he rang me crying hysterically begging me to tell the staff he'd tried to nick some tablets. He said he had also rung Lindsay to try to convince her to get some on the black-market and then called Jimmy to ask him to bring them down and pass them to him through the window – Paul had been moved to a downstairs room where the windows opened wide enough to push a packet of tablets through.

It was news to me that they'd started talking again. As far as I was aware, Paul had stopped all communication with Jimmy for at least six months. Over the years we all got blamed for the state he was in, whether it was because I had called him up out of the blue after he'd been clean and serene for months and demanded huge amounts of money, or that every time he was back on his feet I'd find a way to derail his rehabilitation programmes. He's said as much in interviews, but no one who was ever close to him was exempt from these accusations. It was always other people getting him the drink and drugs who got the blame. Jimmy's and Paul's friendship was just as destructive as my relationship with Paul. Jimmy had been shot at with an air rifle, tricked into eating human faeces, hit many times and insulted over and over again by Paul.

I tried to calm Paul down and said how pleased I was that he'd told me: it was a big step forwards. I called the staff, who seemed quite offended: it was impossible for Paul to do such a thing, they said – and maybe it was. Truth is a mirage with Paul. It all confirmed to me that Paul was not ready to be released. He knew it too. On 11 July he sent a text, saying he felt he was going crazy and like he couldn't get out of the rut he was in.

We had a final meeting at the Priory, at which I was told that Paul would be released to come to my house in a couple of days' time. He would still be under section so if he ran away the police would pick him up and take him back to the Priory. The week after that he would have to go back to the Priory for assessment, and if everything was all right, they'd take him off the section. I said that if they took him off the section, he'd be gone and Mason would be proved right that it had all been a waste of time. Paul got narky and said we wanted him condemned for ever.

'No, Paul, just long enough to get better.' And he hadn't been there long enough. If they had him under section, why were they letting him out? He'd done just over a month there, and it had made no difference. But I was overruled. On 17 July his in-patient treatment came to an end. I needed accounts for all of his treatments so that I could find out what the trust was and was not paying for.

17 July

Me: Task of the day! Go to account office ask you for yr accounts up to date and copies of previous accounts X.

Paul: you have been very supportive in the last couple of months and I LOVE YOU XXX

Me: im supportive because i live in hope we can all live happy ever after x

Paul: Ah thats nice darling xx

And so he came home, to our house, so that we could all live happily ever after.

17. Iron Maiden

On 18 July 2008, after six weeks and three days in rehab, Paul came home to live with me and the kids. I was still in the middle of a major refurbishment and the builders, who'd seen him serenading me in his shorts and turning up unconscious in the back of taxis, were still there. His therapists were concerned the work would make it difficult for him – but, builders or no builders, Paul didn't want to go anywhere else. He knew it was the only way that the section would be lifted and he would be out of the Priory for ever.

David Clews, of Spun Gold, came over and arranged with Paul to leave a camera for him to make a post-rehab video diary: they wanted Paul to record his thoughts and antics in his first days at home. After that they would come in to film. Paul loved it – if nothing else, he's a showman. Regan has the same characteristic, and he certainly didn't get it from me.

Having the camera in the house was fun – it was a good ice-breaker and helpful at disguising how odd it was to have Dad back after five broken years. Paul seemed optimistic, and the kids were positive too, Mason in particular: all he had wanted for years was to have his father back, safe and alive. Paul said to the camera, 'It's great to be back home with Sheryl and the kids. Let's hope everything works out. We'll just try and live a normal life.'

He asked if he could buy Regan a tent, which Regan had said he'd always wanted, and since we weren't going on holiday because of the refurbishment, I agreed that it could be a very early – or maybe a forgotten – Christmas present. So we went to the local camping shop and bought one. Not just any tent: as ever with Paul, it was the best possible tent, big enough for two double beds, and there was plenty of room to stand up. Regan was very excited about getting it home and building it in the garden.

While I was queuing to pay, Paul stole a snack bar from a shelf. A joke, or was he looking for another form of buzz? He was seen and didn't like being snitched on. He got nasty, then stormed out of the shop and sat in a huff in the car. We were all on edge. Great! Was this the family life I'd been pinning all my hopes on? I wondered for the millionth time whether it could ever work.

Paul wouldn't go out for lunch, so we went home. Regan and I made the tent with the help of Bianca's boyfriend while Mason soothed Paul. It was so tense that I decided to go out and get some food for a barbecue – it might cheer everyone up. Paul took it as a snub that I was going to the supermarket without him and tried to stop me going. I was in the car on the drive when he yanked the door open and put his foot in the way so I couldn't drive. Then he started shouting in my face. It had been a long time since he'd done that and he accused me of sleeping with every man I came into contact with.

But the children were sure that having Paul at home was the only way to save him. I think they believed their love alone would stop him killing himself with drink. At least, Bianca and Mason thought so. For Regan it was different. This wasn't the prodigal father returning home after a long truancy: suddenly there was a man in the house he was supposed to call Dad, but he knew him less well than the postman. And the memories he did have of Paul were not pleasant.

Paul was sleeping in Mason's room so that he could have the en-suite, but he wasn't happy about it. Mason had wanted to do anything to accommodate his dad and had moved into Regan's room and Regan had moved into mine. Paul was not happy, but I had told him straight that he wasn't coming anywhere near me.

On Wednesday, 23 July, Paul and I had a meeting with Colin

Blowers back at the Priory, during which we discussed Paul's relationship with the children. It was another fraught and difficult session. Paul couldn't get it. He thought the children should have more respect, regardless of what he had put them through. I don't think Paul will ever understand that respect is something a father has to earn.

On Friday Paul had an appointment booked with our dentist, Jeremy Hill, and got stroppy when he realized a bill was still outstanding for his dental work in 2003. He cancelled the appointment – 'F— that.' His buoyant mood was slipping. He was not facing up to his responsibilities or taking responsibility for his actions. Instead he was gearing himself up for a fight. He was increasingly angry that I wasn't sleeping with him.

On Sunday I suggested we had a barbecue because Regan wanted to catch up with his friend Florence. She came over with her mother, Adele. Paul was a bit off. Adele had already kind of sussed that she shouldn't speak to him unless he spoke to her. Now and then he sat and chatted with her over a cigarette, but as the day progressed he seemed to be sinking into a darker, quieter mood. I had popped to the shops and bought the food, including tuna and salmon steaks for Paul – he was still so paranoid about his weight that he was barely eating, except for sweets. But Paul made a great big roll full of fish with mayo then tomato ketchup then mustard, you name it the sauce went on it. This used to happen at the Priory. Nobody could have avoided seeing all the sauces and gunk spreading round his mouth and falling out all over the place as he took a huge mouthful of his sandwich. Eating with his mouth closed was never an option!

I was getting some salads ready when Paul started taking them outside. I told him it was a bit too hot and to wait until Mason had got the barbecue under way. He stormed off, accusing me of talking to him 'like a little kid'. I tried to apologize and told him not to be so silly, but he threw a paddy and went to his room, saying he was going for a sleep. Ten minutes later Mason came to say his dad had taken pills. I did a quick recce of the medications cupboard and decided that everything was in order. I told Mason not to worry: Paul was attention-seeking. Three-quarters of an hour after that, Regan and Florence came to the patio. 'Dad's gone,' Regan said.

'Oh, he's probably in my room being funny. Go and look.'

'No, he isn't,' they said. 'We've looked all over the place.' In fact they'd known for a while he wasn't in his room or mine because apparently they'd gone to spy on him.

Mason and Bianca went into panic mode. Nick, Bianca's boyfriend, jumped into my car and drove them round all the local pubs looking for him. I sat down with Adele and said, 'Can you believe it? He isn't centre of attention for five minutes so he has to cause a scene.' Knowing Paul, he could have been hiding somewhere watching me, testing my reaction, so we sat there pretending neither of us was bothered – if he wanted to throw a tantrum he had to learn it would get him nowhere. Except it was.

Regan and Florence took off on their bikes. 'We'll go over the golf course looking for him,' they said. It was a bit of drama to enliven the peaceful Sunday barbecue, and maybe an adventure for them.

I checked upstairs and quickly discovered he'd taken no money or phone, not even his beloved medicine bag, which usually had to be surgically removed from him. 'He's not gone far,' I said, hoping I was right.

Mason and Bianca had no luck with the pubs, so then they started on the hotels. Finally Florence pedalled up to me. 'We found him – he was lying on the golf course with no top on! He was going to give us fifty pounds each for finding him!' Regan was next to appear, with Paul behind him. I couldn't even bring myself to make eye-contact with him, let alone acknowledge the fact that the wanderer had returned. I rang Mason, Bianca and Nick and told them to come back.

The next day he had his section review meeting with Dr

257

Collins. I didn't go. I was still furious about the previous day's events, so Mason and Bianca went instead. They explained to Dr Collins what had happened, and Mason said again, 'If you take him off section he'll be gone and everything will have been for nothing.' All Dr Collins said was that if he slipped back he could always come to the Priory for a couple of days and took him off the section.

On the way home the kids asked Paul if he was going to leave again. Paul laughed, said no, and laughed again. That night he became quite cocky: Gazza had won again. But Paul had lost, and he didn't even know it. Now he just needed an excuse to leave, and a drink was practically in his hand.

The next morning we were in the kitchen and Paul was on the sofa watching TV. Megan, Regan's friend from across the road, came to the window with her three-year-old niece, Ellie. It was Ellie's birthday: she was dressed up like a princess and wanted to show us. Paul was on the phone to Anna, giving her our address so she could invite us to her wedding. The rest of the Gascoigne family wouldn't be there: I discovered that all the time Anna and I had been in contact over Paul and the sectioning, his family hadn't been speaking to her. Paul felt sorry for her because they weren't going to her wedding.

I believed the coast was clear so Megan and Ellie came into the kitchen. I was singing 'Happy Birthday' and telling Ellie how gorgeous she looked when Paul suddenly shouted, 'Oi, you ignorant f—ing woman, I'm talking to you.' Megan picked up Ellie and ran.

Something in me snapped. For eighteen years I had been the proverbial camel being loaded with straw. Each taunt, insult, smack, hit and kick, each bite, yank, spit, swear word, put-down and humiliation had been another straw piled on my back. I'd taken them all, carried them all, lumbered under the weight of them all, but 'Oi, you ignorant f—ing woman, I'm talking to you,' was the last straw. It broke the camel's back and I reared up in its place.

'How dare you? You've just embarrassed those children. How dare you talk to me like that?'

'Who are you, then? A f—ing princess?' he screamed.

'That's it. You're out! I'm not having you speak to me like that again!' Remembering that I'd put up with it for so many years just made my resolve stronger. It was iron-clad.

Now Mason and Bianca ran in from the garden, ready to break up the fight. But there was nothing to break up. It was over. I apologized to them and told them I couldn't put up with it any more.

Everything went into fast forward: people ran round the house, chasing and cajoling Paul, trying to undo what had been done. I remained strangely still in the middle of it all. Paul threw together his meagre belongings, stuffed his medicine bag with medication and papers, then stood defiant. He had got what he wanted: he was leaving, and it was my fault because I had told him to go. His attempt at normal, family life had lasted twelve days.

Mason begged to go with him.

'No, mate,' said Paul. 'I'll be mortal drunk in an hour.'

He called a taxi and went to the Royal Kensington Gardens Hotel. True to his word, he rang a few hours later, pissed. Mason spoke to him and offered to stay with him and keep him clean.

But Paul refused his help. 'I'm pissing off out of this country.' We'd heard the threat before. He was always leaving for America or Australia.

The next day I rang my agent to tell her what had happened. There would be no documentary. The production company thought he'd be back, but I wouldn't have him. He was drunk now and, to be honest, it was bad enough when he was sober.

Paul started texting me and ringing at all hours of the night and day, each more incoherent than the last. He was claiming he'd left because he couldn't sleep in my bed, and that seemed to be the extent of it. He wouldn't tell us where he was or who he was with. Mason barely slept, fearful, as he had been for the previous five years, that he would miss Paul's drunken call in the early hours and with it his chance to save him. But when Paul did phone, he was abusive and threatening. Mason was gutted.

The next thing we knew Paul was on tour with Iron Maiden – we only found out because it was in the press. When he called he said he was with the biggest band in the world – or as he called it the 'biggest bandstand in the world', he was clearly drunk – and they'd fly us all out free of charge on their private jet. The children were desperate to get him back, terrified that we would next see him in a box. I tried to convince him to come home, but my heart wasn't in it. 'Where are you?' I kept asking.

'I'm not f—ing telling you!' he would say or, more ominously, 'I'm not allowed to talk or discuss that.'

'Just come home, Paul.'

On top of all that, Spun Gold were going bananas. I told him they wanted to film us while he was away, but I couldn't see the point. It was his documentary, not ours, and I had enough problems in the house with upset children and building work to want to deal with being filmed too. I was more than happy to tell them it was off and that they should cancel the whole thing. My agent Jan spoke to him and he told her he wanted to do it but only if I was involved. But his drunken rants were becoming increasingly unpleasant and I thought the project was doomed. The director and head of production spoke to Paul and he said they should go on filming us, then come out to film him. But when they asked for a date, place and time, he would either hang up or demand either £100,000 or a convertible Bentley for his dad. They saw for themselves how impossible it was to live with that sort of erratic, unpredictable, selfish behaviour. Then he was texting me: I'd cancelled the documentary because I didn't care about him any more – I knew how much he'd wanted to do it. It was Paul's usual manipulative nonsense. The only good thing was that this time I knew it.

Then one night Paul rang from the back of a taxi. As usual, he wouldn't tell me where he was, just that the band had moved on. The children and I were trying to work out where he was by following the band's movements through their fan site. He was so drunk he started swearing at the taxi driver. I tried to calm him down – I had visions of him being attacked and left in a ditch in a foreign country. Then I heard the taxi driver say, 'Where do you want to go?'

'I don't give a f—. Get me women – yeah, prostitutes!'

I stayed on the phone listening until he hung up. I tried calling him back but he didn't answer. I rang Jimmy, who had also heard from him and thought he was close to seriously harming himself. Paul had been calling him, shouting abuse, then hanging up.

About an hour later, crying hysterically, Paul rang again, begging me to tell him where he was. But I couldn't because he'd refused to tell me while he was sober enough to remember. He got into another taxi and started shouting at the driver – I tried to work out from the poor man's accent where they might be. Then Paul told me he was in trouble, he had no money to pay the taxi. When he got to his hotel he was repeating, 'I'm in trouble,' over and over again. Then he freaked out because his watch and bracelet were missing. I told him to go straight to his room, but he put some guy on the phone, telling him to tell me, his wife, that he was fine, just fine. I asked the man where he was, but Paul was in the background, saying, 'Ssh, don't say where we are.' So drunk and yet so lucid – it defies understanding.

It turned out that the watch and bracelet were in his room, and once I knew he was back there, I texted Jimmy to let him know, and that, contrary to what he wanted us to believe, he was not alone. Yes, Iron Maiden had moved on, but they'd left a minder with him. I'd heard the man in the background. At two forty-five I climbed into bed and tried to sleep. He kept calling, kept asking us to go out and meet him, then wouldn't tell me where he was.

The children were running out of patience. Even Mason, who'd been a rock throughout, finally snapped and told him to f— off, which set off another barrage of abuse. We'd spent so much time trying to get him better, but Mason had been right: the meetings, the treatments, the therapy had been for nothing.

And I wouldn't change a thing. Because what came out of the confusion was a new idea for a documentary that evolved before David Clew's eyes. It was about a family in despair trying to live life around an alcoholic. It happened to be about my family, but it was about many others too. I think David began to feel part of the solution and could see for himself that we needed help. He suggested I spoke to an interventionist. I didn't know what that was until he explained that this was someone who helped a family to live with an addict.

I had spoken to Dr Collins on the phone a couple of times in the last week or so and he had said I only had one method left to explore: tough love. 'If you are not there for him, who is? He needs to hit rock bottom.' It was terrifying to think that he hadn't yet.

I had also been speaking to Jimmy and Paul's mum, relaying what Dr Collins had been saying to me since Paul had gone AWOL. Jimmy and I spoke on 9 August about how, as two people who believed they genuinely loved Paul, we were going to help him. We talked about sticking together. Jimmy agreed that Paul had slagged each of us off to the other so that we could never be a force for change in his life. Now Paul's Newcastle family, including Jimmy, and I agreed not to speak to him until he came back to England for help. Then Jimmy told Paul that that was what we were planning to do, which made him too scared to come home. I can't blame Jimmy. Like me, he'd confused love with something else.

During those conversations I gleaned a great deal about

Paul's enigmatic, closed family. I knew that when Paul descended drunk on Newcastle the whole family was disrupted. I discovered that his father stayed in a B-and-B because he couldn't deal with Paul, and let him use his house until he moved on and it was safe to return home. Lindsay protected her son, Cameron, by shutting the curtains of their house. I asked Carol why no one had come to visit Paul while he was at the Priory and she said John wasn't well and she didn't 'go out'. But John had just returned from three weeks' driving through Spain, so I don't think he was that ill. And what about Carl, Lindsay, Anna? Paul explained that it was too far for them to come. My personal feeling was that he had become too much of a liability for anyone else to deal with.

One day Paul's mum rang me to give me the telephone number of Ian Day, Iron Maiden's tour manager. He had got her number from the back of Paul's passport. She was in tears. 'Sheryl, you have to call them, I don't know where they said he was, but ring them. Go and get him, Sheryl – he won't listen to us. We all agree you're the only one who can help him.' Even Dr Collins at the Priory agreed that they could do no more for him if he ever returned than stabilize his medication and dry him out.

I rang Ian. He told me Paul was so devious that they'd had no option but to leave him behind with a minder – I'd been right about that, then. Paul couldn't go to Moscow with them since he didn't have a visa. He said they hadn't meant any harm by taking him along. They'd thought they were helping, but hadn't known how bad he was. They had left him in a hotel in Portugal where they knew the manager, with instructions to watch out for him. When I called the hotel, the manager wouldn't tell me anything since he couldn't be sure it was me talking to him.

Next thing I knew Jimmy was in Portugal, with his girlfriend, so obviously our pact to stick together had been nonsense. Paul repaid Jimmy for coming to his aid by getting drunk and going for him. The people he hates most are those who are foolish enough to love him. Jimmy had to call Paul's dad to buy a flight home as he had no money.

When I spoke to Carol again, she told me she felt sorry for Carl and his wife: they too were on holiday in Portugal a couple of hundred yards down the beach from Paul. Unable to do anything for his brother, Carl had told Paul his mobile didn't work in Europe and switched it off.

I kept calling the hotel, and finally spoke to a receptionist, who told me Paul had checked out and was somewhere in Vale do Lobo. Footage appeared on the Internet of Paul ranting that he knew Gadaffi – 'Ten Downing Street called us up last night, not only that, the White House.' He looked and sounded pitiful.

The film maker asked Mason what he thought was wrong with his dad.

'He doesn't know who he is. If you turned to him and said, "Who are you?" the best he could come up with is "Gazza". That's all he knows of himself. He doesn't know himself as a caring person, a good father, a role model, he only knows himself as this football player. He's lost out there. He doesn't know what to do – he's a lost person.' And we were the only ones who believed we could find him again, find Paul.

Mason had always seen beyond 'Gazza' because Paul had been his dad since he was a year old. He said that if all he had known was the drunk he wouldn't have tried to help him. 'What he used to be like is the reason I've chased him all these years.' We were stuck, waiting to see what Paul would do next.

David Clews watched us, rendered inert, desperate for the phone to ring, but dreading it when it did. He then suggested that I go and talk to the psychologist, Tracy Towner. She wasn't the soft, sympathetic listening ear I was expecting, in fact, she was one serious Iron Lady, and if she was sent from above, as I believe she was, I know by whom. My sister, Vicki.

18. Walk Away

When I was on the way home from that first pivotal meeting with Tracy, David Clews told me he'd sent me to see her on the pretext that it would help Paul, but really he had wanted to help me and the children. I knew then that an interventionist was very different from anyone I'd seen in the world of therapy. It was a far cry from the 'poor Paul' attitude which I'd seen so much of throughout his stays in rehab. Tracy wanted to help us survive the havoc created by having an addict in the family. She told me I had to deliver a solid ultimatum: get help or we're gone. Anything else was complicit. It seemed harsh and a difficult thing to ask the children to do, but I had finally realized that everything else was harmful to them. Knowing that made it easier to keep my resolve, though I was worried about how they would react when I told them I wasn't going to help their dad any more. I will always be indebted to David and Tracy for their help in saving my family.

As predicted, Mason and Bianca were very concerned that Paul would be left to rot without my help. At first they were angry and shocked and couldn't believe what they were hearing. And why would they, after all the years I'd been letting him back in to hurt us again? Why stop now? I hadn't known that what I was doing was hurting them so much. As the saying goes, 'When you live in the sewer, you can't smell the shit' — well, I could smell it now.

Half an hour after I'd told them, Mason came to talk to me. He understood why I was doing it and thought I was making the right decision, but he couldn't envisage himself or Bianca ever turning their back on Paul. He never ceases to amaze, that boy: his heart remains firmly in the right place. I begged them to see Tracy and, after much deliberation, each of them went to see her on their own. They went in under the illusion that it was to help their dad, just as I had.

Bianca went in first. Tracy was very concerned about how much hurt Bianca had buried ever since Colin and I had split up. Then Paul had stepped in as the hero of the hour, but Bianca was old enough to know that behind closed doors he didn't behave heroically at all. He had made her change her name and call him 'Dad', a big sacrifice for a little girl to make. But Paul had not delivered either. Yes, he had schooled her, put a roof over her head, taken her on holiday, fed and clothed her, but he hadn't done the one thing she craved: he hadn't loved her. Little girls are supposed to be the apple of their daddy's eye – but Bianca feels that, through no fault of her own, she has been let down by two fathers. When Tracy asked Bianca to explain how she felt about all of it, Bianca couldn't speak. She just cried. Loving Paul was detrimental to herself, but protecting herself meant not loving him and that made her feel bad. What kind of daughter doesn't love her dad? Especially next to Mason whose love up to that point had been unconditional. Bianca had been in a lose-lose situation for a long time, never able to say, 'I hate this,' and be heard.

Then Mason went in. Tracy was equally worried about him. After hours of talking about how giving up on his father felt like giving up on himself, he admitted that his life had been on hold since Paul had stopped calling him four years ago, and worrying about him had occupied his every waking minute since. Finally he came round to the idea of an intervention. This is not a fun thing to do. The family descend on the addict out of the blue, then each member announces, 'I love you and care about you. I remember [a nice memory] but what you're doing to yourself I can no longer be a part of. If you agree now to get help, after a month I will be there for you, but if you choose not to take the help, I am walking away and will no longer be there for you until such time as you have had proper help.'

If the kids and Tracy found out where Paul was in Portugal, they would go together. Once Mason and Bianca had delivered this ultimatum with love, Tracy was particularly insistent that Mason should be prepared to see it through to the end. Tracy was almost certain that Paul wouldn't accept help, but she had things in place in case, by some miracle, he did. She made Mason promise that if Paul told him to get lost, Mason would get on with his life. I was very worried about both of them being in Portugal, Paul turning nasty and me not being there to comfort them. I decided to go with them and Tracy.

I rang Carol and Jimmy to tell them I had decided I was no longer going to help Paul. It was time to walk away, to protect my sanity and my children's. Carol said she felt Paul was old enough to know better and all he did was keep hurting everyone. Her nerves were shot to pieces, too, she added. When we had been trying to track Paul down, she and I had remained in regular contact. She'd told me she pulled the phone out of the wall, so I would ring, leave messages, then she would call me back. I told her that as soon as I found him I'd let her know. 'But not after nine o'clock. That's when I go to bed.' A far better idea than waiting up all night.

The day before we went to Portugal, Paul had been ringing, still asking the kids to come out. He sent me a text saying I was the only one who could help him, but when I texted back that we'd come and get him, he didn't respond. Regan spoke to him and said a friend of his had seen him at a certain hotel.

When Regan pushed him for an answer on his whereabouts, he hung up. It was then Regan decided he was coming too. This surprised me because Regan was adamant he felt nothing for Paul and just wished he'd go away. Tracy said Regan was the most clued up of all of us, unpolluted with false memories of happy times. He wanted to be reminded, for what he suspected might be the last time, that Paul was not a man to miss, or love or pin his hopes to. If something terrible happened Regan would not be left full of remorse – you can't miss something you've never had. Seeing Paul in that drunken state would confirm what he already knew: that he'd never had a father. In contrast, Mason wanted to go to remind himself that, beneath the mess, there was a father worth saving.

We flew to Portugal early in the morning, a fairly subdued bunch surrounded by happy holidaymakers. We arrived at Vale do Lobo – we'd been told by the Iron Maiden band manager, Ian Day, that Paul was still there. We chose the cheapest hotel to stay in because I knew it was the one place Paul would not be. Mason wanted to go out looking for him straight away, but Tracy sat him down and explained that this was the last opportunity for us to get an answer out of Paul, hopefully to get him help or, failing that, to take our chance to move on. For the moment he could look for him but not approach him.

'But how can I not step in if someone's taking the piss?'

We made him promise or he couldn't go out. I was seeing a glimmer of light at the end of a long, dark tunnel, and was terrified of losing it again. David went with Mason, and the rest of us stayed at the hotel in case someone recognized us and blew our chance.

The surprise element is a big part of an intervention. In Paul's case, as with many addicts, if he'd found out we were coming he would have done a runner.

With twenty-four hours before our flight home, it all got a bit farcical. Mason met a bar owner called Joe, who told him that his ex-wife, Sally, was with Paul in a mountain rehab clinic and that he had spoken to Carol. I wasn't convinced: he'd definitely been pissed when Regan had spoken to him only the day before. At hotel after hotel the staff denied that he was there – we were thrown out of one, but I didn't care: I was on a mission now and my children would get to say what they'd come to say. Then we saw a world-class English footballer who had played with Paul so I just barged into his golfing party and asked if he knew where Paul was. Everyone was suspicious. I don't have the best reputation, but the children and Tracy were with me, and we all said the same thing. We were there to help Paul or, at least, help the children jump off the not-so-merry-go-round and get closure. The footballer said that was the most sensible thing he'd heard in years and offered to help in any way he could.

Finally one of the hotel managers agreed to talk to us. Paul had been there and, under instruction from Iron Maiden, they'd not replenished the mini-bar. Things had turned bad when Jimmy and his girlfriend had shown up. Paul had thrown them out. Then the manager rang around the other local hotels. Meanwhile the footballer had located Paul and called Tracy. Within minutes we had two confirmations: Paul was at the Don Pedro in Vilamoura. But there were three Don Pedros.

I called Joe again to ask if Sally would tell us where Paul now was. He insisted that nothing was going on between her and Paul – but he didn't know Paul like I did and I thought his confidence was misplaced: Paul only hung around with women for one reason. Through Joe, I begged Sally to give us the information, but she didn't relent.

However, luckily for us Paul's dad had spoken to Paul, who had let slip his room number: 427.

When we got to Vilamoura we went to the first Don Pedro we found, walked straight to the lift and up to room 427. The atmosphere was very tense, and no one was talking. We were just hoping it was the right room and we'd be able to say what we'd come to say. Tracy repeated again to us that if Paul turned nasty, we had to leave. She would not condone any violence. The kids agreed.

We came out of the lift on the right floor but the room number didn't exist. We left straight away in fear of being recognized. The second Don Pedro was an apartment block, so I dismissed it and we headed off to the third, a hotel and golf resort. Again we went straight up to room 427. This time there was one. We walked past the door. Then, just as we'd decided to go back and knock, a bellman arrived with a note in his hand.

The kids and I stayed back, but Tracy went closer and thought she saw the name 'Gascoigne' on it. No one came to the door and the bellman left.

We followed him downstairs. Mason went to check the pool and Tracy followed the bellman until she was sure the name was Gascoigne. It was an IOU with a local number clipped to a receipt. She would do whatever it took to track down wayward alcoholics and drug addicts and set their families free. She copied down the number, grabbed us and we ran out as the footballer called again to tell us the golf resort we were standing in was where Paul was and the room number we had was correct.

My heart was in my mouth as we went across the road to calm down before we returned to find out if Paul was in the room or not. Mason was ready to bang the door down if Paul didn't open it but Tracy suggested we deliver notes instead. Then Regan piped up. 'No way. I've gone through all this to let him hear how I feel. I want him to suffer like he makes us suffer!'

I think Tracy was quite shocked – so much for Regan not feeling anything. Our goal was reset. We called the number Tracy had seen on the IOU and discovered it belonged to a taxi driver. Paul had been picked up from the police station in Albufeira earlier that morning, having been held overnight for drunk and disorderly behaviour; he'd told the driver he'd been mugged and had no money, hence the IOU. The driver said Paul was in a very bad way – so much for the rehab clinic in the mountains.

Tracy, moved by Regan's plea, went across to the hotel although she was now feeling nervous about the violent, un-predictable, bullying, angry alcoholic we were trying to get in to see. She told the hotel we were there to help, but nothing moved them until she said we could also sort out the financial situation. Ker-*ching*! Money moved another mountain. Appar-ently Paul had been asked to leave if he couldn't pay his bill, but had become aggressive and refused. She rang me and told me to come over to her with the kids – and suddenly it was as though we were in a movie, 'Go, go, go!' except it was real. We crossed the road quickly, then stopped outside the front entrance. I couldn't remember whether Tracy had said to come straight in or wait for her. She telephoned again and summoned us in. Terrified, we forced ourselves to go through the hotel doors, and reality hit home. Tracy was waiting with a security guard. As the lift doors closed behind us, we all felt sick.

Tracy reiterated our promise to her. If he got violent, we walked away. If he got nasty, we walked away. We would deliver our message: if our help was refused, we walked away. Tracy had said many times that it was very common for an addict when confronted by an intervention to refuse it, but once the family started to walk away, they shouted for help. But, and this was paramount, if that happened, we had to keep walking. Then it was up to the addict to choose.

The lift doors opened. The stairs down were directly in front of us and Paul's door was across the corridor to the left. We knocked on the door. We knocked again. Paul was on the phone. Tracy suggested I call out his name. But I couldn't. Then she said, 'He's not going to open the door,' and told the kids to shout their messages through the closed door. Suddenly, from deep inside me, all the anger exploded, leaving behind the cold, hard strength to save my children once and for all.

I shouted, 'Paul, open the door! Paul, it's Sheryl! Open the door! We're here to help you!'

'Sheryl? Sheryl who?'

'Open the door, Paul. The children need to speak to you.'

He opened the door. He was wearing just a pair of blue shorts, which were covered with white powder. Wide-eyed, his pupils dilated and fixed, he glared at me. He was horribly, painfully thin. He grunted, then slammed the door. Bianca and Regan were crying uncontrollably – the sight of him had been so shocking.

We heard Paul slam the phone down in his room and then he yanked the door open again. Mason was closest to it, so he started speaking first. He couldn't really look at Paul: he felt terrible delivering an ultimatum to such an emaciated creature.

'Dad, I love you. I can't do this any more. I don't sleep, I wait up for hours for you to ring, but unless you accept our help today, I can't be there for you any more.' Paul got aggressive and squared up to Mason, shouting in his face, 'F— off! I don't need you!'

I put my arm out to protect them, then Bianca and Regan delivered their own messages through gulps and sobs. I love you, get help, we can't do this any more. I love you, get help, we can't do this any more. Each of them added a personal memory of better days with Paul.

Listening to them would have melted a frozen heart, but Paul didn't falter. In fact, he smirked. Perhaps he didn't have a heart to melt any more.

It was my turn to speak. 'Paul,' I said, 'this lady is amazing. I believe she can truly help you. We have an amazing place lined up for you. You need serious help and you know it.'

His eyes stared at me, but I don't know what he was looking at. He shouted, 'F— off! F— off, the lot of you! I don't need you, I don't need my f—ing son telling me my wife's sleeping with loads of men.' He went into his list of the men I'd sup-posedly slept with – none of whom I had, of course – which demonstrated again how lucid he was in that he could recall all the names, and how ridiculous it was to imagine he could be anything else. 'A f—ing twelve-year-old sleeping with his mum! F— off, you bunch of c—s!'

I held out Tracy's card to him. He wouldn't take it so I put it in the top of his shorts. He snatched it out, stood in front of his desperate children and tore it up slowly into tiny pieces with a hideous smirk on his face. Then he shouted, 'F— off!'

We were riveted to the spot, watching him.

Tracy said, 'Right, you've done it. Let's go.' Then she turned to Paul. 'Paul, when you're sick of this life, living in hotels, getting arrested drunk and taking drugs, and you want serious help, call me any time. I will come and get you.'

We turned away. I didn't want to wait for the lift so headed for the stairs and started going down them. I wanted to get away. I wanted the pain to end. Paul had always been able to do anything to me, but now that I knew how much our relationship had hurt the kids, I couldn't leave fast enough.

Tracy kept saying to Mason, 'Don't look back, keep walking.'

Then Paul started shouting: 'Sheryl! Sheryl! Come back, Sheryl!' just as Tracy had said he would. Bianca and Regan were in front, then Tracy, me and Mason. I was keeping my eye on Mason, in case he ran back up the stairs. 'Come on, keep walking, it's what we agreed,' I said. 'Don't look back.' But he couldn't stop glancing over his shoulder.

We must have looked a right state, charging down the stairs with Paul shouting after us. We were all in tears, and I think the security man was in a state of shock. We walked through the reception area and out to the car park. The footballer rang to find out if we'd seen Paul and whether everyone was all right. Tracy told him Paul looked terrible and that he had reacted as predicted, but she was praying we could all move on. Again, he said it was the best thing he'd heard and sent his support. For years I'd felt the football industry was against me, against my family, but that day I changed my mind. I'd like to thank him: he knows who he is and he was pivotal in helping us.

Everyone was in shock, reeling from the sight of Paul, the smirk on his face, the void in his eyes, but we were calm.

Within twenty minutes Paul's mum was on my phone. She asked me to call her back so, with Tracy standing next to me, I did. She told me Paul wanted me to go back to the hotel. I explained I wouldn't but that Tracy would and we would leave another card at Reception so he could call her. 'He loves you, Sheryl. Please, only you can help him – he won't listen to us but he will listen to you.'

Tracy took the phone. 'This family is done now. You would have been very proud of your grandchildren. They told Paul they loved him and asked him to get help. He refused, so they're done now. They have to live their lives. If Paul is ready, I'll be there.'

Carol took Tracy's number to give to Paul. 'He wants Sheryl to go to the hotel and bring him to London.'

That wasn't going to happen. The Priory wasn't strict enough, as well she knew.

In the age-old fashion, Paul soon called Tracy's number. 'Put Sheryl on!'

How many friends had he called before to demand that very thing? Well, Tracy was different. She wasn't a friend. She was a saviour.

'No.'

'Put her on now!'

'No.'

'Put her on. I just want to talk to her.'

'No. They're done, Paul. When you truly want to stop living like this, call me any time. I'll help you and I'll go with you.'

'Put Sheryl on first, then I will.'

'No. This is not negotiable. I'm going to hang up now, Paul, but call me when you're truly, truly sick of this lifestyle.'

She was fantastic – kind, strong and blunt. She had shielded me and I was grateful.

We made our way slowly back to the hotel, trying to take in the enormity of what we'd done, what had happened, and get used to life without responsibility for Paul. The future looked empty and open. For me, that was exciting. I'd lived for a long time with the misery of Paul strewn across my path, blindly unaware that I could choose something else. I was exhausted, drained and punch-drunk but I felt free. I wasn't rejoicing yet – my children were too distraught for that – but I could see a time when I would, not long from now.

*

274

At the airport during check-in I had missed some calls from Joe, the bar owner. He had left messages.

'Paul is ready for you to come and get him.'

'Paul has to be picked up. The hotel's going to chuck him out. He has no money. Come and get him.'

Then Joe rang again to tell me more bad news. Immediately I fell back into my old pattern without even realizing it: Paul was being kicked out of the hotel and had nowhere to go!

Tracy said, 'Good. I told you he has to have *his* moment of clarity, which is when he reaches rock bottom. He may have just done that. It's usually once they've lost everything and have no money.'

Then Joe told me the hotel were going to call the police.

'Even better!' said Tracy. 'Twenty-four hours in a cell to sober him up. But he needs to call me himself. Give Joe my number.'

I felt sorry for Joe: he'd tried to help, but he couldn't. I knew the feeling well enough. I didn't want to be dragged back into it all. Only twelve hours previously, I had walked away, and I wanted to keep on walking. I told Joe to call Tracy.

I hadn't heard anything from Anna for five weeks, since 6 August when she'd texted that she was going to America on holiday. The night we arrived home, exhausted, she texted to tell me she'd just got back and wanted to know where Paul was. I replied:

Try the Don Pedro Hotel, room 427, he was there this
morning. He is in a very bad way, your mum has been talking
to him.

Twenty minutes later she asked me where in Portugal the Don Pedro was, the town or the area. I was too tired to reply.

The next day Joe texted to inform me that Paul was in

275

hospital in Faro. I thanked him, and said Paul would have to sober up before he flew anywhere. Another text informed me it wasn't likely Paul was going anywhere: he didn't have a credit card and he had a huge bill to pay. I repeated the mantra that Paul had to call Dr Tracy Towner if he wanted help. Joe said he would try, but since Paul had been in an alcoholic coma, it had been impossible. After a few more texts, Tracy took over. Guilt would drag me back in if I wasn't careful and I was determined to keep on our mission.

On my birthday, 24 September, we had a gathering of the usual mates at the Grove Hotel. The three kids were there and I was really happy. David from Spun Gold had come too. At one point his phone rang. Someone told him that a body had been found in Newcastle, and was believed to be Paul's. He didn't want to spoil my party so he told Adele, but then Bianca's agent called. Adele was worried that Bianca would hear before I did so she ran over to me and told me. I'd been expecting this call for years. Calmly I went into protection mode, my first thought for the children, my second, It's over. Paul had always said he wouldn't go without me and we would be buried alongside one another, and I felt a fleeting relief that I was still alive.

We put a call through to the powers-that-be and were told that the rumour was nonsense. My birthday party resumed.

Three days later the story of Paul and Sally Mulholland broke in the *Sunday Mirror*. Poor Joe: his caring ex-wife had been a little more hands-on than he'd imagined. When someone had asked if the blonde woman Paul was with was me, he had allegedly said, 'Sheryl who? Who's she?' Sally did look weirdly like me, *circa* 1990, from behind. Identikit hair. I sent Joe a message of support and hoped he was bearing up over the press coverage. He replied, 'I was wrong and well fooled, but that's life. The press is a small problem. My kids are the big one.'

Paul was wreaking havoc elsewhere and another pretty

blonde was letting him do it. I felt sorry for Sally: I knew only too well how convincing he was, making her believe she was the only one who could help him. He probably said he'd never felt the way he did with her, no doubt the sex was out of this world, and she was his new princess. I may have felt a little satisfaction that I was right, but it was hard earned.

The article hurt Bianca and Mason more than it did me: there were pictures of Paul with bags of presents for Sally's kids, but it wasn't that – if they couldn't save him, how or why could she? Joe had already hinted Paul had turned nasty and frightened her – hadn't she fled from the golf resort because he was so angry and out of control? Part of me wanted to reach out to her. She didn't know what I knew and I doubt she would have believed me anyway.

It was around this time that David Clews, having held out to the last moment that Paul would see sense and return home for treatment, gave up on the notion of the documentary being Paul's and went to Channel 4 with another idea. He suggested it was no longer *Loving Gazza*, but *Surviving Gazza*: the intervention and our subsequent 'rehabilitation' would form the main theme. They agreed, and after I had spoken at length with the kids, we decided to go ahead. David drew up the contracts, paid us £40,000 and Spun Gold left £10,000 on deposit for Paul. I thought that was fair in the circumstances.

David had wanted to take me back to Gleneagles for a sequence to end the film and exorcize some ghosts, but when we got there the hotel wouldn't give us permission to film. That was fine: I wasn't that keen to go back anyway – but I resented being made to feel like a social leper again.

The transformation in Mason was extraordinary, and when the filming ended and the cameras left us, I knew we had done the right thing. While David disappeared into an editing suite, we spent a shell-shocked few weeks contemplating every-thing we'd been through. It was strange but enlightening that we could live in a home where the phone didn't ring incessantly. Our message had got through. I was done. We were done.

There were constant rumours about Paul – he was in one rehab place, he was out drinking, he was in another rehab place, he was out drinking. He couldn't stand up, he was living off Special Brew, he'd gone missing over Christmas, he was found off his face. On New Year's Eve he walked out of the rehab centre that uses horses to treat patients, and Regan and I had a quiet night at home on our own. It was 2009. I had lost almost twenty years. The thought made me cry.

The documentary was due to be screened in January. I became increasingly nervous about it being shown. I was worried about all the things that I'd always worried about – money, the school fees, the mortgage, the children – and now the documentary: when it had been aired there would be no going back. I was acutely aware that Paul would see it as the ultimate betrayal and he would sever his links with us for ever.

Maybe for that reason it was worth doing. The pull to go back always lingered and my new-found freedom sometimes felt like a mirage. Had I left that door open just a crack? Was the lure of my idealized, long-hoped-for happy ending still so powerful that it could trick me again? I kept my head down during post-production but had agreed to do *This Morning* to publicize the documentary. I felt happy doing live television because my words couldn't be distorted: I'd had so many lies written about me in the press that speaking for myself was of the utmost importance to me. I had no idea how the film would be received, but I was amazed when I was told that on Monday, 5 January, 2.4 million people had watched it, not quite *Britain's Got Talent*, but pretty good for a documentary.

I got a really hideous text from one of Paul's sisters, but that didn't bother me so much because a few days later I was receiving letters from men, women and children who'd lived and were still living with addiction. I knew from their desperate tone that it had been a worthwhile thing to do, not just for my children, not just because it had closed the door for ever, but for the children I would never meet.

As for Mason, Bianca and Regan, they were relieved that it was finally 'out there'. Paul wasn't the great dad everyone had been led to believe, the one photographed holding babies, kicking a ball with eager lads, the man whom Denise Welch had described on *Loose Women* as 'fantastic and thoughtful' because he'd taken care of her boys by putting on a limo full of sweets and drinks for them when they'd missed their train. That was Gazza, not the monstrous, manipulative, divisive, bullying drunk my children knew as Dad. For a while people stopped asking them how he was.

My former sister-in-law Lindsay has set up a 'We dislike Sheryl Gascoigne for being a money-grabbing hound' group on Facebook, which was perhaps a little childish, but no doubt Paul was back in their lives, controlling everyone through fear and money, as he always had. I'm sure they would benefit from a visit from Tracy. They can blame me for everything as long as they live, but it won't keep Paul alive.

After the documentary, I was approached about writing this book. The money was good and I thought it was a brilliant way to put on record what I knew to be true against the many lies that had been written about me and continue to be written and told. Anger and years of pent-up resentment prompted me to agree to the book deal, but I'm not so angry now.

As I write, it was reported only recently that I was suing Paul for £100,000 pounds' maintenance and that he'd paid me £17.5 million over the ten years since we divorced. That is simply not true – and neither was it true that I called his mother a 'whore' at Gleneagles. I did not fly to Florida with an empty suitcase to fill with shopping, and I did not start to make notes on our relationship a week after it had begun. I did not contact Paul out of the blue after he'd had seven successful weeks in treatment. I am not a wicked vulture who has been making money out of him over a relationship that only lasted three months, and I certainly did not go to Italy only when I fancied a holiday. I have a whole list of things that he and his family have said about me, but suddenly it no longer seems so important.

If you've read this far, you pretty much know my side of the story. Paul can keep his. I don't need to tell you that lying is a compulsion Paul uses to protect himself from the consequences of his actions, and until he admits otherwise he will never get better. He may have been right about one thing. Perhaps I didn't know what love was: love had been a dream I'd been chasing since early childhood, a fantasy I had built up that could never be matched. Love is much more mundane than that. Funnily enough, Ami had described it to me at my wedding. But then I hadn't grasped what the words meant. I have now.

> *Love is patient and kind.*
> *It is not jealous or conceited or proud.*
> *Love is not ill-mannered, selfish or irritable.*
> *Love does not keep a record of wrongs.*
> *Love is not happy with evil but is happy with the truth.*
> *Love never gives up, and its faith, hope and patience never fail.*

I love my children fiercely and would defend them with my life. I am sorry, so sorry, from the bottom of my soul, for everything I have put them through. All I can do now is ask for their forgiveness. I had no idea what I was doing to them, none. I honestly thought I was doing the right thing. That was what I told myself anyway. Not only did I fear I was not enough for them and that I couldn't provide the wonderful things Paul could, I had a desperate need to be needed that played right into the hands of a young footballer who wanted to be wanted, the biggest and the best. Paul's mother may have been right about that: it was a toxic mix and I'm sorry.

I hadn't realized any of this until I wrote this book. It has been an exhausting, soul-searching, painful exercise, but now that I understand why I put up with the beatings and abuse, and why I went back, I can forgive myself. I've been surviving for a long time. It's time to start living. And that's what I intend to do. I'm going to do what I should have done years ago when Paul first dragged me by my hair and held me over a balcony in a hotel in Florida, spitting and screaming in my face. I'm going to hold my head high and walk away.

Acknowledgements

My fantastic 'team', Jan, Julie, Lorraine, Adele and Florence. I love you all. Each of you in your own unique way kept me sane, made me laugh and backed me up even when I'm sure, at times, you all thought I was mad. Your support has been immeasurable. Thank you from deep within my soul.

Tommy and Margaret and all my friends in Scotland, you are such lovely people and have always made me so welcome.

The Andersons, Gary, Julie, Lauren, Daniel and Josh, a loyal and lovely family.

My beautiful sister Vicki, who I only got to share a very short time with, but who has a huge place in my heart.

My children ... the reason I'm still here. The reason I go on. The ones I am so very proud of and whose approval I seek in too many things. The ones I apologize to for continually putting them through a perpetual nightmare of a rollercoaster. You are my world. xxx

The most elegant and kindest lady ever, Nanny, you were my inspiration, my angel, my all. I miss you and think of you daily, and in all that I do and the decisions I face I always ask 'Would you approve?' first.

My handsome godson Sam and his two beautiful sisters, Ellie and Skye.

My brothers Gaylord and David. It saddens me that we missed our childhood together. I respect and love you both.

My agents, the elegant Jan, Vicki and Jonathan, thank you for helping me to start on this formidable and life-changing episode.

Debbie: we have missed out on a lot of our childhood together but, boy, we can make up for it now.

To Gay, a hugely talented and inspirational lady, for taking this journey with me: one that would not have been the same without you, and has been far better with you. I thoroughly enjoyed working with you, even though you put me through the wringer a few times! You have given me immeasurable inner peace. I thank you, my children thank you. xxx

To all at Penguin, those I've met and those I haven't, thank you for being so supportive. In particular Katy, Clare, Paulette, Louise and Tom for wanting to hear my story and for releasing me in the process.

To David Clews and Tracy Towner for throwing me a lifeline and for having the insight and knowledge to realize 'we' needed the help. What a difference you made to our lives. Thank you.

To all of the above, I am the person I am today because of you. The continuing ripples of your friendship and support will leave me indebted to you all for the rest of my life. x

Picture Credits

'My first attempt at modelling, aged fifteen.'
Photograph by Chris Dawes

'Photo taken for the local newspaper in Hertford.'
'Another picture for the local newspaper'.
Photographs by Mike Poultney for the Hertfordshire Mercury

'My one and only beautiful daughter, Bianca.'
'And then there were three.'
'Three going though a western phase.'
Photographs by Ray Lowe, Cheshunt

'My amazing wedding dress.'
'My wonderful friend Isabell, who designed my dress.'
'I was very proud of my handsome family that day.'
'The Zodiac Room. Hanbury Manor, 1996. The setting
    was stunning.'
'Me, Paul and his father.'
'Me, Paul, my two fabulous children and the infamous
    Jimmy 'Five Bellies'.
'Paul and me with my dear friend Rebekah and her partner
    Ross.'
'The three stooges.'
Photographs courtesy of Hello! Syndication

'I was asked to be the face of a new jewellery line called
    Joy.'
Photography by Steve Burden, Post Studios Photographic

'My stunning daughter in her way to Love Island.'
Photograph by Nicky Johnston, Camera Press London

'Trying to change attitudes and reaching out to society at the
    fifth Annual Domestic Violence conference in London,
    November 2007. I was honoured to speak alongside the
    Rt Hon. Harriet Harman, QC MP.'
'Bianca and I, pictured here with Cherie Blair and Sandra
    Horley, OBE, were honoured to be invited to Chequers.'
Photographs by Julian Nieman